Greek Prose Composition

Greek Prose Composition

M. A. NORTH, M.A.
Late Assistant Master at Clifton College

AND

THE REV. A. E. HILLARD, D.D.
Late High Master of St. Paul's School

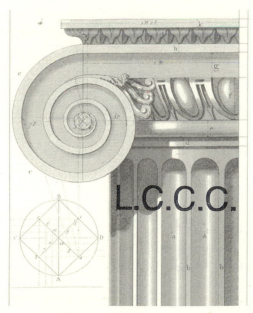

LIBRARY
Focus Classical Reprints
Focus Publishing
R Pullins Company
Newburyport MA 01950

PREFACE

THIS book follows the lines of the same authors' Latin Prose Composition. It is intended to cover the work of Fourth and Fifth Forms in Public Schools, and is carefully graduated throughout. Every exercise has been expressly written for the place in which it stands, and no construction is introduced which has not already been learnt. Connected pieces are given together with sentence exercises from the beginning, and exercises for revision occur at regular intervals. As in the Latin book each exercise is marked (*A*) or (*B*). This is to divide the section assigned to a form into two terms' work. Either the (*A*) exercises or the (*B*) exercises will make a complete course and contain sufficient practice in constructions, but it is recommended that the Vocabularies of both (*A*) and (*B*) exercises should be learnt in any case.

The Vocabularies for the separate exercises are placed at the end of the book and are meant to be learnt. The authors regard this as an important point, for there is no doubt that ignorance of common words is a constant source of weakness in Composition. A General Vocabulary has been added collecting all the words given in the Special Vocabularies (p. 246). This is meant to assist short memories, but not to supply again Genders, Genitives, etc., which should have been learnt in the Special Vocabularies.

v

The Principal Parts of the Irregular Verbs required are given in an Appendix (pp. 223-229). Other Appendices contain (1) a list of the Compounds of some of the commonest verbs (pp. 230-232); (2) a list of Prepositions with their prose usages (pp. 233-237); (3) a table of the commonest Particles (pp. 238-239); (4) the chief rules for Accentuation (pp. 240-245).

The authors have obtained a great deal of help from Goodwin's *Moods and Tenses*, Thompson's *Syntax of Attic Greek*, and other books too numerous to mention. Their thanks for valuable suggestions and criticisms are specially due to their colleagues, the Rev. H. J. Wiseman and Mr. W. W. Asquith; also to the Rev. W. A. Heard, Head-master of Fettes, the Hon. and Rev. E. Lyttelton, Head-master of Haileybury, the Rev. Dr. W. A. Fearon, Head-master of Winchester, Mr. F. E. Thompson of Marlborough, Mr. R. Whitelaw of Rugby, Professor Gilbert Murray of Glasgow University, and Mr. C. H. Garland of Haileybury.

M. A. NORTH.
A. E. HILLARD.

CLIFTON COLLEGE.

CONTENTS

THE ARTICLE

1. The Article is used sometimes in Greek where it is not used in English :—

(*a*) **With Nouns denoting whole classes.**

> *e.g.* οἱ θῆρες, *wild beasts*; οἱ ἄνθρωποι, *mankind.*

(*b*) **Often with abstract Nouns and proper names,** especially the names of countries.

> *e.g.* ἡ ἀνδρεία, *courage*; ἡ Ἑλλάς, *Greece.*

2. The Article used with an Adjective or Adverb, or with an Infinitive, makes it a Noun.

> *e.g.* τὸ ἀληθές, *truth*; οἱ ἀνδρεῖοι, *brave men*; τὸ λέγειν, *speech*; τῷ λέγειν, *by speaking*; οἱ πάλαι, *the men of old.*

3. Participles, like Adjectives, when used with the Article, are equivalent to Nouns.

> *e.g.* οἱ λέγοντες, *speakers,* or *those who speak.*
> οἱ τεθνηκότες, *the dead,* or *those who have died.*

This is constantly the Greek equivalent for an English Relative clause.

> *e.g.* τιμῶμεν τοὺς στρατιώτας τοὺς ὑπὲρ τῆς πόλεως τεθνηκότας.
> *We honour the soldiers who have died for their city.*

Exercise 1 [*A*].

1. Greeks are always brave.

2. Greece was formerly free

3. Brave men are honoured.

4. Hope gives men courage.

5. Truth is often strange.

6. Speaking is difficult to me.

7. He thinks lying base.

8. A rich man has many friends.

9. A brave man conquers difficulties.

10. Victory harms many men.

11. Men of the present day are braver

12. Men here do not believe me.

Exercise 2 [*B*].

1. Wise men honour truth.

2. Greeks are not willing to obey barbarians.

3. Speaking well is difficult.

4. Ships are safe in harbours.

5. We wish to free Greece.

6. Good men admire wisdom.

7. By obeying wise men we become wise.

8. By victory we become free.

9. Free men do not admire slavery.

10. The men of old used to admire wisdom.

11. The people here do not honour courage.

THE POSITION OF THE ARTICLE

4. (*a*) An Adjective as an ordinary attribute comes usually between the Article and the Noun.

e.g. ὁ ἀγαθὸς ἀνήρ, the brave man.

But this may also be expressed by—

ὁ ἀνὴρ ὁ ἀγαθός

(*b*) In any other position the Adjective is a Predicate.

e.g. ὁ ἀνὴρ ἀγαθός (ἐστιν),
ἀγαθός (ἐστιν) ὁ ἀνήρ, }   The man is brave.[1]

5. All attributive phrases naturally take the same position as the Adjective in 4 (*a*).

e.g. ἡ τῶν ᾿Αθηναίων[2] πόλις, the city of the Athenians.
οἱ ἐν τοῖς τείχεσι στρατιῶται, the soldiers on the walls.

So also οἱ εὖ λέγοντες, *those who speak well, good speakers.*

---

[1] Notice that this rule applies to such sentences as—

ἡδεῖαν ἔχει τὴν φωνήν, *he has a pleasant voice.*

ἅπαντες θνητὸν ἔχομεν τὸ σῶμα, *we all have a mortal body.*

The adjective here adds a fresh assertion or predicate, *e.g.* ' *We all have a body and it is mortal.*'

The Article often distinguishes the Subject from its Complement—

e.g. νὺξ ἡ ἡμέρα ἐγένετο, *day became night.*

[2] Notice that the dependent Genitive (unless a proper name) generally has the Article, if the Noun on which it depends has the Article, *e.g.* τὸ τῆς ἀρετῆς κάλλος.

Exercise 3 [*A*].

1. The soldiers of the Athenians died bravely.

2. Men of old used to honour good speakers.

3. The army in the city was not willing to fight.

4. Those who fled came to the city.

5. Those who said this were lying.

6. Those who stood[1] in the streets escaped.

7. The herald had a loud voice.

8. Many of the noblest Athenians perished.

9. They destroyed the walls which had just been made.

10. They used to bring out into the streets those who were sick.

11. The women have graceful hands.

12. They sent back the Athenians who were in the army.

---

[1] Perf. Part. of ἵστημι.

Exercise 4 [*B*].

1. We always honour good speakers.
2. Those who have died for their [1] city are worthy of honour.
3. The ships which are in the harbour are safe.
4. Greeks will not obey the soldiers of the king.
5. Those who fled from the city are not brave.
6. Hope gives courage to those who are fighting for the city.
7. Lions have sharp teeth.
8. The sons of wise fathers are not always wise.
9. Good citizens give money to the wives of soldiers who have died for their country.
10. The general whom we obey is brave.
11. We honour the men who freed Greece.

Exercise 5 [*A*].

1. Men of the present day honour the heroes of old.
2. Rich men give money to those who are poor.
3. Truth is not always easy for clever speakers.
4. The wives of the citizens did not honour those who fled from the battle.
5. The leaders of the Greeks destroyed the walls of the city.

---

[1] The Possessive need not be expressed where there is no ambiguity. The Article here is sufficient.

6. The soldiers who escaped to the city are now safe.

7. The citizens wished to destroy the ships which had come (*Aorist*) into the harbour.

8. Those who fight bravely on behalf of their[1] country are worthy of the greatest honour.

9. Soldiers are saved by fighting bravely rather than by flying.

10. We honour the orators who wish to save Greece.

Exercise 6 [*B*].

1. Those who fight best will conquer.

2. They conquered men who fought more bravely.

3. They made the walls of the city stronger.

4. Wild beasts obeyed him.

5. The enemy's victory destroyed[2] the hope of the citizens.

6. They became rich by lying.

7. The general of the enemy freed the soldiers who fought bravely.

8. The ships that sailed never arrived.

9. The Athenians killed the women who betrayed the city.

10. I think fighting wrong.

---

[1] See page 6, note.   [2] καταλύω.

AGREEMENT

6. The rules for agreement both of Adjectives and of Verbs are the same as in Latin,[1] except that :

(a) **Neuter Plural subjects have their verbs in the Singular,** unless they represent a number of *persons.*

> *e.g.* ταῦτα παύσεται, *these things will cease.*
>
> but τὰ τέλη κελεύουσι, *the magistrates order.*

(b) **Greek has a Dual Number, but in speaking of two persons or things the Plural may be used as well as the Dual, and a Dual subject may have a Plural Verb.**

> *e.g.* ἀπέθανον οἱ δύο στρατηγοί.
>
> *The two generals were killed.*

The Dual is scarcely used except of things considered as a pair : *e.g.* τὼ ὀφθαλμώ, *the eyes.*

---

[1] Therefore in dealing with a Predicate that has two or more subjects—

(a) **with regard to Person**—the 1st is preferred to the 2nd and the 2nd to the 3rd ;

(b) **with regard to Number**—the Predicate may be plural or may be singular in agreement with the nearest subject ;

(c) **with regard to Gender**—if the subjects are persons the masculine is preferred to the feminine ; if the subjects are things the predicate may agree with the nearest subject, or, if the plural be used, is put in the neuter.

> *e.g.* καὶ ὁ ἀνὴρ καὶ ἡ γυνὴ ἀγαθοί εἰσιν.
>
> καὶ ὁ ἀνὴρ ἀγαθός ἐστι καὶ ἡ γυνή.
>
> *Both the man and his wife are good.*
>
> τῶν κακῶν ἡ στάσις καὶ ὁ πόλεμος αἴτιός ἐστι.
>
> *Both sedition and war are the cause of our troubles.*

Observe also that with disjunctives ἤ . . . ἤ (*either . . . or*) οὔτε . . . οὔτε (*neither . . . nor*), the Predicate should agree with the nearest subject.

Exercise 7.

1. Living creatures are not always beautiful.

2. Both the men and the women are small.

3. Trees and flowers grow in this island.

4. The two generals were killed by the enemy.

5. The two armies were fighting.

6. Gold and silver are brought to the market.

7. Many missiles were thrown by the enemy.

8. Two friends gave me the present.

9. Children are dear to their fathers.

10. Corn and wine are useful to men.

11. I gave them the money, the gift of the king.

12. Nicias and Demosthenes, two brave soldiers, were (both) killed.

13. These are the gifts of Callias, the Athenian general.

TENSES IN THE INDICATIVE

7. The Imperfect and Aorist tenses of the Indicative both express actions as having occurred in past time; but the Imperfect expresses the action as continuing or being repeated, while the Aorist simply states that it occurred.

> *e.g.* ἔγραφον, *I was writing, I used to write, I wrote.*
> ἔγραψα, *I wrote.*
> πᾶσαν τὴν ἡμέραν ἐπορεύοντο καὶ ὀψὲ ηὐλίσαντο.
> *They were marching (marched) all day and encamped late.*

8. The Aorist is frequently used where English uses the Pluperfect, so long as a single action and not a *state* is implied. This is especially the case in Relative and Temporal sentences.

> *e.g.* ἐπειδὴ ἦλθον ηὐλίσαντο.
> *When they had come* (or *Having come,*) *they encamped.*

9. The Perfect expresses a state resulting from completed action.

> *e.g.* ὁ Κῦρος τέθνηκε, *Cyrus is dead.*

Many perfects are therefore equivalent to English Presents, *e.g.* ἕστηκα, *I stand* (literally, *I have placed myself*), μέμνημαι *I remember* (literally, *I have called to mind*).

Exercise 8 [*A*].

1. The soldiers were killed by the missiles.
2. The citizens used to give many presents to the king.
3. The women and the children are standing on the wall.
4. The ships always brought corn into the harbour.
5. When the army had been conquered, the city was taken.
6. Many men and women were standing in the market-place.
7. When the ships had sailed into the harbour, they were safe.
8. We always honoured speakers.
9. The Greeks often conquered the Persians.
10. Cyrus was killed by his brother's soldiers.

Exercise 9 [*B*].

1. The enemy destroyed the army of the Athenians.
2. The men of old honoured the brave.
3. When the general arrived, he was killed.
4. When the sailors arrived, they used to remain in the city.
5. The Athenians and their wives are standing in the market-place.
6. The man and his wife are dead.
7. The women and children were killed by the missiles.
8. The heroes of old always fought bravely.
9. The ships remained all day in the harbour.
10. We used to honour those who fought bravely.

TENSES IN THE PARTICIPLES

10. The Present Participle denotes an action as going on at the same time as the action of the Principal Verb.

e.g. ἀπέθανε καθεύδων, he died while sleeping.

The Aorist Participle generally represents an action as having occurred before the action of the Principal Verb. It will therefore frequently translate the English Perfect Participle.

e.g. ἐλθὼν οἴκαδε ἀπέθανε, having returned home, he died.

The Perfect Participle, like the Perfect Indicative, denotes a Present state as the result of action in the Past.

e.g. οἱ τεθνηκότες τιμῶνται, the dead are honoured.

Compare with this—

ἔθαψαν τοὺς Μαραθῶνι ἀποθανόντας.
They buried those who died at Marathon.

Exercise 10 [*A*].

1. The enemy attacked them while marching.
2. Being always attacked, the citizens were in distress.
3. They were not willing to march.
4. The general ordered them to attack, but they did not obey.

5. When they had made a camp, they awaited the enemy
6. He was killed while crossing the river.
7. Hearing this they fled.
8. They were often seen entering the town.
9. Those who had been asked answered.
10. When they had arrived at the town, they were caught.

Exercise 11 [B].

1. The ships which had arrived were destroyed.
2. The enemy attacked the soldiers as they were marching.
3. The soldiers always fought bravely, and they were never [1] defeated.
4. The enemy destroyed the ships which had sailed out of the harbour.
5. The army, having come to the walls of the city, encamped.
6. The city was being destroyed, and the citizens were flying.
7. The Greeks defeated a great army of the Persians.
8. The Greeks often fought bravely against [2] the Persians and defeated them.
9. Many ships were taken as they were coming from the harbour.
10. Having conquered the enemy, the soldiers were marching to the city.

---

[1] *And . . . never,* οὐδέ *. . .* ποτε.
[2] *Against* is expressed by the Dat. here.

THE MIDDLE VOICE

11. The Middle Voice is Reflexive, but not so often in the sense of doing a thing to oneself as in the sense of doing a thing for oneself or getting a thing done for oneself. It is generally equivalent therefore to the Active Voice with the *Dative* of the Reflexive Pronoun.

e.g. φέρω, *I bring.*

φέρομαι (*I bring for myself*), *I win.*

e.g. φέρομαι τὸ ἆθλον. *I win the prize.*

διδάσκω, *I teach.*

διδάσκομαι τὸν υἱόν. *I have my son taught.*

παύω, *I stop (transitive).*

παύομαι, *I stop myself.* *I stop (intransitive).*

e.g. ἔπαυσαν τὸν πόλεμον. *They ended the war.*

e.g. ἐπαύσαντο τοῦ πολέμου. *They desisted from the war.*

ἀμύνω τῇ πόλει. *I keep off* (*the enemy*) *from the city.* *I defend the city.*

ἀμύνομαι τοὺς πολεμίους. *I resist the enemy* (*i.e. keep him off myself*).

εἷλον ταύτην τὴν πόλιν. *They took this city.*

εἵλοντο ταύτην τὴν βίβλον. *They chose this book* (*i.e. took it for themselves*).

Exercise 12 [*A*].

1. They saved their wives and children.

2. They sold the house of Demosthenes.

3. Alcibiades won many prizes.

4. They put an end to the battle.

5. Socrates taught the sons of the Athenians.

6. The sun appeared.

7. He showed the present to his father.

8. They ceased from the battle.

9. The Athenians were resisting the Persians bravely.

10. They ransomed the citizens who had been captured.

11. They chose Nicias general.

Exercise 13 [B].

1. The storm quickly stopped the battle.

2. The sailors sold the fish to the citizens.

3. We will ransom the sons of the general.

4. We will defend our city against the enemy

5. You win many prizes at the games.

6. These presents appear to me most beautiful.

7. We will show this to the citizens.

8. We will now desist from the war.

9. They resisted the enemy bravely.

10. I kept my money safe.

11. I gave back the money to the judge.

12. They chose the best men as leaders

Exercise 14 [*A*].

1. The soldiers chose Nicias (as) general.
2. The books were chosen by the children.
3. The battle was stopped by the general.
4. Having been often conquered, they desisted from the war.
5. These things were heard by the citizens.
6. Those who had perished were buried.
7. The army was saved by Callias.
8. Those who attacked us were taken.
9. They were seen by the enemy (when) crossing the river.
10. The presents were given back to the children.

Exercise 15 [*B*].

1. Having sailed away, the Athenians were saved.
2. The battle was stopped by a storm.
3. The Athenians were set free, and ransomed their slaves.
4. The walls were taken.
5. They were ordered to attack the enemy.
6. Having attacked the enemy, they were beaten.
7. The army was increased as it entered the country.
8. The messengers who had been sent brought back much corn.
9. The city was destroyed and the citizens perished.
10. They stopped fighting.

AGENT AND INSTRUMENT

12. The person by whom a thing is done is expressed by ὑπό with the Genitive Case.

The instrument by which or the cause through which a thing is done is expressed by the Dative Case.[1]

e.g. ἡ γέφυρα ἐλύθη ὑπὸ τῶν πολεμίων·

The bridge was broken down by the enemy.

διώλεσε τὸν ἄνδρα τοῖς φαρμάκοις.

She killed her husband by poison.

Exercise 16 [*A*].

1. The camp was besieged by the enemy with all his forces.
2. They killed him with stones when he was already wounded.
3. By whom were the gates opened?
4. He conquered the Athenians by his skill.
5. They were ordered by the general to cross the river.
6. They crossed the river by means of the bridge.
7. Messengers sent by the king betrayed the town.
8. He ransomed his father with a large sum of money.[2]
9. They saved the citizens by the ships.
10. The country is being destroyed by the Persians.

---

[1] In certain cases the Agent can be expressed by the Dative—
(*a*) after the 3rd Person Perfect and Pluperfect Passive and the Perfect Participle Passive—

e.g. ταῦτα τετέλεσταί σοι, *this has been accomplished by you;*
(*b*) after the Verbal Adjective. See Rule 54, page 130.

The instrument, especially if it is a person, may also be expressed by διά with the Genitive.

e.g. δι' ἀγγέλων ἔπεισε τοὺς 'Αθηναίους.

He persuaded the Athenians by means of messengers.

[2] A large sum of money = πολλὰ χρήματα.

Exercise 17 [B].

1. The great army of the Persians was defeated by the Greeks.

2. The boys pelted the orator with stones.

3. The traitor was killed by stones hurled by the citizens.

4. Many of the soldiers were wounded by the arrows.

5. The Athenians, having been caught by the enemy, were killed.

6. They were defeated many times, and desisted from the war.

7. The bravest of the soldiers were killed by the missiles of the enemy.

8. Those who win prizes in the games are honoured by the citizens.

9. The Athenians wished to ransom the soldiers who had been taken by the enemy.

10. The bridge was broken by the storm.

PLACE

13. Place is usually expressed in Greek by Prepositions.
'Place whither' generally requires a Preposition with the
Accusative, 'place whence' a Preposition with the Genitive,
and 'place where' a Preposition with the Dative.[1]

e.g. to ⎫
    into ⎬ *the city* ⎰πρὸς⎱ ⎰εἰς ⎱ τὴν πόλιν.
    against⎭   ⎰ἐπὶ⎱

    to the king   ὡς τὸν βασιλέα
                  (ὡς of persons only.)

    from ⎫ *the city* ⎰ἀπὸ⎱ τῆς πόλεως.
    out of ⎭   ⎰ἐκ ⎱

    from the king   παρὰ τοῦ βασιλέως
                (παρά is used especially of persons.)

    in the city   ἐν τῇ πόλει.

    at ⎫ *the city*   πρὸς τῇ πόλει.
    near ⎭

But Greek has remains of certain old cases expressing
place :—

(1) The Locative Case expressing *place where* with the
termination -ι, *e.g.* οἴκοι, *at home*; Μαραθῶνι, *at
Marathon*.

(2) The termination -θεν signifying *place whence, e.g.*
οἴκοθεν, *from home*; ᾿Αθήνηθεν, *from Athens*; ἄλλοθεν, *from elsewhere*.

(3) The termination -δε *or* -σε signifying *place whither,*
e.g. οἴκαδε, *homewards*; ᾿Αθήναζε, *to Athens*; ἄλλοσε, *to another place*.

---

[1] But the uses of ἐπί to express place require special notice—
    e.g. ἐπὶ τῆς τραπέζης, *upon the table.*
    ἐπὶ τῆς Νάξου, *towards Naxos.*

Exercise 18 [*A*].

1. The ships sailed from Athens towards the Hellespont.

2. The soldiers who had been captured by the enemy were sent home.

3. The soldiers on the walls were killed by the arrows.

4. Messengers were sent by the Greeks to the king.

5. The messengers who had come from Thebes announced these things to the Spartans.

6. Those who remained at home saw the soldiers who had arrived from the island.

7. The general and his followers were killed by the traitors.

8. The ships arrived at Athens bringing many presents from the king.

9. The army which was marching against the city was destroyed by a great storm.

10. The soldiers who died at Marathon were greatly honoured by the Athenians.

Exercise 19 [*B*].

1. The traitors who had come from the king were put to death at Athens.

2. Those who sailed from the city reached the mainland safely.

3. An army was sent from Plataea to the Athenians at Marathon.[1]

4. Many Greeks marched with Cyrus from Sardis against the King of Persia.[2]

5. The Spartans killed the messenger who was sent to Sparta from the king.

6. The enemy kept attacking the soldiers as they were marching homewards.

7. The ships which had been sent against Greece by the Persians were destroyed.

8. Money was sent to Athens from the islands.

9. The slave was sent from Sparta to the Thebans.

10. Those who had come to the island from the mainland were put to death by traitors.

11. The ships were sailing towards Greece.

---

[1] Translate '*being at Marathon.*'

[2] βασιλεύς (without the Article)=*the King of Persia.*

TIME

14. The cases in Greek are used to express time without any preposition.

'Duration of time' is expressed by the Accusative.

e.g. τρεῖς μῆνας ἐνόσει, he was ill for 3 months.

'Time when' is expressed by both Genitive and Dative, but with a difference, the Genitive expressing 'the time within which' something occurs, the Dative 'the point of time at which' it occurs.

e.g. ταύτης τῆς νυκτὸς ἐνόσησε,   he fell ill in the course of
                                                    (during) this night.
τῇ τετάρτῃ ἡμέρᾳ ἀπέθανε,   he died on the 4th day.

SPACE

15. Extent of space is expressed, as in Latin, by the Accusative case.

e.g. δέκα στάδια ἐπορεύθησαν.
They marched 10 stades.
δέκα στάδια ἀπέχει (ἀπὸ) τῶν Ἀθηνῶν.
It is distant 10 stades from Athens.

Height, breadth, etc., are generally expressed by the Genitive and an Accusative of Respect.

e.g. τεῖχος εἴκοσι ποδῶν τὸ ὕψος.
A wall twenty feet in height.

Exercise 20 [*A*].

1. Having encamped all the night, they set out at daybreak.

2. He was killed at night while sleeping.

3. The army having set out by night reached the city before morning.

4. In the course of the day the army marched 95 [1] stades.

5. On the fourteenth day the army encamped near the city.

6. They crossed a river 105 feet broad.

7. On the second day he ran twelve parasangs.

8. The camp was distant many stades from the city.

9. The Greeks set out early and came to the camp towards evening, having marched all day.

10. In the winter the armies encamped for a long time.

11. Three times in the year we used to see them.

12. He was carrying a spear 12 feet long.

---

[1] In Greek, compound numbers after 20 may be expressed in three ways :—

    (1) The larger precedes the smaller without καί.
    (2) The larger precedes the smaller with καί.
    (3) The smaller precedes the larger with καί.

Exercise 21 [B].

1. Having marched 25 stades they remained all night near the river.

2. On the 14th day they reached Sardis.

3. They started from Sparta at dawn and reached Athens in the evening on the following day.

4. In this summer the Athenians were defeated both by land and sea.

5. The harbour is five stades from the city.

6. Having ruled eight years he died.

7. On the 29th day of this month, the Persians entered Athens.

8. Here there was a wall 75 feet high.

9. He came to my house in the course of the night.

10. On the return of spring another battle took place.

11. In winter war ceases.

12. He has a meadow 2 stades broad.

COMPARISON

16. Where two things are directly compared with one another by means of a Comparative Adjective, use the **Genitive of Comparison in Greek** where in Latin you use the Ablative.

> *e.g.* οἱ Ἕλληνες ἀνδρειότεροί εἰσι τῶν Περσῶν.
> *The Greeks are braver than the Persians.*

In all other forms of Comparison, as in Latin *quam* is used, so in Greek ἤ is used for *than*, and the case of the noun following it will be the same as the case of the noun which corresponds to it in the first part of the sentence.

> *e.g.* οἱ Πέρσαι ἔχουσι μεῖζον στράτευμα ἢ οἱ Ἕλληνες.
> *The Persians have a bigger army than the Greeks.*
>
> μείζω δῶρα ἐμοὶ ἢ τῷ ἀδελφῷ ἔδωκεν.
> *He gave greater presents to me than to my brother.*

Exercise 22 [*A*].

1. They gave more money to the sailors than to the soldiers.
2. The Athenians sent out more ships than the Spartans.
3. Commanding is much[1] easier than obeying.
4. Gold is often more useful than force.
5. The Athenians were far more powerful by sea than by land.
6. The islands sent more money than ships.
7. The men at Sparta were not braver than the women.
8. Ships used to be more beautiful than those of the present day.[2]
9. We win more prizes at the games than the Thebans.
10. We love liberty no less than life.

Exercise 23 [*B*].

1. The Athenians were more clever than the Spartans.
2. The Athenians had greater power than the Spartans.
3. The second ship sailed faster than the first.
4. You have a finer house than I.
5. He loved nothing more than glory.
6. Xenophon wrote more books than Thucydides.
7. It is easier to write well than to speak well.
8. They have made the wall broader than the ditch.
9. Aristides was a juster man than his enemies.
10. They have given a more beautiful prize to him than to me.

---

[1] πολλῷ. In Greek the Dative is used to express the measure of difference, corresponding to the Ablative in Latin.

[2] See Rule 2, page 1.

Exercise 24 [*A*].

REVISION.

1. Speaking well was more easy for the Athenians than for the Spartans.

2. Having marched many stades in the course of the day, the army encamped towards evening.

3. Greeks did not consider lying disgraceful.

4. The traitors who had entered the city were pelted by the citizens with stones.

5. They set out at daybreak and continued to march the whole day.

6. At the approach of spring the ships which had sailed in the winter came to the island.

7. Men are not always braver than women.

8. Many of the soldiers were killed by the weapons of the enemy.

9. The enemy attacked the army which had set out from the camp at daybreak.

10. Cyrus was killed as he was attacking his brother.

Exercise 25 [*B*].

REVISION.

1. The Athenians always won many prizes at the games.

2. One thousand hoplites having set out from Plataea marched against the Persians.

3. We ransomed the soldiers who had been captured by the enemy.

4. I had my son taught to speak well.

5. The soldiers were willing to obey the general, and they did not desist from the battle.

6. Three hundred soldiers were killed in the night by the arrows of the barbarians.

7. The women wished to persuade the general to stop the battle, but he would not obey them.

8. Courage always was greatly honoured by the Greeks of old.

9. Money is not less useful to men of the present day than to those of old times.

10. Those who win prizes in the games are sometimes[1] honoured more than those who fight for their country.

---

[1] ἐνίοτε.

Exercise 26 [*A*].

REVISION.

1. The messengers who had been sent to Athens by the King of Persia were put to death by the citizens.

2. Many gifts were being brought in ships from those in the islands.

3. During the winter the ships remained in the harbour, and sailed out at the approach of spring.

4. The king wished to enslave the Greeks who had fought against the Persians.

5. The Plataeans being attacked by the Thebans sent messengers at once to Athens.

6. The soldiers, not having obeyed the general, were put to death.

7. We marched many stades, and reached the city towards evening.

8. We were not willing to ransom the citizens who had betrayed the city to the enemy.

9. Themistocles having fled from Greece to the King of Persia remained with (παρά) him for many years.

10. Jason sailed out wishing to win a great prize.

Exercise 27 [B].

REVISION.

1. The power of the rich is much greater at Thebes than at Athens.

2. The city, not being able to save itself by arms, was saved by the skill of one citizen.

3. Thermopylae was betrayed by Ephialtes, persuaded by a great sum of money.

4. Those who were left fought again on the following day.

5. The Athenians, having freed the islands, were greatly honoured by all the Greeks.

6. In summer the city is less pleasant than in winter.

7. The Persians, having set out from Sardis, attacked Greece with a large army.

8. Men of old gave the greatest honour to those who won prizes in the games.

9. The leaders of the Greeks, having been seized by the Persians, were put to death.

10. Clever speaking is much more useful for orators than for soldiers.

Exercise 28 [A].

REVISION.

1. The slaves were carrying food into the house.

2. Those who said this were condemned by the judges.

3. Having been captured by the Persians, he remained at Sardis for twenty years.

4. They were conquering, but the night stopped the battle.

5. After three days I shall come home bringing many prizes.

6. Men of those times used not to love money more than honour.

7. They were caught while crossing a broad river.

8. I have more friends now than I had then.

9. In spring I always wish to be in Athens.

10. The messengers who came from the king told us these things.

Exercise 29 [B].

REVISION.

1. Those who announce evil tidings are not loved.

2. The army of Demosthenes perished in the river.

3. Greece is distant a journey of many days from Persia.

4. Messengers sent to Cyrus kept asking for money.

5. Archimedes defended his city from the enemy.

6. By bravery we win renown.

7. Fighting is better than staying at home.

8. Poor men do not always obey the rich.

9. Having heard these things, the general led his army quickly towards Thebes.

10. The slaves, having been set free by the soldiers, at once left the island.

GENITIVE ABSOLUTE

17. Just as Latin uses an Ablative Absolute so **Greek uses a Genitive Absolute** ; *i.e.* a participle may be used in agreement with a noun in the genitive case, the whole phrase being independent of the construction of the rest of the sentence.

> *e.g.* οἱ Ἀθηναῖοι ἔπλευσαν ἡγεμονεύοντος τοῦ Νικίου.
> *The Athenians sailed under the leadership of Nicias.*
>
> ληφθέντων τῶν τειχῶν οἱ πολῖται ἐξέφευγον.
> *The walls having been taken, the citizens tried to escape.*

But if the participle can agree with the subject or object of the sentence, the Genitive Absolute must not be used. *e.g.* we must write :

> νικηθέντες οἱ Ἀθηναῖοι ἔφυγον.
> *The Athenians, having been conquered, fled.*

And

> οὐκ ἀπολογουμένους τοὺς Πλαταιέας οἱ Λακεδαιμόνιοι ἀπέκτειναν.
> *As the Plataeans did not defend themselves the Spartans put them to death.*

Note that in Greek, participles may often be used to translate English adverbial clauses, *e.g.* 'When the messengers arrived' may be 'the messengers having arrived,' 'As the army had no food' may be 'the army having no food.' See further page 122.

Exercise 30.

1. When the soldiers arrived they encamped in the market-place.

2. When the army entered the city the citizens fled.

3. They took the messengers and put them to death.

4. The Spartans, under the command of the king, defeated the Athenians.

5. Having marched for many days, we reached a river ninety feet broad.

6. The traitor having been taken was put to death.

7. While we were marching homewards the enemy attacked us.

8. Though they were few, they attacked the enemy.

9. Though we are few, no one despises us.

10. When Cyrus was killed the soldiers fled.

11. We gave back the presents at his bidding.

12. Having ransomed the citizens, we returned home.

Exercise 31 [*A*].

1. The cavalry having been routed, the army retreated.

2. The army, having been routed, fled.

3. Being allowed to escape, they did not remain.

4. When the messengers arrived the king had already died.

5. The city having been betrayed to the enemy, all the men were killed.

6. The army crossed the river when the general ordered them to advance.

7. Having reached the river, the army crossed at once.

8. We remained in the city though we were able to depart.

9. The king being weak, no one was willing to obey him.

10. Having captured the messengers, the Thebans put them to death.

Exercise 32 [*B*].

1. When the Athenians had arrived, the army fought more bravely.

2. Being commanded by the general, the soldiers retreated.

3. The ship having set sail was away for twenty-one days.

4. The ship having already sailed, Socrates was not put to death for nineteen days.

5. The citizens having been condemned, the Spartans put them to death.

6. Being compelled to retreat, the soldiers were ready to march.

7. The soldiers having no food did not wish to attack the enemy.

8. The general did not wish to attack the enemy as the army had no food.

9. Though able to escape, Socrates stayed in the city.

10. When they had entered, the judge asked the slaves many questions.[1]

---

[1] *many questions* = πολλά (n. pl.).

PRONOUNS

αὐτός.

18. (a) αὐτός used by itself in the oblique cases = *Lat.* eum,
eam, id, *etc.*, *him, her, it.*[1]

(b) Used in the Nominative by itself, or used with
nouns (or pronouns) in any case, αὐτός = *Lat.* ipse,
self. In this sense it must not come between the
Article and the Noun.

(c) ὁ αὐτός (αὐτός) = *Lat.* idem, *the same.*

e.g. (a) ἀπέκτεινεν αὐτούς.
He slew them.
ἀφειλόμην τὸ ξίφος αὐτοῦ.
I took away his sword.

(b) αὐτὸς ἀπέκτεινα τὸν βασιλέα.
I myself slew the king.
ἀπέκτεινα αὐτὸν τὸν βασιλέα **or** τὸν βασιλέα αὐτόν.
I slew the king himself.

(c) πάντες τὸν αὐτὸν μισθὸν ἔλαβον.
They all received the same reward.

---

[1] In this sense do not place the Pronoun first in the sentence.

Exercise 33 [A].

1. The king himself gave me the money.
2. They all obey the same master.
3. We ourselves gave the money to the poor.
4. The storm seemed dangerous to the sailors themselves.
5. I gave them the same reward.
6. I consider the citizens themselves traitors.
7. She herself was braver than they.
8. The soldiers themselves flew from the city.
9. The same men do not always say the same things.
10. I myself saw his wife in the house.

Exercise 34 [B].

1. Truth itself is not always pleasing.
2. I received the same reward from the king himself.
3. I sent their money to the king.
4. He himself said it.
5. The rich men gave them the same presents.
6. Who will ransom the general himself?
7. In the same battle the general was killed.
8. They killed the citizens, women and all.[1]
9. I myself sent them to Athens.
10. The son has greater power himself than the father.

---

[1] αὐταῖς ταῖς γυναιξί.
So ἡ ναῦς ἀπώλετο αὐτοῖς τοῖς ναύταις.
The ship perished, sailors and all.

PRONOUNS

19. Demonstrative Pronouns.

οὗτος, *this, that*. It sometimes corresponds to Lat. *iste*.

ὅδε is a more emphatic *this*, generally meaning *this near me*, *this here*, like the Lat. *hic*.

ἐκεῖνος = *that, that yonder*, corresponds generally to the Lat. *ille*.[1]

These three pronouns when used with nouns require the article, but take the Predicative position, *i.e.* they *must not come between the article and the noun*.

e.g.　ταῦτα τὰ δῶρα
　or τὰ δῶρα ταῦτα　} *these gifts.*

　ἐκείνη ἡ νῆσος
　or ἡ νῆσος ἐκείνη　} *that island (yonder).*

　ἥδε ἡ ὁδός
　or ἡ ὁδὸς ἥδε　} *this street here (where we are).*

20. The Article as a Pronoun.—The Article was originally a Demonstrative Pronoun, and one or two uses of it as a Pronoun remained in Attic Greek. The most important was its use with μέν and δέ for 'one . . . the other,' 'some . . . others.'[2]

e.g.　οἱ μὲν ἔμενον οἱ δὲ ἀπῆλθον.
　Some remained, but others went away.

　ὁ μὲν φιλεῖ τὴν δόξαν ὁ δὲ τὸ ἀργύριον.
　One man loves glory, another money.

---

[1] Other differences between these Pronouns are explained on p. 133.
[2] Another use of the Article as a Pronoun is explained on p. 134

21. Possessive Pronouns. These generally require the article

1st *Person.*   ὁ ἐμός, *my*   ὁ ἡμέτερος, *our.*

2nd *Person.*   ὁ σός, *thy*   ὁ ὑμέτερος, *your.*

3rd *Person.*—Attic Greek has no Possessive Pronoun of the 3rd Person, but uses the Genitive of the Reflexive ἑαυτοῦ for *Lat.* suus, *his own,* and the Genitive αὐτοῦ from αὐτός for the *Lat.* eius, *his.*

It is possible in the same way to use the Genitives ἐμοῦ, ἡμῶν, etc., for the Possessives of the 1st and 2nd Persons.

Of these Genitives the Reflexives ἐμαυτοῦ, ἑαυτοῦ, etc., are placed between the Article and the Noun. The rest generally follow the Noun.

e.g. ἀπῆλθον εἰς τὴν ἐμὴν οἰκίαν.
I went away to my own house.

ἀπῆλθεν εἰς τὴν ἑαυτοῦ οἰκίαν.
He went away to his own house.

ἦλθον εἰς τὴν οἰκίαν αὐτοῦ.
They came to his house.

ἀπέλθετε πρὸς τὴν οἰκίαν ὑμῶν or πρὸς τὴν ὑμετέραν οἰκίαν.
Go away to your house.

Exercise 35 [*A*].

1. The general himself was not willing to attack this army.

2. Truth is good, but men do not always love what is good.

3. These masters set their own slaves free.

4. Some had already arrived and others were setting out.

5. The king himself announced these things to all the citizens.

6. He gave them his own horse.

7. I was not willing to take his horse.

8. The Greeks were victorious three times in the same war.

9. The Thebans saved their own city, but they were not willing to fight for Greece.

10. We ourselves always wished to receive the same presents.

11. We all went away to our own houses.

12. I did not wish to give him my own sword.

Exercise 36 [*B*].

1. Some remained in the city and others went out against the enemy.

2. We ourselves willingly gave the poor our own money.

3. Those soldiers are worthy of the greatest honour.

4. He gave the general his sword, but he was not willing to give him his horse.

5. I reported these things to the king himself.

6. I consider these traitors worthy of the same punishment.

7. He gave them his ships and sailors.

8. Some love gold more than honour; others consider this disgraceful.

9. I willingly gave a large sum of money to these poor men.

10. He did not wish to send his son, but he sent a slave.

11. We will give you our gold and you will send us food.

12. That money I myself received from my father.

CONNECTION

22. In writing Greek it is most important to notice the use of Participles and Particles in connecting sentences.

Participles, as in Latin, are mainly used to make several statements in one sentence, where in English we should use several verbs.

> *e.g.* ἀναστὰς ἐξῆλθε.
>> *He got up* and *went out.*
>
> συλλαβὼν τὸν δοῦλον ἀπέκτεινεν.
>> *He arrested the slave* and *put him to death.*

Particles are used to connect sentences and clauses with each other.

The commonest are καί, *and* ⎫
ἀλλά, *but* ⎬ first word.

δέ, *but* or *and* ⎫
οὖν, *therefore* ⎪
γάρ, *for* ⎬ second word.
μέντοι, *however* ⎭

---

[1] Notice that Relative Pronouns are rarely used in Greek, as they are in Latin, to connect sentences.

> **e.g.** *Quae cum ita sint* would in Greek be
> ἐπεὶ δὲ ταῦτα οὕτως ἔχει or τούτων δ' οὕτως ἐχόντων.

. . . μέν . . . δέ are used to point to a contrast between two co-ordinate clauses or sentences.

e.g. τὸ μὲν στράτευμα διεφθάρη, νῆες δὲ δώδεκα ἐξέφυγον.
The army was destroyed, but twelve ships escaped.

(*N.B.*—μέν must not be used unless there is a δέ to follow.)

. . . τε . . . καί, *both . . . and*   ⎫ connect words
οὐ μόνον . . . ἀλλὰ καί, *not only . . . but also* ⎬ or clauses.

e.g. ἀπώλεσεν τούς τε ἵππους καὶ τὰ ὑποζύγια.
He lost both horses and beasts of burden.

βούλεταί τε καὶ ἐπίσταται.
He both wishes and knows.

Exercise 37 [*A*].

The Greek army left the harbour on the following day. When they had sailed for four days in the direction of Lemnos, a storm arose and destroyed five of the ships. Not many of the hoplites in these vessels were saved. On the eighth day, however, they reached Lemnos, and immediately sent messengers to all the cities. Some of the cities were persuaded, and sent five hundred of their hoplites into the Athenian camp. But the rest brought in all their property into the towns and defended their walls.

Exercise 38 [*B*].

The Athenians wished most of all to conquer the citizens of Mytilene, they being the bravest and the richest of all the Lesbians. But when they had attacked the walls of this town three times and had done nothing, they retreated to the place where they had made their first camp. This camp was on a spot where there was no water, and as winter was beginning, the army was already suffering terribly; for their own provisions, brought from Athens, had been in the ships which perished in the storm. It seemed best, therefore, to the generals to return home at once, and start again in the following spring.

Exercise 39 [*A*].

At the approach of spring the army of the Thebans left behind all the baggage and marched out of camp. Having crossed the mountains, they came down into the plain where the enemy were already awaiting them. The soldiers wished to attack at once, but the general thought it safer to wait, the enemy having a strong position. Therefore he sent out the cavalry, wishing to persuade the enemy to fight, but he himself remained with [1] the infantry in the camp. But the enemy, seeing the cavalry advancing, at once came out of their camp and attacked the Thebans with all their force.

---

[1] Say *having*.

Exercise 40 [*B*].

When the Persians reached Marathon, ten thousand Athenians were drawn up on the mountains, under the command of Miltiades.[1] When they were about to attack the Persians, an army of one thousand infantry arrived from Plataea, the other states sending no soldiers. These Plataeans came, being grateful to the Athenians, who had helped them of old. Therefore eleven thousand Greeks were ready to attack the great host of the Persians. It was possible for them to remain in the mountains, but Miltiades ordered them to fall upon the Persians at once, whilst they were disembarking from their ships, and not fearing an attack.

---

[1] Miltiades being general (Gen. Abs.).

INDIRECT STATEMENT

23. Verbs of *saying* and *thinking* are followed by two constructions :

I. Clauses introduced by ὅτι or ὡς (that).　Negative οὐ.

(*a*) **After Primary tenses the verb retains the mood and tense of Direct speech.**

(*b*) **After Historic tenses also the Verb generally retains the mood and tense of the Direct Speech.**[1] **But an Indicative of the Direct Speech may be changed to the same tense of the Optative.**

Notice (1) that the tense of the Direct Speech is never changed ; (2) that *Sequence* in Greek is a sequence of *mood*, not of tense, the Optative practically corresponding to the Historic tenses of the Latin Subjunctive.

(The Imperfect and Pluperfect having no tenses in the Optative are generally kept in the Indicative.)

EXAMPLES.

Direct.　　　ὁ Κῦρος πάρεστι, *Cyrus is present.*

Indirect (*a*) λέγουσιν ὅτι ὁ Κῦρος πάρεστι.

　　　　　　They say that Cyrus is present.

(*b*) ἀπεκρίνατο ὅτι ὁ Κῦρος παρείη ⎰ *He answered*
　　　　　　　　　　　　　　　　　　　⎱ *that Cyrus*
　　,,　　　　,,　　　　,, πάρεστι ⎰ *was present.*

εἶπεν ὅτι ⎰πάρεσται⎰ *He said that he would be present.*
　　　　　　⎱παρέσοιτο⎱

---

[1] This is known as a *Graphic* or *Vivid* Construction, because it keeps as closely as possible to the exact words of the speaker.

E.g. In ' He said that the general was present,' where the exact words of the speaker were ' The general is present,' Greek prefers εἶπεν ὅτι ὁ στρατηγὸς πάρεστι, though εἶπεν is Historic, and we might say εἶπεν ὅτι ὁ στρατηγὸς παρείη.

Exercise 41.

1. The messengers announced that the ships of the enemy were approaching.

2. He replied that the ships would speedily come into the harbour.

3. It is reported that the enemy have fled.

4. They reported that the army had fallen into a marsh.

5. It was reported that Cyrus was dead.

6. They said that the army would not encamp for the night.

7. Say that I will come to their assistance.

8. It was reported that the Athenians were fortifying their city.

9. Demosthenes said that Philip could not conquer the Athenians.

10. Answer that you will not be present yourself.

INDIRECT STATEMENT (*continued*).

24. II. Verbs of *saying* and *thinking* may also be followed by the **Accusative with the Infinitive,** as in Latin.

But in Greek if the subject of the Infinitive is the same as the subject of the principal Verb, it is expressed only where emphasis or contrast is required, and, if expressed, it is in the **Nominative.**

The **tense** of the Infinitive is the same as the tense of the Indicative used by the speaker, the Present Infinitive including the Imperfect, and the Perfect including the Pluperfect.

The Negative with the Infinitive in Indirect Statement is οὐ.

(1) Of the verbs of *saying*, φημί takes only the Infinitive construction, while λέγω and εἶπον prefer a clause with ὅτι or ὡς.

(2) οὔ φημι is used like *nego* in Latin for the English 'I say that . . . not . . .'

EXAMPLES.

ὑπέλαβε τὸν Κῦρον οὐ παρεῖναι.
He answered that Cyrus was not present.
οὐκ ἔφη ἀπιέναι.
He said he would not go away.
ἐνόμιζεν (αὐτὸς) εἶναι κριτής.
He thought he (himself) was judge.

N.B.—The verbs *hope* (ἐλπίζω), *promise* (ὑπισχνέομαι), *swear* (ὄμνυμι), form a class by themselves. They do not

INDIRECT STATEMENT (*continued*).

take Construction I. at all; on account of their sense they generally require the *Future* Infinitive; and the negative after them is μή.

> ὑπέσχοντο μὴ τοῦτο ποιήσειν.
> *They promised not to do this.*

Exercise 42.

Turn all the sentences of Exercise 41 by the Infinitive construction.

INDIRECT STATEMENT (*continued*)

25. Verbs of *knowing* **and** *perceiving* **take a Participle instead of an Infinitive.**

The Participle may belong either to the subject or the object of these verbs and agree with it in case. The negative is *οὐ*.

Thus 'I know that he has arrived' takes in Greek the form 'I know him having arrived,' where the Participle agrees with the object. 'I am conscious that I have made a mistake' takes the form 'I am conscious having made a mistake,' where the Participle agrees with the subject (or with the Indirect Object).

Thus—

οἶδα αὐτὸν ἀφικόμενον.
σύνοιδα ἐμαυτῷ ἁμαρτών (or ἁμαρτόντι).

Also—

ᾔσθετο τῶν πολιτῶν οὐκέτι ἀμυνουμένων.
He perceived that the citizens would resist no longer.

Such verbs are οἶδα, γιγνώσκω, αἰσθάνομαι, μέμνημαι, ἐπιλανθάνομαι, ἀκούω. Many others *may* take this construction instead of the Infinitive, *e.g.* ἀγγέλλω, πυνθάνομαι.

Exercise 43 [*A*].

1. The messenger said that he had not seen the camp of the Persians.

2. I perceived that I had come to the house of my friend.

3. He knew that no one had gone out of the house.

4. He knows that not he himself but his friend is being sought for.

5. The scouts announced that the enemy had fled.

6. He says that the army will not arrive immediately.

7. We saw that the enemy would attack us immediately.

8. I promised not to go into the town.

9. I confessed that I myself did this deed.

10. Aeneas perceived that Troy was burning.

11. I think he spoke the truth.

12. We think it right to honour those who fell at Thermopylae.

Exercise 44 [B].

1. I saw that the city was already burning.

2. They knew that the general himself would be present.

3. The Athenians all declared Aristides to be the justest of men.

4. Miltiades promised to bring money to Athens.

5. They admitted that they had fled from the battle.

6. Who has not heard that Greece was once free?

7. They hoped that no one had seen them.

8. He said that not he himself but his wife had betrayed the city.

9. The prisoners said that they had not done wrong.

10. We thought that we should find you here.

11. They perceived that the gates had been opened.

12. Wise men think that the soul is immortal.

Exercise 45 [*A*].

After this, messengers arrived at Athens saying that the whole army had been destroyed, and that the generals themselves had perished. At first no one believed that this was true. Some said that the messengers were traitors and wished to deceive the people ; others declared that they knew the enemy had been defeated. But at last they perceived that the news was true. They did not however despair, but began to [1] fortify the walls of the city, for they believed that the Spartans, having heard the tidings,[2] would speedily attack them.

Exercise 46 [*B*].

News came to Athens [3] that the Persians had already crossed the mountains, and were advancing into Attica. Many of the chief men speaking in the senate said that they would be unable to defend the city, and that they thought it better to take refuge in the Acropolis ; but on the advice of Themistocles [4] the majority determined to embark on the fleet,[5] for they hoped that there they would be safe, thinking that the ships were the wooden walls spoken of [6] by the god.

---

[1] *Began to fortify*—Imperfect of *fortify*.
[2] The things which had been announced.
[3] It was reported to (εἰς) Athens.
[4] Themistocles advising (Gen. Abs.).
[5] Ships.   [6] εἰρημένα

Exercise 47 [*A*].

REVISION.

1. These things having happened, I think it is better to have no general than this one.

2. I told them plainly that I would not assist them.

3. My house is in this street.

4. They saved the citizens, but destroyed their city.

5. Having captured Athens, the Persians thought they had finished the whole war.

6. When their army has been conquered the Athenians punish the generals.

7. You and I have the same books.

8. He himself does not think that he acted wisely.

9. The ship not having sailed, we can stop it.

10. I think these men themselves are worthy of honour.

Exercise 48 [B].

REVISION.

1. Conon being general, the soldiers thought that they could always conquer the enemy.

2. We promised to set free our own slaves.

3. The general himself said that we could not conquer.

4. He promised to give me his sword.

5. The leaders having been killed, Xenophon was made general.

6. I saw that these ships came from the same harbour.

7. We perceived that we should be captured ourselves.

8. Themistocles himself was willing to help the Persians.

9. Those scouts report that the enemy are crossing the mountains.

10. They said that barbarians would never invade their country.

DIRECT QUESTIONS

26. Single Questions in Greek may be asked in three ways—

1. With Interrogative Pronouns or Adverbs τίς, ποῦ, πῶς, etc.

2. With the Interrogative particle ἆρα.

3. Without any interrogative word at all.

In 2 and 3, if the negative οὐ be used, the question expects the answer 'yes,' like questions asked with *nonne* in Latin.[1] If the negative μή be used, the answer 'no' is generally expected, as when *num* is used in Latin.

> *e.g.* πόθεν ἦλθε;
>> *Whence did he come ?*
>
> ἆρα φιλόσοφός ἐστιν ἐκεῖνος;
>> *Is that man a philosopher ?*
>
> ἆρ' οὐ φιλόσοφός ἐστι;
>> *Is he not a philosopher ?*
>
> ἆρα μὴ φιλόσοφός ἐστι;
>> *He is not a philosopher, is he ?*

27. Double Questions are asked with the conjunctions πότερον ... ἤ ...; but πότερον may be omitted.

> *e.g.* πότερον πλούσιος ἢ πένης ἐστί;
>> *Is he rich or poor ?*

---

[1] Another way of expressing this form of question is by the use of πῶς οὐ. *E.g.* πῶς οὐ φιλόσοφός ἐστι; *Is he not a philosopher ? Surely he is a philosopher* (literally. ' How is he not,' etc.).

28. Deliberative Questions (*i.e.* questions in the 1st person where the speaker asks *what he is to do*) are always put in the subjunctive. They may be preceded by θέλεις, βούλει, etc. The negative is μή.

> *e.g.* [βούλεσθε] εἴπω τοῦτο ; *Shall I say this?   Do you wish that I should say this?*
>
> τί εἴπω ;   *What am I to say?*
>
> μὴ ἀποκρίνωμαι ;   *Am I not to answer?*

The following is a list of the commonest Interrogative Pronouns and Adverbs with the corresponding Relatives and Demonstratives :—

INTERROGATIVE.		RELATIVE.	DEMONSTRATIVE.
Direct.	Indirect.		
τίς ;	ὅστις ; *who?* quis?	ὅς, *who*, qui.	οὗτος, ὅδε, etc., *that, this,* hic, etc.
πόσος ;	ὁπόσος ; *how great?* quantus?	ὅσος [*as great*] *as,* quantus.	τοσοῦτος, *so great,* tantus.
πόσοι ;	ὁπόσοι ; *how many?* quot?	ὅσοι [*as many*] *as,* quot.	τοσοῦτοι, *so many,* tot.
ποῖος ;	ὁποῖος ; *of what kind?* qualis?	οἷος [*such*] *as,* qualis.	τοιοῦτος, *such,* talis.
ποῦ ;	ὅπου ; *where?* ubi?	οὗ, ὅπου, *where,* ubi, qua.	ἐκεῖ, *there* (ibi), ἐνθάδε, αὐτοῦ, *here* (hic).
ποῖ ;	ὅποι ; *whither?* quo?	οἷ, ὅποι, *whither,* quo.	ἐκεῖσε, *thither,* eo.
πόθεν ;	ὁπόθεν ; *whence?* unde?	ὅθεν, *whence.* unde.	ἐκεῖθεν, ἐνθένδε, *thence, hence,* illinc, hinc.
πότε ;	ὁπότε ; *when?* quando?	ὅτε, *when,* quo tempore.	τότε, *then,* tunc.
πῶς ;	ὅπως ; *how?* quomodo?	ὡς, *as,* ut.	οὕτως, ὧδε, *thus,* sic.

Either Direct or Indirect Interrogatives may be used for asking Indirect Questions.

Exercise 49.

Who said that?

How many were present?

What sort of books?

How great is the wall?

Where is the money?

Where did they come from?

Shall I not do this?

Where shall you go?

Whom do you obey?

Whither am I to go?

When did you arrive?

How did you do this?

Did you see him?

Did they not arrive?

Are we to go away?

Did they send **money** **or** ships?

He is not dead, is he?

Where is the harbour?

Do you wish us to remain?

Whose books have you?

Surely he knows this?

Exercise 50 [*A*].

1. Do these citizens obey the king willingly?
2. How many cities in Greece have tyrants?
3. When was it announced that he was dead?
4. Is this the country which you wish to set free?
5. What sort of reward did you promise them?
6. Are not these the fields which you tried to sell?
7. Whither is the army to march?
8. Did they encamp where there was a river?
9. Do you wish to go away or to remain here?
10. How many oxen did you send to the army?
11. How large was the ship in which you came?
12. What am I to ask him?

Exercise 51 [*B*].

1. How many ships were sent by the Athenians?

2. This is the ship in which they came.

3. Who brought the gold from the continent?

4. Did the orator try to save the city?

5. Were there not many oxen in these meadows?

6. We tried to save the citizens whose houses were burning.

7. Surely you did not send your children there?

8. What kind of presents did you give to these boys?

9. Where was that man going to whom you were speaking?

10. Were you trying to save others or to escape yourself?

11. Do you think soldiers or sailors more useful to a city?

12. Do you wish us not to ask?

INDIRECT QUESTIONS

29. The construction of an **Indirect Question** in Greek is the same as that of an Indirect Statement introduced by ὡς or ὅτι [see p. 48], and has the same preference for the *graphic* form.

It is introduced by Interrogative Pronouns and Adverbs (of the Direct, or Indirect form) or by Conjunctions.[1]

The regular negative is οὐ, but after εἰ, and in the second part of alternative questions, μή can be used as well as οὐ.

EXAMPLES.

βούλεται γνῶναι ὁπόσοι ⎫
                 πόσοι ⎭ πάρεισι.

He wishes to ascertain how many are present.

ἠρώτησεν εἰ ὁ στρατηγὸς παρείη ⎫
                          πάρεστιν ⎭

He asked if the general were present.

εἰπέ μοι πότερον τὴν οἰκίαν θέλεις ἔχειν ἢ οὐ ⎫
                                         μή ⎭

Tell me whether you wish to have the house or not.

30. Deliberative Questions becoming Indirect may always remain in the Subjunctive, but after a Historic tense they may become Optative.

Remember that the Subjunctive can only be used in *deliberative* questions, never in other Indirect Questions.

EXAMPLE.

ἠπόρει ὅτι ποιήσῃ ⎫
         ποιήσειε ⎭ *He was at a loss what to do.*

(Direct, τί ποιήσω; Aor. Subj.)

---

[1] εἰ is used to translate *if* or *whether*. ἐάν must never be used.

Exercise 52 [A].

1. I was asking if you were here.
2. He taught me how a book is made.
3. Tell me by what way you came.
4. I am wondering whether we shall find the gates opened.
5. When he died I cannot say.
6. They asked to whom they were to surrender the city.
7. They did not know who would come to their assistance.
8. I asked why this had not been done.
9. I asked where they were fighting.
10. They told me how broad the river was.
11. I asked if no one had come.

Exercise 53 [B].

1. These boys will tell us where the road leads.
2. We tried to find out where the enemy had encamped.
3. Do you know who said that?
4. Tell me if the enemy will attack us or not.
5. It was difficult to discover how great were the numbers of the enemy.
6. We learnt how Spartan boys were trained.
7. We did not know whether these men were friends or enemies.
8. Tell me what I am to answer.
9. We wondered how they could be saved.
10. We are trying to discover if there is not a river here.
11. It is not easy to know if it is better to fight or fly.

Exercise 54 [A].

1. Tell me how you learnt this?

2. The scouts informed the general how large the Persians' camp was.

3. These men told us who were in the house.

4. No one seemed to know where we were.

5. We were asking what he had done.

6. They asked us if we were willing to come to their help.

7. I do not clearly know whether the army had set out or was remaining in the camp.

8. I wonder why they are no longer friendly to us.

9. We learnt why the Spartans were so strong.

10. I do not know whither I am to flee.

Exercise 55 [*B*].

1. I enquired of him why he had fled to the Persians.

2. I cannot tell whither he has gone.

3. They told me how big the city was and how many citizens there were in it.

4. I asked how many archers he had.

5. Ask him whether he hopes to obtain the reward or not.

6. I wondered how they crossed so great a river.

7. I asked the breadth of the river.

8. I wondered how we were to save the fleet.

9. I did not know the greatness of the danger.

10. I am trying to find out who that man is.

11. I tried to find out what kind of a man he was.

Exercise 56 [*A*].

The messengers having returned, the general asked them what kind of a country they had seen. They replied that it was a good land where fruit is gathered from the trees twice in the year, and that there were many rivers in it. When asked if the people had received them kindly, they answered that they had passed through the country and had suffered no harm; but that the people spoke a strange language, and they were not able to understand what they were saying. When the general asked how large the army of this people was, the messengers said they had not seen a soldier in all their journey.

Exercise 57 [*B*].

The ambassadors then informed the king why they had come. They declared that many cities wished to be independent, and they asked him if he were willing to permit this. Therefore the king demanded how many states had already revolted. On learning that few were any longer [1] willing to obey his rule, he became enraged, and asked why no one had informed him of these things before. 'They shall soon learn,' he said, 'how great my power is, for I will destroy all their cities and bring the inhabitants here as slaves.'

---

[1] ἔτι.

Exercise 58 [*A*].

When the ship came near the land, a great many of the inhabitants assembled on the shore and asked the heroes where they came from and what they wanted. They replied that they were going to Colchis in search of the golden fleece.[1] On hearing this, the inhabitants received them kindly, and their king came down to the shore and sent for many oxen and great skins of wine. The next day the heroes sailed away, but a great storm came on and they could not see where they were going. At last, while it was still night, they disembarked on an island, but the inhabitants attacked them, thinking that they were pirates, and many were killed. When the day dawned, the heroes discovered that they had killed the very king who had received them so kindly the day before.

Exercise 59 [*B*].

Medea now knew that her father would never permit her to come home again ; for she had not only deceived him but had shown the stranger how he could steal the golden fleece.[1] She therefore fled with Jason to the Greek ship, taking with her her young brother only. But when the ship had not yet sailed a journey of one day, they perceived another vessel, faster than their own, pursuing them. As this ship drew near, Jason was at a loss what to do, but Medea killed her brother with her own hand, and cast his limbs into the sea, hoping thus to stop the pursuers.

---

[1] πόκος *m*.

31.   GENITIVE CASE AFTER VERBS

1. A genitive of 'the object aimed at or desired' follows such verbs as—

   τυγχάνω, *hit*; ἁμαρτάνω, *miss*; ἅπτομαι, *touch*; ἄρχω, *begin*; ἐπιθυμέω, *desire*; δέομαι, *need*.

2. A genitive of 'separation' follows such verbs as—
   ἀπέχω, *to be distant from*; παύω, *make to cease from*; ἀπαλλάσσω, *separate*.

3. A genitive of the 'ground of accusation' follows verbs of accusing, etc., as αἰτιάομαι, *accuse*. But compounds of κατά, such as καταγιγνώσκω, *to condemn*, take a Genitive of the person, an Accusative of the ground of accusation or the penalty.

   e.g. $\begin{cases} κατηγορεῖν \ τινος \ τὴν \ δειλίαν. \\ αἰτιᾶσθαί \ τινα \ τῆς \ δειλίας. \end{cases}$
   To accuse some one of cowardice.

   καταγιγνώσκειν τινὸς θάνατον.
   To condemn a man to death.

4. A genitive follows verbs implying 'perception' as—
   αἰσθάνομαι, *perceive*; μέμνημαι, *remember*; ἐπιλανθάνομαι, *forget*. ἀκούω, *to hear*, takes a Genitive of the person (the source of sound), an Accusative of the thing heard.

   e.g. ἤκουσα σοῦ ᾄδοντος.
   I heard you singing.

   ἤκουσα τὴν τοῦ ῥήτορος φωνήν.
   I heard the orator's voice.

Exercise 60.

1. They were in want of food.

2. They condemned him for cowardice.

3. They accused him of cowardice.

4. They said they would not listen to him singing.

5. They said they had heard a noise.

6. Remember the things done by your ancestors.

7. They enquired how many stades Marathon was from Athens.

8. They made the Thebans cease from the battle.

9. The separated the cavalry from the hoplites.

10. They forgot the words of their father.

11. The judges passed sentence of death on the traitor.

12. Will they not accuse us of folly?

GENITIVE CASE AFTER VERBS (*continued*).

5. A genitive of 'Price' follows such verbs as—
ὠνέομαι, *buy* ; πωλέω, *sell.*

> *e.g.* ἐπρίατο τοῦτον τὸν οἶκον τριῶν ταλάντων.
> He bought this house for three talents.

6. A **Partitive** Genitive follows—
μετέχω, *share in* ; μεταδίδωμι, *give a share of.*

> *e.g.* μετέδωκέ μοι τοῦ μισθοῦ.
> He gave me a share of the reward.

7. A genitive, which is really **Comparative**, follows verbs
expressing 'superiority to' or 'power over'—
κρατέω, *conquer, be master of* ; ἄρχω, *rule* ;
περιγίγνομαι, *be superior to, overcome.*

8. A genitive of **Cause** follows such verbs as—οἰκτίρω,
pity ; ζηλόω, *envy* ; θαυμάζω, *admire* ; also χάριν ἔχω
or χάριν οἶδα, *feel gratitude, thank* (dat. of person).

> *e.g.* ζηλῶ αὐτὸν τῆς εὐτυχίας.
> I envy him his good fortune.

> χάριν ἔχω τῷ βασιλεῖ τῆς εὐεργεσίας.
> I am grateful to the king for his kindness.

Exercise 61.

1. They forgot the message.

2. Have you sold the house?

3. He promised not to touch the money.

4. I hope to begin the work myself on the fourth day.

5. I am thankful to you for your assistance.

6. They said they would not themselves share in the work.

7. They asked whether I remembered them.

8. Did you not perceive that they wished to condemn him?

9. Nicias was accused by Cleon of cowardice.

10. Give me a share of the money.

11. We envy you your leisure.

12. They desisted from the battle.

13. They bought a house at Athens for 1200 drachmae.

14. Did we not share your danger?

15. I admired him for his bravery.

16. I pitied you for your folly.

DATIVE CASE

32. The following are important uses of the Dative after
Verbs :—

(1) **Dative of Possessor** with εἰμί or γίγνομαι.

  e.g. πολλαὶ νῆές εἰσι τοῖς ᾿Αθηιαίοις.
  The Athenians have many ships.

(2) **Dative after certain Verbs used impersonally.**

  e.g. δοκεῖ, *it seems* (*good*); συμφέρει, *it is expedient*;
  πρέπει, *it becomes*; προσήκει, *it befits*; ἔξεστι, *it
  is possible.*

(3) Dative denoting '**Association with**' or '**Advantage to**'
after such verbs as—

  ἕπομαι, *I follow*; χράομαι, *I use*; ἐντυγχάνω, *I
  meet*; βοηθέω, *I help*; μάχομαι, *I fight*; ἐπιτίθεμαι, *I attack*; πείθομαι, *I obey*; ἥδομαι, *I have
  pleasure in.*

Also notice

(4) **Dative of Respect.**

  πόλις Θάψακος ὀνόματι.
  A city, Thapsacus by name (*called Thapsacus*).

For Dative expressing **Instrument** or **Cause** see page 18.

  „   „   **Place** and **Time** see pages 20 and 23.

Exercise 62 [*A*].

1. We will now go to the help of the allies.
2. It is expedient for you to obey the king.
3. I know that the Athenians have many ships.
4. It is possible for us to attack the enemy, but it is wiser to wait.
5. It seemed good to the generals to send forward the cavalry.
6. We saw that the Persians had many cavalry but few infantry.
7. Are you willing to obey those who took our city by force?
8. They were fighting bravely against the enemy.
9. Apollo had a temple in an island called Delos.
10. We will attack the enemy who are following us.

Exercise 63 [*B*].

1. Socrates had no money but much wisdom.
2. Tell me how many are following us.
3. The Athenians promised to help the Plataeans, but they forgot their promise.[1]
4. To most of them it seemed best to fight at once.
5. It is expedient for us to use the help of the Spartans.
6. By birth he is a Spartan.
7. I shall not try to kill him with the sword.
8. Are we allowed to share in your good fortune?
9. They did not obey the general though he gave the order many times.
10. They fought the same enemy bravely before, and I think they will fight him again.

---

[1] the things promised, τὰ ὑπεσχημένα.

ACCUSATIVE CASE

33. (1) Some Verbs, such as *ask* (αἰτέω), *teach* (διδάσκω), and *conceal* (κρύπτὼ), take **two Accusatives**, one of the Person, the other of the Thing.

> *e.g.* τὸν πατέρα σῖτον ᾔτησεν.
> *He asked his father for food.*

A similar construction is found with κακὰ λέγειν, ἀγαθὰ ποιεῖν, etc.

> *e.g.* κακὰ (or κακῶς) λέγει τοὺς ἐχθρούς.
> *He speaks ill of his enemies.*
>
> ἀγαθὰ (or εὖ) ποιῶ τοὺς φίλους.
> *I do good to (confer benefits on) my friends.*

(2) (*a*) **The Accusative of Respect** limits the meaning of a Verb or Adjective.

> *e.g.* ἀλγῶ τὴν κεφαλήν.
> *I have a pain in the head.*
>
> παρθένος καλὴ τὸ εἶδος.
> *A maiden beautiful in form.*
>
> ὁ ποταμὸς εἴκοσι πόδας εἶχε τὸ εὖρος.
> *The river was twenty feet broad.*

(*b*) Under this head come the so-called **Adverbial Accusatives.**

> *e.g.* οὐδέν, *in no respect*; πολύ, *by far*; τί; *why?* τὸ πᾶν, *altogether*; τἆλλα, *in other respects.*

For the Accusative denoting **Time** and **Space**, see page 23.

Exercise 64 [A].

1. I knew that they had much money.

2. He was an Athenian by birth, but lived at Plataea.

3. Whom did you meet there?

4. Have not the Persians more ships than the Athenians?

5. I concealed the gold from them.

6. For many days they could not use the water.

7. I believe that this river is fifty feet broad.

8. He is in no respect better than his father.

9. He was taught music by a certain Athenian.

10. We were following the guide who had been sent to us.

11. They were willing to do good to their friends, but they tried to injure their enemies.

12. Why did you not ask the rulers for money?

Exercise 65 [*B*].

1. Those who are fighting us are brave.

2. Bring help quickly to the allies.

3. Do not speak evil of rulers.

4. A Spartan called Lysander took Athens.

5. We admire those who speak well of us.

6. In other respects they injured us.

7. He was pleased with the presents which I gave him.

8. Did you use the money which you received?

9. We met him near the city.

10. Having marched many stades, their feet were very painful.

11. We used often to ask the king for pay.

12. They were not willing to do good to us in any way.

Exercise 66.

1. Will you not send help to the Greeks?

2. I think it is expedient for us to obey the laws.

3. Mycenae has no harbour.

4. I ask you whether it is possible for us to overcome the Persians.

5. Having formerly conferred many benefits on the king, I shall not now attack him.

6. Have you forgotten his name?

7. Why do you think it will be easy to conquer this country?

8. He was slain by a man named Harpax, a Thracian by race.

9. He said he had no money.

10. We perceived that three men were following us to the city.

11. They had no house, but were using mine.

12. I wished to know whether the Athenians or the Thebans were in possession of Plataea.

13. It is fitting for a slave to use few words.

14. On the following day he told me that he had already forgotten my words.

15. He says he will not sell it for 150 drachmae.

16. I know that I am in no way superior to him.

COMMANDS, EXHORTATIONS, WISHES

34. *Commands* **are always expressed in the Imperative.**

e.g. μάχεσθε ἀνδρείως, *fight bravely.*

ἐλθέτω δεῦρο, *let him come here.*

Prohibitions (*2nd Person*) **may be expressed either in the Present Imperative or the Aorist Subjunctive.**[1]

μὴ ποίει τοῦτο = *Do not do this habitually.*

         or *Do not go on doing this* (*stop doing this*).

μὴ ποιήσῃς τοῦτο = *Do not do this.*

Negative always μή.

35. *Exhortations* (which are equivalent to commands in the 1st person) **are expressed by the Subjunctive. Negative μή.**

e.g. μαχώμεθα ἀνδρείως, *let us fight bravely.*

μὴ ἀφῶμεν αὐτόν, *let us not release him.*

36. *Wishes for the Future* **are always to be expressed by the Optative** with or without the particles εἴθε or εἰ γάρ. **Negative μή.**

e.g. ἀπόλοιο, *mayest thou perish !*

μὴ γένοιτο, *may it not be so !* or *Heaven forbid !*

εἴθε τοῦ πατρὸς εὐτυχέστερος εἴη.

May he be happier than his father.

---

[1] The *2nd Person Aorist Imperative* must not be used in prohibitions.

Exercise 67 [*A*].

1. Children,[1] obey your parents.
2. Let the slave carry these presents to the king.
3. May the army always be victorious in the war!
4. Let them not think that we are afraid.
5. My son, may you be more fortunate than your father!
6. Let us find out what the others are doing.
7. May they not discover that we deceived them!
8. Do not conceal this money, but give it to the poor.
9. Citizens, do not obey a tyrant.
10. Let us bravely attack the enemy.

Exercise 68 [*B*].

1. Let us ransom those who were captured by the robbers.
2. May he never[2] know that his father was a slave!
3. Let him not try to deceive the general.
4. Basest of men, may you perish miserably!
5. Do not think that courage is easy for all.
6. May he always speak the truth!
7. Let him give back the money which he stole.
8. Soldiers, fight bravely and do not fear these enemies.
9. May you win many beautiful[3] prizes at the games!
10. Do not try to persuade men so foolish.

---

[1] The Interjection ὦ is generally used with Vocatives in Greek.

[2] μηδέποτε.

[3] In Greek *many and beautiful*. So always when a noun is qualified by two adjectives.

NEGATIVES

37. οὐκ and all its compounds are used to negative statements and questions (except deliberative questions). In
commands and wishes μή and its compounds must be used.

In statements, etc.	In commands, etc.	
οὐδείς	μηδείς,	*no one.*
οὐ . . . ποτέ ⎫ οὐδέποτε ⎭	μὴ . . . ποτέ, μηδέποτε,	⎫ ⎬ *never.* ⎭
οὐκέτι	μηκέτι,	*no longer.*
οὔπω	μήπω,	*not yet.*
οὐδέ	μηδέ,	*and not, not even.*
οὔτε . . . οὔτε	μήτε . . . μήτε,	*neither, nor.*

Compound negatives which follow another negative confirm
it, not cancel it as in English.

> *e.g.* μὴ δεῦρο ἔλθῃς μηδέποτε.
> *Never come here again.*

But if the simple negative follows the compound the two
together make an affirmative.

> *e.g.* οὐδεὶς οὐχ ὁρᾷ.
> *Every one sees.*

Exercise 69 [*A*].

1. Never yet have I seen a more powerful army.
2. My son, may you never become a traitor !
3. No one will come here again while we remain.
4. Let them no longer hope to persuade any one.
5. Obey your parents and do not think you are wiser than they.
6. I have not seen either fruit or flowers in this island.
7. Do not be afraid or think that this storm will destroy the ships.
8. O that we may never be more cowardly than the heroes of old !
9. Let none of the Greeks ever believe that there are no gods.
10. Have you not yet heard why the judge condemned them ?
11. My friends, be brave and never despair.

Exercise 70 [*B*].

1. Let no one ever try to persuade me.
2. My friends, no longer try to become rich.
3. Let us not desire either riches or honour.
4. The sailors had not yet landed from the ships.
5. May you never wish to leave your friends !
6. Let these traitors no longer be honoured by the rulers.
7. O that I might see my native land again !
8. No one ever yet found any fruit in this island.
9. Do not hope to persuade one of these barbarians.
10. Citizens, defend the walls and do not yield the city to the enemy.
11. Let no one make any answer to this judge.

INDIRECT COMMANDS

38. Indirect commands and petitions are expressed by the Infinitive as in English.   Negative μή.

> *e.g.* ἐκέλευσεν αὐτοὺς εἰς τὴν οἰκίαν εἰσιέναι.
> *He bade them enter the house.*
>
> παρεκελεύσατο τοῖς στρατιώταις μὴ ἀναχωρεῖν.
> *He exhorted the soldiers not to retire.*

Exercise 71 [*A*].

1. Nicias always advised a general setting out for war not to despise the enemy.
2. The general first[1] exhorted his men to remember the glorious deeds of their ancestors,[2] then[1] bade them charge the enemy.
3. Nothing will induce me to set him free.
4. Philip by this message persuaded the Athenians to make peace.
5. Let us warn Philip not to enter the territory of Olynthus.
6. Themistocles tried to persuade the Greeks not to destroy the bridge.
7. I forbid your using this money.

---

[1] *First . . . then,* πρῶτον μὲν . . ἔπειτα δὲ . . .
[2] The things nobly done by their fathers.

8. The ambassadors of the Samians begged the Athenians to spare their country.

9. I beseech you not to condemn the innocent.

10. I advised you, being so few, not to resist the enemy.

Exercise 72 [B].

1. The general ordered his men to wait no longer, but to charge the enemy boldly.

2. No one could persuade these youths not to journey to foreign lands.

3. I shall advise all my friends to return home.

4. With difficulty the general persuaded the troops not to break the treaty.

5. The other states tried to induce the Thebans not to make peace with the Persians.

6. The authorities at home commanded the general to stop the war.

7. Order the men to return to the ships and not to remain any longer in the town.

8. I could not induce them not to use these books.

9. We vainly tried to persuade the rulers to spare the captives.

10. We do not know why they forbade us to return home.

SUBORDINATE CLAUSES
IN INDIRECT SPEECH

39. Clauses dependent on indirect statements, commands, or questions, follow these rules :—

(*a*) **If the principal verb is Primary, the mood of the verb in the dependent clause is unchanged.**

(*b*) **If the principal verb is Historic, the verb in the dependent clause may be put into the Optative, but frequently the mood of direct speech is retained. The Historic tenses of the Indicative should not be changed to the Optative.**

e.g. Direct. χρῶμαι ταῖς βίβλοις αἷς ἔχω.
I use the books which I have.

Indirect. (*a*) φησὶ χρῆσθαι ταῖς βίβλοις αἷς ἔχει.
He says he uses the books which he has.

(*b*) ἔφη χρῆσθαι ταῖς βίβλοις αἷς ἔχοι.
　　　　,,　　　,,　　　,,　　　,,　　ἔχει.
He said he used the books which he had

Exercise 73 [*A*].

1. He said he would not obey a general who treated the soldiers badly.

2. He ordered them to bring the prisoners whom they had arrested.

3. He said he would lead us to a city where we could get provisions.

4. The young man said he did not like sophists who made a display of wisdom.

5. He asked if we had received the money which he had sent.

6. I will tell him to read the letter which you wrote.

7. The judge threatened to condemn the prisoners whom he was trying.

8. The generals promised to pardon the soldiers whom they had taken.

9. Surely you knew that we should remain where we were?

10. He has been ordered to report what happened.

Exercise 74 [B].

1. I am surprised that[1] he does not read half the books which he has.

2. They were ordered to bring into the camp the provisions which they had found.

3. They said they would not pardon the men who betrayed the city.

4. I have persuaded them to pardon the prisoners whom I considered innocent.

5. Do you think they will condemn to death the young man whom they arrested?

6. I asked them where they had hidden the money which they had found.

7. He declared that he would not remain in the city where his enemies could find him.

8. I know that it is Aristides whom you consider the most upright of the Athenians.

9. We knew that we should reach an island where there were many rivers and mountains.

10. I do not suppose that they will pardon the citizens whom they believe to have betrayed the city.

---

[1] θαυμάζω εἰ μή.

Exercise 75 [*A*].

REVISION.

Erginus, king of the Minyae, made war upon the Thebans and killed a great number of them. He also ordered them to give him every year one hundred cows, and sent messengers to receive[1] them. But Hercules, seeing these messengers, asked them who they were and where they were going. When he heard that they were sent by the Minyae, he told them to return to the city from which they had been sent and not to come again. When they refused, he bound their hands and cut off their ears and noses, bidding them take these as tribute to the king. Then the messengers returned and entreated the king to avenge them ; and Erginus swore that he would destroy the Thebans and raze their city to the ground.

---

[1] Fut. Part.

Exercise 76 [*B*].

REVISION.

Alcmaeon, being commanded by the god to leave his native land, set out, not knowing whither he was going. At Delphi, however, the Pythia told him not to despair because he was sent to another country, but to go to Achelous and ask the river-god to help him. When Alcmaeon came to the river, Achelous asked what he wanted. Alcmaeon replied that he was not allowed by the gods, who wished to punish him, to remain in his own land, and that the foreign lands to which he went were not willing to receive him. Then Achelous commanded the river to bring down sand and earth from the mountains, and in this way made a new land in which he allowed Alcmaeon to live.

Exercise 77 [A].

REVISION.

In the middle of the feast Phineus came into the hall at the head of a large band of his slaves, and said that he would kill Perseus and all who helped him. For he said that Perseus had stolen Andromeda, whom the king had promised to give to himself. Then they fought in the hall, and Perseus slew many of his adversaries; but the fight was not equal, for there were twenty against one.[1] At last, Perseus, drawing forth the Gorgon's head, displayed it to Phineus and his followers, and instantly they were all turned into stone.

Exercise 78 [B].

REVISION.

After this the Trojans came at sunset to the land of the Cyclopes. Here they met a Greek who had been left behind by Ulysses. Aeneas bade him tell who he was and what had befallen him. The man replied that he was one of the sailors who were returning home from Troy after the war, and that when his comrades escaped he alone had been left in the cave of the Cyclops. He begged Aeneas not to leave him in the island, where he ran the risk of being killed or dying of hunger. While he was speaking, the Trojans saw the shepherd Polyphemus coming down to the shore, and taking the suppliant, they speedily embarked on their ship and sailed away.

---

[1] But they did not fight on equal terms—twenty against one.

GPC–G

CAUSAL CLAUSES

40. The Cause of an action is frequently to be expressed in Greek by the Participle [see page 34]; but it may be expressed by Causal Sentences introduced by ὅτι, διότι, ὡς, *because*; ἐπεί, ἐπειδή, *since*.[1]

The Verb in these clauses is regularly in the Indicative; but if the speaker implies that the cause is one assigned by others, the clause is virtually in Indirect Speech and may have its Verb in the Optative if it is after a Historic tense.

Compare in Latin *quod* with the Subjunctive.

e.g. οἱ Ἀθηναῖοι τὸν Περικλέα ἐκάκιζον ὅτι οὐκ ἐπεξῆγεν.

> *The Athenians abused Pericles because he did not lead them out.*

In this sentence the writer gives the cause as his own statement. But if he wished to give it merely as the cause assigned by the Athenians, he would have written ἐπεξάγοι or ἐπεξάγει (which latter form would be marked as Virtual Indirect Speech by *its tense*).

Exercise 79 [*A*].

1. They appointed Cleon general because those who had been appointed before could not take the island.
2. They accused Miltiades because, as they said, he had received bribes.
3. The allies revolted because they were unwilling to pay tribute.
4. They threw away their arms because they could no longer resist the enemy.

---

[1] ὅτι and διότι explain what has *preceded*.

5. He caused these islands to revolt from the Persians as they had treated them badly.

6. For my own part I believe he was angry because he was not appointed general.

7. They were angry with Themistocles for persuading them to leave the city.

8. They were honoured by all because they served the state both in public and private to the best of their ability.

9. The island was reduced because it had revolted from the Athenians.

10. They blamed the general for not giving orders to punish the tribes which had revolted.

Exercise 80 [B].

1. The Milesians revolted because they were oppressed by the Persians.

2. The Milesians revolted on the ground that they were oppressed by the Persians.

3. They do not suffer because they remain in their ranks.

4. He was made general because he had saved the army in the former war.

5. The Milesians resisted bravely because they knew the Persians would not spare them if defeated.

6. A plague sprang up in the Greek army because the gods were angry with them.

7. Since for a long time they gave me no answer, I delayed.

8. Do not reproach him for being unfortunate.

9. Since he did his duty, you ought not to reproach him.

10. Homer praised Agamemnon because he was a good king.

USE OF TENSES IN THE MOODS

41. Except in the Indicative and Participles (and the Infinitive and Optative when these stand in Indirect Speech for the Indicative of the Direct) there is no distinction of time between the Present and Aorist. When they differ, it is only in that the Present expresses the action as *going on* or *repeated*, while the Aorist expresses simply the fact of its occurrence. (Compare the difference between the Imperfect and Aorist Indicative, page 10.)

EXAMPLES.

εἰ γὰρ σὺ λέγοις ὡς ὁ Δημοσθένης.
May you be a speaker like Demosthenes !
ὄλοιο.   *May you perish !*

βούλομαι νικᾶν ἀεί.
I wish always to be victorious.
βούλομαι νικῆσαι τήμερον.
I wish to gain a victory to-day.

N.B.—The Future Optative should only be used in Indirect Speech after Historic Tenses to represent the Future Indicative of the Direct Speech ; and it is more usual to retain the Future Indicative.

e.g. εἶπεν ὅτι τἆλλα αὐτὸς {πράξοι.
πράξει.

He said that he himself would manage the rest.

Exercise 81 [*A*].

1. May we always remain faithful to our king!
2. May the Greeks and Persians immediately desist from the war, and may the peace last for a long time!
3. Let us not now stop the voyage, but let us sail on to the island.
4. The master commanded the slave to give him a sword.
5. Let us not remain here, but go out at once.
6. May he never see his native land again!
7. May this plague never come to our city!
8. Let us kill the slaves who betrayed their master.
9. O that the war would cease and the soldiers remain at home!
10. Let them try to be braver than the men of old.

Exercise 82 [*B*].

1. Let us loose the horses and set out at once.
2. Cyrus commanded the soldiers to remain in the camp.
3. They were all willing to die for their country.
4. We thought that he was dying, but suddenly he stood up.
5. May they never find out that he died (as) a slave!
6. Let us always give money to the poor.
7. O that our soldiers may conquer the enemy in this battle!
8. Tell your slaves to give these beautiful prizes to the boy.
9. They seemed to speak the truth now, but I thought they lied before.
10. Do not now go out of the house, and do not always wish to be seen by the people.

FINAL SENTENCES

42. Purpose may be expressed in Greek in three ways—

(a) **By the particles** ἵνα, ὅπως, **the verb in the Final Clause being in the Subjunctive if the Principal Verb is Primary, in the Optative if the Principal Verb is Historic. Negative** μή.

But, by the 'Graphic Construction' (see page 48), **the Subjunctive may also frequently be used instead of the Optative even after an Historic tense.**

> *e.g.* μάχονται ὅπως τὴν πόλιν λάβωσι.
> *They fight in order to take the city.*
> ἀπέφευγον ἵνα μὴ ληφθεῖεν⎫
> 　　　　　　　ληφθῶσι⎭
> *They were running away that they might not be caught.*

(b) **By the Future Participle. Negative** οὐ.

> *e.g.* ἦλθον λυσόμενοι τοὺς πολίτας.
> *They came to ransom the citizens.*

ὡς **may be used with this Participle, implying that it expresses the alleged purpose or presumed purpose of the subject of the Principal Verb.**

> *e.g.* παρεσκευάζοντο ὡς πολεμήσοντες.
> *They made preparations with the intention of going to war.*

(c) **By the relative** ὅστις **with the Future Indicative even when dependent on an Historic tense. Negative** μή.

> *e.g.* πρέσβεις ἔπεμψαν οἵτινες ταῦτα ἀπαγγελοῦσι
> 　　　τῷ βασιλεῖ.
> *They sent ambassadors to announce this to the king.*

Exercise 83 [*A*].

1. I sent messengers to announce this.
2. You must use all means to deceive Brasidas.
3. Call Brasidas to the Senate that we may consult him.
4. I hope Demosthenes will be here to speak on my behalf.
5. I made haste in order to be present.
6. The victors returned to set up a trophy.
7. We accused him in order that he might not be allowed to leave the city.
8. Three hundred were left to bury the dead.
9. We will go home by another way in order that there may be food for us on the march.
10. We must make the camp bigger, to receive all the allies.

Exercise 84 [*B*].

1. In order not to be deceived, watch Brasidas carefully.
2. That poet wrote in order to win prizes.
3. Send slaves to inform him of these things.
4. They summoned the doctor to attend to him.[1]
5. Themistocles sent ambassadors to deceive the Spartans.
6. He does all this to appear wise.
7. Let us send out scouts everywhere to learn what is going on.
8. We sent messengers to ascertain what had happened.
9. He burnt the ships, so that Cyrus might not cross the river.
10. Send a Spartan to command the army.

---

[1] θεραπεύω with Accusative.

Exercise 85 [*A*].

1. The general sent out messengers to discover where the enemy had encamped.

2. We must advance quickly, that no one may see us.

3. We are come to make peace.

4. Brasidas went to Thrace to fight against the Athenians.

5. In order not to break the truce, the Greeks remained all day in the camp.

6. They said this not to deceive us but to persuade the rulers.

7. Soldiers were sent by the general both to bury the dead and erect a trophy.

8. They accused us falsely, that they might obtain our money.

9. The Spartans destroyed the walls of Athens, that the Athenians might never be powerful again.

10. These ships have come to bring wine and food to Athens.

Exercise 86 [B].

1. Many men went to Delphi to consult the god.

2. Did you not send these men to find out what we were doing?

3. They made a trench and a wall to defend the city.

4. We sent for the doctor, that we ourselves might not seem to have killed him.

5. In order not to receive the presents, he went away from home.

6. We hid the money to deceive the judge.

7. They sent out messengers in all directions to discover where we were.

8. The satrap sent for Alcibiades, to learn what was happening at Athens.

9. We will set out in the ships to discover new lands.

10. He does not often come to Athens, lest the Spartans should consider him a traitor.

VERBS OF FEARING

43. **(1)** **Fear for the Future**—μή or **(if negative)** μὴ οὐ **with Subjunctive or Optative as in the Final construction.**[1]

e.g. δέδοικα μὴ ἁμάρτῃς, $\left\{\begin{array}{l}\text{\textit{I fear you will (may) make a}}\\ \text{\textit{mistake.}}\end{array}\right.$

     ἐφοβούμην μὴ οὐκ [1] $\left.\begin{array}{l}\\ \end{array}\right\}$ *I was afraid he would*
     ἀφίκοιτο (or ἀφίκηται), $\quad$ *not arrive.*

(2) **Fear for the Present or Past**—μή or μὴ οὐ **with Indicative.**

e.g. φοβοῦμαι μὴ ἁμαρ- $\left.\begin{array}{l}\\ \end{array}\right\}$ *I fear you are making a mistake.*
     τάνεις,

     ἐφοβούμην μὴ ἥμαρ- $\left.\begin{array}{l}\\ \end{array}\right\}$ *I was afraid you had made a*
     τες, $\qquad\qquad$ *mistake.*

(3) **Where English uses the Infinitive after** *fear,* **Greek also does.**

e.g. φοβοῦμαι εἰσιέναι, *I am afraid to enter.*

VERBS OF PRECAUTION ('take care,' etc.)

44. These may take construction **(1)** above, but **their commonest construction is** ὅπως **or** ὅπως μή **with the Future Indicative.**

     e.g. ἐφυλάσσοντο ὅπως μὴ κακοὶ φανοῦνται.

     They took care not to appear cowardly.

The governing verb (if it is an Imperative 2nd Person) is usually omitted in this construction, if the dependent verb is also in the 2nd Person.

     e.g. ὅπως ἀνδρεῖοι φανεῖσθε.

     See that you show yourselves brave men.

---

[1] Translate μή by ' lest ' and there will be no difficulty with the negatives after Verbs of Fearing.

Exercise 87 [*A*].

1. I was afraid the judges would condemn him.
2. I am afraid that no one will come to our help.
3. There is danger that they will attack us unexpectedly.
4. They obeyed him, fearing they would be punished.
5. I am afraid I appear very cowardly to you.
6. Take care you do not speak evil of the judges.
7. I wrote it down, for fear I might not remember it.
8. I am afraid he is not becoming more prudent.
9. I was afraid to ask him for money.
10. I was afraid we might suffer the same again.
11. Are you not afraid he will do you some harm?

Exercise 88 [*B*].

1. I am afraid that we shall not be able to return home.
2. They took care that no one should deceive them.
3. We were afraid to march by night.
4. They are afraid that the general is dead.
5. We ought to be on our guard lest the orator should accuse us.
6. We were afraid that they would wish to injure us.
7. We must take precautions that the enemy may not attack us unawares.
8. Were you not afraid that you would lose all the money?
9. I am exceedingly afraid that this is true.
10. Perseus was afraid that his friends would see the Gorgon's head.
11. Do not be afraid to do good to the strangers.

CONSECUTIVE CLAUSES

45. Consecutive Clauses are generally expressed by the Conjunction ὥστε followed by the Infinitive (negative μή): but when stress is laid on the actual occurrence of the consequence, they are expressed by ὥστε with the Indicative (negative οὐ).

EXAMPLES.

οὐχ οὕτω μῶρος ἦν ὥστε ἐκείνῳ πείθεσθαι.

I was not foolish enough to obey him.

οὕτω ταχέως ἔδραμον ὥστε μηδένα αὐτοὺς λαβεῖν.

They ran so quickly that no one could catch them.

They ran too quickly for any one to catch them.

οὐκ ἦλθεν· ὥστε πάντες ἐθαύμαζον.

He did not come, so that all men wondered.

N.B.—(1) ἐφ' ᾧ and ἐφ' ᾧτε, *on condition that*, take either the Infinitive like ὥστε, or the Future Indicative. Negative always μή.

e.g. συνέβησαν ἐφ' ᾧτε $\begin{Bmatrix} ἐξιέναι \\ ἐξίασιν \end{Bmatrix}$ ἐκ Πελοποννήσου.

> *They made an agreement on condition that they should leave the Peloponnesus.*

(2) Notice the use of a Comparative with ἢ ὥστε to represent the English 'too' with an Adjective.

e.g. μεῖζόν ἐστι τὸ κακὸν ἢ ὥστε φέρειν δύνασθαι.

> *The evil is too great for me to bear.*

Exercise 89 [*A*].

1. The Spartans were so poor that they were always willing to receive money.

2. The war came to an end, so that all the soldiers returned home.

3. I will do this on condition that you speak to no one.

4. He was wiser than to speak evil of the judge.

5. They escaped from the house so as not to be burnt.

6. The general was so careless that he often let slip an opportunity.

7. They were too brave to fear death.

8. I will let you use these books on condition that you return them to me quickly.

9. He was so strong that he could himself endure all the hardships.

10. He was clearly a traitor, so that the general gave orders to put him to death.

Exercise 90 [*B*].

1. Few are so bold as not to dread Philip.

2. The army was so afraid that the general did not dare to attack.

3. They made peace on condition that the Athenians gave back the prisoners

4. He is too clever not to know this.

5. Demosthenes spoke so well that he often persuaded the Athenians against their will.

6. The fleet was too weak even to set sail from the harbour.

7. On condition that you give me back the money, I will not accuse you.

8. He is too lazy to learn anything.

9. The danger was so great that the Thebans wished to return home.

10. I hope you will speak so as to persuade them.

11. They brought enough provisions into the town to hold out for three years.

Exercise 91 [*A*].

1. Philip besieged Olynthus so closely that the citizens could no longer get provisions.

2. They tried to obtain allies so as not to fight the Persians alone.

3. He chose the best soldiers to defend the walls.

4. He made his own army weaker so that he might send help to the Thebans.

5. The citizens were so disheartened that they summoned Alcibiades home.

6. The Syracusans were building a new wall so that they might not be surrounded.

7. The Athenians spent so much money at home in the time of Demosthenes that they had no pay for the soldiers.

8. In order to provide pay for the soldiers the Spartan generals begged money from the Persians.

9. To defeat them we must attack them unawares.

10. We are too near the enemy to encamp here.

Exercise 92 [B].

1. Go away quickly so that no one may see you.

2. They were so wise that many came to consult them.

3. The ships were saved, so that all the city rejoiced.

4. We will go to the help of the Spartans on condition that they give us a larger sum of money.

5. Cyrus led a Greek army to overthrow his brother's empire.

6. He was too honourable to speak evil of the judge.

7. He gave a large bribe to the rulers that he might never be banished from the city.

8. They remained at home so that they might not see the enemy enter the city.

9. So good a leader was Xenophon that the Greeks came safely to the sea.

10. So many men had perished that we could not bury the dead.

Exercise 93 [*A*].

One day, when the Cretans were on the seashore offering sacrifices to Poseidon, King Minos begged Poseidon to send him a bull out of the sea, that the Cretans might know how greatly the gods honoured him ; and he promised to sacrifice it to Poseidon. Immediately there came, borne on the waves, a most beautiful bull. But Minos admired it so much that he sacrificed another bull and kept the one which had come out of the sea. Poseidon thereupon punished him by making the bull mad ; he escaped into the forest so quickly that no one could catch him. Then Minos was so terrified that he wished he had kept his word, for he feared that many would be destroyed by the monster.

Exercise 94 [*A*].

Whilst the king was wondering what ne ought to do, Heracles arrived and promised to capture the bull ; for Eurystheus had commanded him to bring it to Thebes. Minos was so rejoiced that he willingly gave him ropes and spears ; and having received these Heracles went out into the forest to seek for the bull. It was not difficult to find him, for he was making so loud a noise that it was heard in all directions. When Heracles approached, the bull ran towards him so swiftly that it was impossible to avoid him. But Heracles, standing firmly, seized his horns and held them so that the bull could not raise his head again. After a short time he became so exhausted that Heracles led him to the city to show him to all the citizens.

Exercise 95 [B].

REVISION.

Thus the Athenian fleet won a victory, and the Lacedaemonians were so disheartened that they no longer tried to besiege Mytilene. But in the battle a great number of the Athenians had perished, and when the Lacedaemonians sailed away many were still seen clinging to the wrecks. The generals therefore, determining themselves to pursue the enemy, left certain ships behind and gave orders that these men should be saved. But a storm immediately arising, the officers of these ships, fearing that their own vessels might suffer harm, sailed away. When the news of this came to Athens the people ordered that the generals should be put on trial, and they were too enraged to listen to their defence. To escape the penalty two of the generals never returned, but those who had returned were put to death.

Exercise 96 [*B*].

REVISION.

After the death of Cadmus many more people came to live in the Cadmea. Here they built many houses, so that at length they made a large city which they called Thebes. The Cadmea became the citadel of Thebes, and the king bade the citizens fortify it with very strong walls, in order that when an enemy attacked the city the inhabitants might take refuge in the citadel. There was once a king of Thebes called Amphion, who sang so beautifully that all things were compelled to obey him, and even the stones used to follow him. Knowing this, he began to sing in the middle of the city, and so many stones came together to hear him sing that in a short time a stone wall was built round the city.

Exercise 97 [*A*]

REVISION.

1. May they never be base enough to betray the city !

2. I was afraid they would come to attack us.

3. Do not suppose that they did not see you.

4. So great was their wisdom that people came to see them from all sides.

5. At the approach of spring we will set out to besiege the town.

6. Those who sought refuge in the Acropolis were too few to resist the enemy.

7. May you never discover who told me this !

8. Let them not fear that we shall do them harm.

9. We sent many messengers to find out where you had gone.

10. I will go to the king on condition that you give me a large reward.

Exercise 98 [*B*].

REVISION.

1. We must be on our guard lest they should deceive us.

2. They were surrounded by the mountains so that they could not escape.

3. Let us fly for refuge to the mountains that the enemy may not catch us.

4. So closely was the city besieged that the citizens could get no provisions.

5. They resisted a long time, so that even the enemy marvelled at them.

6. Do not be afraid to speak.

7. I know that he is ill, and I am afraid he is dead.

8. These men were too brave to fly, and they were all killed.

9. Would that I might perish, so as not to see the enemy in our city.

10. We will spare you on condition that you throw away your arms.

Exercise 99 [*A*].

REVISION.

1. They were ordered to march all day.

2. I am not afraid they will attack us unprepared.

3. The general sent forward cavalry to get information.[1]

4. Let us persuade them not to run[2] into danger.

5. Do not tell me that they have chosen Cleon.

6. Why do you forbid our remaining here?

7. May we always be allies and never enemies!

8. He is too good to do harm to any one.

9. He commanded them to find out how many the enemy were.

10. Take care not to acquit the guilty.

---

[1] To find out what was being done.
[2] *Say* come into danger.

Exercise 100 [*B*].

REVISION.

1. Do not return here.

2. They promised to acquit me on condition that I accused my friends.

3. He exhorted the soldiers not to fear danger.

4. The scouts went forward in order to perceive the enemy approaching.

5. They asked why Cleon was general.

6. Those who returned to Athens were put to death, but those who remained in Asia escaped.

7. I knew the enemy would conquer us.

8. I was afraid the enemy would conquer us.

9. I think that, with Brasidas for general, we shall be victorious.

10. Do you know how long the battle lasted?

CONDITIONAL SENTENCES

46. Conditions may be divided into two classes :—
    A. Conditions relating to the Present or Past.
    B. Conditions relating to the Future.

A. PRESENT AND PAST CONDITIONS.

In these conditions the question of fulfilment is already decided, but we may or may not wish to imply anything with regard to this.   Present and Past Conditions, therefore, fall into two classes :—

(1) **Where we simply assume the condition without implying anything as to its fulfilment.**   Such conditions are—
    'If the well is full, it rained yesterday.'
    'If Gracchus conspired against the state, he was justly slain.'
    'If the gods do base actions, they are not gods.'
    'If you know this, you are wiser than I.'
    'If a triangle has equal sides it has also equal angles.'[1]

The construction of these is—
    Protasis—εἰ **with the Indicative.**
    Apodosis—**generally the Indicative.**[2]
    e.g. εἰ ἐβρόντησε, καὶ ἤστραψεν.
    If it thundered, it also lightened.

(2) **When we imply that the condition is not or has not been fulfilled.**
    'If you were not helping us, we should not try.'

---

[1] Observe that all hypotheses in Euclid are of this kind.   They simply assume a certain condition for argument's sake, and show what the result is if the condition be fulfilled.

[2] But the apodosis may often take the form of a command, a wish, or a question.

'If he had taken my advice, he would have recovered.'
'If he had taken my advice, he would now be well.'
The construction of these is—

Protasis—εἰ with a Past tense of the Indicative.

Apodosis—A Past tense of the Indicative with ἄν.

The Aorist is to be used of a simple occurrence in Past time, the Imperfect of the Present time or of an act continued or repeated in Past time.

e.g. εἰ μὴ ἐπλούτουν οὐκ ἂν ἦρχον.

If I were not rich, I should not be ruling.

εἰ ἥμαρτον ἀπέθανον ἄν.

If I had made a mistake, I should have been put to death.

εἰ εὖ ἐπαιδεύθης, οὐκ ἂν ἠγνόεις.[1]

If you had been well educated, you would not be ignorant.

B. Future Conditions.

We may state Future Conditions in two ways :—

(1) **We may make a distinct supposition of a future case—**
'If he does this,' *or* 'If he shall do this.'
The construction is—

Protasis—ἐάν with the Subjunctive or *less frequently* εἰ with the Future Indicative.[2]

Apodosis—naturally a Future Indicative.[3]

e.g. ἐὰν ζητήσῃς εὑρήσεις.

If you seek you will find.

εἰ κλέψεις δίκην δώσεις.

If you steal you will be punished.

---

[1] In this example the protasis contains a condition relating to the *Past* (and hence uses the Aorist), while the apodosis expresses what would have been the *Present* consequence (and hence uses the Imperfect).

[2] As being a stronger and more precise form of expression, εἰ with the Future Indicative is especially used in threats and warnings.

[3] But the apodosis may often take the form of a command, a wish, or a question.

(2) We may put the case less vividly, more 'remotely,' *i.e.* in a form which represents the condition as less likely to be fulfilled—'If he should do this,' *or* 'If he were to do this,' *or* 'If he did this.'

> *Protasis*—εἰ with the Optative.
>
> *Apodosis*—Optative with ἄν.
>
> *e.g.* εἰ ζητοίης, εὕροις ἄν.
>
> *If you were to seek, you would find.*

Further Examples of Conditionals—

A. (1) εἰ τάδ' ἀγνοεῖς, κακῶς ἐπαιδεύθης.

> *If you do not know this, you were badly educated.*
>
> εἰ πέπραχε τοῦτο, καλῶς ἕξει.
>
> *If he has done this, it will be well.*

(2) εἰ ταῦτα ἤκουσε, τὰ αὐτὰ ἂν ἔπραξε.

> *If he had heard this, he would have done the same.*
>
> εἰ τότε ἔζης, καὶ σὺ τὸν Περικλέα ἂν ἐθαύμαζες.
>
> *If you had been living then, you too would have been an admirer of Pericles.*
>
> εἰ τότε ἐν τῇ Περσικῇ ἔζης, τῷ σεισμῷ ἂν ἀπέθανες.
>
> *If you had been living in Persia at that time, you would have been killed by the earthquake.*

B. (1) ἐὰν ἔλθῃς νῦν, πότε ἔσει οἴκοι;

> *If you go now, when will you be at home?*
>
> εἰ ταῦτα λέξεις κακὸς φανεῖ.
>
> *If you are going to say this, you will appear a coward.*

(2) οὐ γὰρ ἄν με ὁ βασιλεὺς ἐπαινοίη, εἰ ἐξελαύνοιμι τοὺς εὐεργέτας.

> *For the king would not praise me if I banished my benefactors.*
>
> εἰ ταῦτα λέγοις, κακὸς ἂν φαίνοιο.
>
> *If you were to say this, you would appear to be a coward.*

Exercise 101.

1. If you say this you are ignorant.

2. If you do this you will suffer.

3. If you had done this you would have suffered

4. If you were to do this you would suffer.

5. If you had done this you would be suffering.

6. If they come I shall see them.

7. If they had come I should have seen them.

8. If they said this they were mistaken.

9. If I do not see you I will write.

10. If I had seen you I should not have written.

11. If I were not here they would have written.

12. If I were to see them I should not write.

Exercise 102 [A].

1. If the army had not arrived the city would have been taken.

2. If we do not march at once the city will be taken.

3. If I had been present myself these things would not have happened.

4. If there are gods there are also works of gods.

5. If they had been acting thus they would not now be safe.

6. If I write to you, set out at once.

7. If this is so I was mistaken

8. If they were to come we should all rejoice.

9. If they do not come, let us keep the gifts ourselves.

10. If you had been present no one would have dared to speak.

Exercise 103 [*B*].

1. If they send Brasidas they will defeat the Athenians.

2. If Brasidas had not been in Thrace the Athenians would have been victorious.

3. If he said that, he lies.

4. If Demosthenes had been speaking I should have listened.

5. If you were to speak I should listen.

6. If you do not come at once I shall not wait.

7. If this was the case they were cowards.

8. If the messengers had arrived, all would have been well.

9. If you plotted against the city you would be banished.

10. If you plotted against the city you were a traitor.

Exercise 104 [*A*].

1. We shall acquit you if you accuse your comrades.

2. If you had not banished Alcibiades, Athenians, you would not be suffering these evils.

3. If Philip took Potidaea without our help, is he not able also to take Olynthus?

4. If a Spartan were to do such a thing, he would be punished.

5. It will be best for us if Philip opposes us at Pydna.

6. If he said that, he made a mistake.

7. If you have any one able to give better advice, choose him general.

8. If he were to learn where this money is hidden he would steal it.

9. If I knew, I would tell you.

10. If I had not sought for it I should never have found it.

Exercise 105 [B].

1. If you help this man, you will appear base.

2. You would be very unjust if you blamed me.

3. If Harmodius slew the tyrant he benefited the Athenians.

4. If Philip is now master of Thermopylae, he is able to march without hindrance [1] into Attica.

5. The Athenians will be glad if Alcibiades be banished.

6. If you had been taught by Socrates you would not think thus.

7. If peace were made all would be well.

8. If they have received my letter they will welcome you as a friend.

9. If they had not guarded the gates, the city would have been taken.

10. If you are ready at dawn, we will start then.

---

[1] No one hindering.

Exercise 106 [*A*].

A herald went through the city making the following
proclamation to the Thebans :—'If any one dares to bury
Polynices or any of the Argives, he will be put to death.'
But Antigone, the sister of Polynices, loved her brother so
dearly that she resolved to disobey the king, even if she
should lose her life by doing this. Therefore in the night
she went out and buried the body. When the king learnt
what she had done he was very angry, but still he would
have pardoned her if she had been willing to confess that
she had done wrong. But she boldly said, 'If I have acted
rightly, I am not afraid to die.' Then the king, growing
still more angry, commanded his guards to shut her up in a
cave that she might die of hunger.

Exercise 107 [*B*].

Then Demosthenes came forward and spoke as follows :—
'Athenians, if you send ambassadors to Philip to ask for
peace, you will only increase our present danger ; for he
will perceive that you are afraid of him, and will therefore
have greater hopes of conquering you. But why do you
fear him? If he were as powerful as you suppose, he would
have conquered all his other enemies and would be marching
against you. But as it is, he is surrounded on all sides
by enemies, and even if he conquers them his army will
be much weaker than before, so that we shall be able to
attack him with confidence. Do not therefore despair, but
fortify the city as strongly as possible, and collect more
forces to fight against the common enemy of Greece.'

Exercise 108 [A].

Had they not trusted Alcibiades there would have been a panic in the town. But Alcibiades called the garrison together and spoke as follows :—'Comrades, you have heard by what disaster Athens has lost her fleet. It is for us[1] now to consider what it is most expedient for us to do. If I were still your general I would command you. But, as things are now, I can only advise you to take service under the Thracian for the present. If any one of you is in want of money immediately, let him ask for it, and if the opportunity ever comes I will show my thanks to you by gifts many times greater. May you, under some more fortunate general, yet render service to[2] the Athenians and all Greece.'

Exercise 109 [B].

When the army had been drawn up for battle, the general thus addressed the soldiers : 'If we were now about to fight in a foreign country to increase our own possessions, the gods would perhaps be on the side of the enemy. But if the gods help men who are defending their native land, they ought now at least to be helping us. In the days of our fathers the Greeks would never have conquered the Persians if the gods had not been on their side ; and our present enemies have shown themselves even more impious than the Persians. If, then, we fight bravely, believing that the gods themselves will help us, we shall conquer.'

---

[1] ἡμέτερόν ἐστι.   [2] help.

PARTICIPLES

Certain usages of Participles have been already described on pp. 12, 34, 52, and 94.

To these we may add the following :—

47. The Participle used to express the **cause or ground of an action** is frequently emphasised by ἄτε, *inasmuch as,* or ὡς, *on the ground that.* The latter implies that what is stated by the Participle is given as the thought or statement of the subject of the principal verb. **Negative** οὐ.

> *e.g.* ὁ Κῦρος ἄτε παῖς ὢν ἥδετο τῇ στολῇ.
>
> *Cyrus, as being a child, was delighted with the dress.*
>
> τὸν Περικλέα ἐν αἰτίᾳ εἶχον ὡς πείσαντα σφᾶς πολεμεῖν.
>
> *They blamed Pericles on the ground that he had induced them to go to war.*

48. The Participle may be used as a substitute for the **protasis of a Conditional sentence. Negative** μή.

> *e.g.* τοῦτο μὴ ποιοῦντες (= εἰ μὴ τοῦτο ποιοῖεν) οὐκ ἂν εὖ πράττοιεν.
>
> *Unless they did this they would not prosper.*

49. The Participle may be used concessively. In this sense it is frequently emphasised by καί or καίπερ. **Negative** οὐ.

> *e.g.* ἐποικτίρω αὐτὸν καίπερ δυσμενῆ ὄντα.
>
> *I pity him though he is my enemy.*

Where '*although*' means '*even if,*' introducing a condition and not an admitted fact, it should be translated by καὶ εἰ or καὶ ἐάν with the suitable form of conditional sentence.

50. Comparative Clauses are expressed by ὥσπερ, *as if,* with the Participle. **Negative** οὐ.

e.g. οὐκ ἐθέλετ' ἀκούειν, ὥσπερ ἤδη εἰδότες.

 You are unwilling to listen, as if you knew it all already.

51. The Participles ἔχων and ἄγων are constantly equivalent to the English *with.*

e.g. ἀφίκετο ἄγων (ἔχων) τριακοσίους ὁπλίτας.

 He arrived with 300 *hoplites.*

Notice that a Participle follows these verbs :—φαίνομαι, *I appear* ; χαίρω and ἥδομαι, *I am pleased* ; παύομαι and λήγω, *I cease* ; ἄρχω, *I begin* ; διατελέω, *I continue* ; τυγχάνω, *I happen* ; λανθάνω, *I remain hid, escape notice* ; φθάνω, *I anticipate.*

e.g. φαίνεται σοφὸς ὤν.	*He is manifestly wise.*[1]
διατελεῖ ὀργιζόμενος.	*He continues angry.*
ἔτυχεν ἐλθών.	*He happened to have come.*
ἔφθασεν ἡμᾶς ἀφικόμενος.	*He arrived before us (He anticipated us arriving).*
ἔλαθεν αὐτοὺς φυγών.	*He escaped without being seen by them {He was hidden escaping).*
ἔλαθεν (ἑαυτὸν) ποιήσας.	*He did it unawares.*

The last two verbs may also have their construction inverted, *e.g.* ἀφίκετο φθάσας, ἔφυγε λαθών.

---

[1] *i.e. Being wise he is made manifest.* φαίνεται σοφὸς εἶναι has a slightly different sense, ' he appears to be wise.'

Exercise 110 [*A*].

1. We happened to be present while the orator was speaking.
2. They ceased from fighting at the command of the general.
3. They escaped from the city without being observed by the guards.
4. They were put to death on the charge of plotting against the city.
5. It is our duty to obey the king although he is not always just.
6. We reached the city first.
7. We pardoned him because he did not know what he was doing.
8. The general advanced with an army of 12,000 men.
9. They killed all the prisoners, and that too though they knew they were innocent.
10. We got to the mountain before the enemy

Exercise 111 [*B*].

1. This boy came in first in the race.[1]
2. The ships came into the harbour without being seen by the enemy.
3. The Athenians blamed Miltiades on the ground that he had received bribes.
4. As he was a boy, the judges pardoned him.

---

[1] *say* running.

5. Those who happened to hear him were greatly surprised.

6. We dismissed the prisoners, and that too though we knew they had plotted against us.

7. They blamed the generals for not saving the sailors.

8. They said this as if they knew that we should believe them.

9. They ceased from the war because both the generals had been killed.

10. The slaves came with many splendid presents from the king.

Exercise 112 [*A*].

1. I was delighted to welcome your friends.

2. Though he was not my brother I treated him as if he were.

3. Why do you keep on asking me the same questions?

4. He was plainly very much ashamed.

5. He came to me with no money ; but I gave him all that he needed because he was my father's friend.

6. If you stop threatening me I will listen to you.

7. They banished Thucydides on the ground that he had lost Amphipolis by his carelessness.

8. The Athenians and Spartans began striving for the leadership of the Greeks in the time of Cimon.

9. They happened to have sent the fleet to Lemnos.

10. Get there before him, if you can.

Exercise 113 [*B*].

1. He continued to live at Athens though he was hated by all the citizens.

2. They were put to death on the charge of plotting against the government.

3. I believe that Brasidas and his men will reach the city first.

4. Although the Athenians knew that Aristides was just, they were not pleased at always hearing this.

5. They escaped unobserved from the city and embarked in the ship.

6. We all rejoiced to hear that you had arrived safely.

7. They carefully preserved the shield as it had been sent by the gods.

8. The general resolved to advance cautiously though the enemy had left their camp.

9. They were plainly Greeks, though we could not understand what they said.

10. We reached the mountains before the enemy, and pitched our camp in a strong position.

Exercise 114 [*A*].

When many years had passed, there came a messenger to Thebes to tell Oedipus that King Polybus was dead, and to beg him to return to Corinth and be king of the city. But Oedipus would not return on account of the oracle ; for though the king was dead, the queen was still alive, and he feared that some madness might compel him to desire to marry her. He told this to the messenger, who happened to be the herdsman who had found Oedipus in the forest when he was a child. Then the old man, as if he were doing the king a service, informed him that he was not the son of Polybus, but had been found on Mount Cithaeron with his feet tied [1] with a string.

Exercise 115 [*B*].

When Jocasta heard this, she perceived that Oedipus was her son ; and when Oedipus began to enquire about his father, he found out that he was the king whom he had himself killed. Then because he could no longer bear to see his mother, he put out [2] his own eyes, and his mother went to her room and died by her own hand. [3] Thereupon the Thebans banished him, on the ground that if he remained all the citizens would suffer. Oedipus, after wandering for many years in company with his daughter Antigone, at last came to Athens, where he continued to live for the future.

---

[1] tied as to his feet.   [2] ἐκκεντέω.   [3] αὐτοχειρί.

IMPERSONAL VERBS

52. The following verbs take the Dative and the Infinitive :—

δοκεῖ μοι	*it seems (good) to me, I am resolved.*
πρέπει μοι	*it becomes me.*
προσήκει μοι	*it concerns me.*
συμφέρει μοι	*it is expedient for me.*
λυσιτελεῖ μοι	*it is profitable for me.*
ἔξεστί μοι ⎱ πάρεστί μοι ⎰	*it is possible for me, I may.*

δεῖ and χρή (Imperf. χρῆν or ἐχρῆν), *it is necessary* (*I ought* or *I must*), take the Accusative and the Infinitive.

χρὴ ἡμᾶς ταῦτα δρᾶν	*we ought to do this.*
χρῆν ἡμᾶς ταῦτα δρᾶν	*we ought to have done this.*

The following take the Dative of the Person and Genitive of the thing :—

μέτεστί μοι τούτου	*I have a share in this.*
μέλει μοι τούτου	*I care for this.*
μεταμέλει μοι τούτου	*I repent of this.*

ACCUSATIVE ABSOLUTE

53. The Impersonal Verbs use an Accusative Absolute, in the Neuter Singular, instead of a Genitive.

e.g. ἐξὸν ἀπιέναι προείλοντο μένειν.

> *It being permitted* (leave being given) *to go away, they preferred to stay.*

So δέον λαβεῖν τὴν πόλιν.

> *It being necessary to take the city.*

δόξαν or δεδογμένον λαβεῖν τὴν πόλιν.

> *It having been determined to take the city.*

ἀδύνατον ὂν σημῆναι.

> *It being impossible to signal.*[1]

---

[1] Also παρόν, *it being possible.*
προσῆκον, *it being fitting.*
παρασχόν, *an opportunity offering.*
εἰρημένον, *it having been stated* or *laid down.*

Exercise 116 [*A*].

1. I hope you repent of your folly.
2. It being necessary to retreat, the soldiers set out at once.
3. These men ought not to have a share in the plunder.
4. We marched with all speed, as it had been resolved to encamp early.
5. Although it was possible for them to ransom the king, they left him in the foreign land.
6. You ought to have given them what they asked.
7. As it was impossible to advance on account of the snow, they halted.
8. I think it is to our advantage to give back the prisoners.
9. The orator spoke as if it were necessary to give up the city.
10. Themistocles wished to equip a fleet on the ground that it was impossible to resist the Persians by land.

Exercise 117 [*B*].

1. We have no part in this matter.
2. Do you not repent of what you have done?
3. He went away after hearing this, as if it was not necessary for him to answer.
4. Surely you ought to have come to our help with a large force?
5. He clearly thought that his friends had resolved to wait.
6. I advised them to surrender on the ground that it was impossible to hold out any longer.
7. I suppose this is not wrong, but I say it is not expedient for us.
8. The Romans were all killed, although they might have escaped.
9. If we have no share in the booty we will never fight again.
10. Let us fight bravely now that we have an opportunity of saving our country.

VERBAL ADJECTIVES

54. The verbal adjective in -τέος implies **necessity.** It has two constructions, Personal and Impersonal. **The Agent is expressed by the Dative.**

(*a*) In the **Personal Construction** the form -τέος, -τέα, -τέον is used. This (like the Latin Gerundive) is always **passive,** and can therefore be used **only with transitive verbs.**

> *e.g.* ὠφελητέα ἐστιν ἡμῖν ἡ πόλις.
> *We must help the city.*

(*b*) In the **Impersonal Construction** the forms . . . τέον (neuter singular of . . . τέος) and sometimes . . . τέα (neuter plural) are used, with ἐστί expressed or understood. This construction is active in sense, and **the objects are in the case governed by the verb.**

> *e.g.* ταῦτα ἡμῖν ποιητέον ἐστίν.
>
> *We must do this* (Note that ταῦτα is the direct object of ποιητέον).
>
> βοηθητέον ἡμῖν ἦν τῇ πόλει.
> *We had to help the state.*

55. The construction (*b*) is equivalent to δεῖ or χρή (*it is necessary*) with the Accusative of the person and the Infinitive. Thus ταῦτα ἡμῖν ποιητέον ἐστί might equally well be rendered δεῖ ἡμᾶς ταῦτα ποιῆσαι.

Exercise 118 [*A*].

1. We must not give up our allies to the Athenians.

2. He told the soldiers that they must not despise the enemy.

3. A share of the booty must be given to the allies.

4. He had to give his daughter in marriage to a poor man.

5. You must not give away so large a sum of money.

6. Surely we must honour those who died on behalf of their country.

7. The general announced that a start must be made at once.

8. They knew that they must undertake the matter themselves.

9. The captains passed the word along that the army was to go to the help of the allies.

10. The Athenians had been told that they must leave their city, and remove to Salamis.

Exercise 119 [B].

1. We must all give up our possessions.

2. We had to remove so as not to fall into the hands of the enemy.

3. The garrison were informed that the city must be surrendered.

4. You must sell your house to provide bread.

5. They were told that they must bring food and clothes for the strangers.

6. They had to set out at once to reach the island in time.

7. As he was once my guest, I thought I ought to help him.

8. They were aware that they must either betray the city or be killed.

9. Word was passed along the lines that an attack was to be made immediately.

10. The men of old, who won this great empire for us, must always be held in honour.

PRONOUNS

(Before this Lesson pages 38-41 should be revised.)

56. Reflexive.

The usual Reflexive of the 3rd person is ἑαυτόν. The Reflexive ἕ with its plural σφᾶς should only be used in a subordinate clause referring to the subject of the Principal Verb.

> *e.g.* ἀπέκτεινε τοὺς ἑαυτοῦ παῖδας.
>
> *He killed his own children.*
>
> ἤροντο διὰ τί σφίσιν οὐκ ἐβοηθήσαμεν.
>
> *They asked why we had not come to their help.*

57. Demonstratives.

Besides the difference explained on page 40, observe that when οὗτος and ἐκεῖνος are opposed they frequently mean ' the latter,' ' the former,' respectively ; and when οὗτος and ὅδε are opposed, they frequently mean ' the preceding,' and ' the following.'

> *e.g.* τῶν στρατηγῶν ἐκεῖνος μὲν ἀνδρειότερος ἦν, οὗτος δὲ εὐτυχέστερος.
>
> *Of the generals, the former was more brave, the latter more successful.*
>
> ὁ μὲν ταῦτα ἤρετο, ὁ δὲ τάδε ἀπεκρίνατο.
>
> *The one asked this, and the other answered as follows.*[1]

---

[1] There is the same distinction between τοσαῦτα and τοσάδε, and between οὕτως and ὧδε.

2. On page 40 the use of the Article as a Pronoun ὁ μὲν ... ὁ δέ, etc., has been explained. It is also used as a Pronoun when ὁ δέ, *but he*, or οἱ δέ, *but they*, begins a sentence; the Article in this phrase must refer to some person or thing mentioned in the previous sentence but not the subject of the previous sentence.

> *e.g.* οἱ Πέρσαι τῶν Μιλησίων ἐκράτησαν· οἱ δὲ μετῴκησαν.
>
> The Persians conquered the Milesians, and they (*the Milesians*) migrated.

Also observe the phrase πρὸ τοῦ, *before that*.

58. Relatives.

The Relative ὅς is equivalent to the Latin *qui*, but cannot be used interrogatively.

The word ὅστις is both a General Relative (Latin *quicunque*, whoever) and an Indirect Interrogative, *i.e.* it is used in asking *Indirect* questions.

59. Attraction of the Relative.

Where the Relative would naturally be Accusative, and the antecedent Genitive or Dative, the latter frequently attracts the Relative to its own case.

> *e.g.* ἐχρῆτο ταῖς βίβλοις αἷς εἶχεν.
>
> He used the books he had.

Or still more commonly—

> ἐχρῆτο αἷς εἶχε βίβλοις.

Sometimes when the antecedent ıs governed by a Pre position, the antecedent is omitted and the Preposition governs the Relative.

> *e.g.* ἐξήγγειλεν αὐτῷ περὶ ὧν ἐποίει.
>
> He informed him of what he was doing.

60. Other Pronouns.

Greek has a Reciprocal ἀλλήλους, *one another*, but may also use ἄλλος . . . ἄλλον like the Latin *alius* . . . *alium*. *e.g.* ἄλλος ἄλλῳ ἔλεγεν, *one was saying to another*. Like Latin, it also used such contracted phrases as ἄλλος ἄλλο λέγει, *one says one thing, another says another thing*; ἄλλοι ἄλλοθεν, *some from one place, others from another*.

$\begin{cases} \text{ἄλλος} = \text{Lat. } alius, \text{ one of any number.} \\ \text{ὁ ἕτερος} = \text{Lat. } alter, \text{ one of two.} \end{cases}$ (In this sense it must always have the article.)

οἱ ἕτεροι = one of two *parties of people*.

ἕκαστος = Lat. *quisque*, each of any number.[1]

ἑκάτερος = Lat. *uterque*, each of two (taken singly)

ἑκάτεροι, each of two parties.

ἀμφότεροι = Lat. *ambo*, both (taken together).

οὐδέτερος
μηδέτερος $\Big\}$ = Lat. *neuter*, neither.

61. Position of Pronouns.

When used with Nouns, οὗτος, ἐκεῖνος, ὅδε, ἑκάτερος, ἀμφότεροι, regularly take the Predicative position, the rest the Attributive position.

e g. ἥδε ἡ χώρα, *this country*.

ἀμφότεροι οἱ στρατηγοί, *both the generals*.

ἡ τοιαύτη χώρα, *such a country*.

The position taken by αὐτός is explained on p. 38 ; that taken by Possessive Genitives ἑαυτοῦ, ἐμοῦ, etc., on p. 41.

---

[1] Notice καθ᾽ ἕκαστον, *singly, each by himself*; ὡς ἕκαστος or ὡς ἕκαστοι, *each by himself*.

Exercise 120.

1. Tell us who said that.

2. I know the man to whom you were speaking.

3. They knew why the citizens hated them.

4. They were both condemned to death, the one justly, but the other unjustly.

5. Before this most of the soldiers had gone away.

6. Some ships came from one harbour, some from another.

7. Neither of these two men is worthy of honour.

8. That is the man whose sons you killed.

9. Tell me about what you heard.

10. Each of the two armies was defeated.

11. Each of the soldiers received a reward.

12. I gave him back his sword

13. They did not obey their own king.

14. We ransomed the citizens, and they came home at once.

15. Wise men should honour one another.

16. We cannot defeat so great a force.

17. Having heard this, he replied as follows.

18. Nicias and Demosthenes were both generals of the Athenians, but the latter was more successful than the former.

19. Let us ask them each by himself.

20. I cannot tell what your friends will say.

Exercise 121 [A].

1. The soldiers were unwilling to obey either of the two generals.

2. When the friends reached the river one crossed and the other went back.

3. We gave him a large sum of money, and he immediately went away.

4. Such soldiers are not capable of bearing hardships.

5. They promised to reward the man who had brought them food.

6. The general came to such a pitch of boldness that he was always ready to fight.

7. In the Senate one party voted for war, the other to keep peace.

8. Before this each of the soldiers received three obols a day.

9. The enemy, advancing at a run, charged both wings simultaneously.

10. I informed the general about what I had heard in the camp.

11. This was what Demosthenes said; and Aeschines replied as follows.

12. Hannibal and Alexander were both great generals, but the latter was more fortunate than the former.

13. When day dawned the survivors looked at one another, wondering how many were still alive.

Exercise 122 [B].

1. One of the brothers became king, the other was killed.

2. Though both my sons were dear to me, I esteemed the elder more highly.

3. Before this we believed that both the towns had been destroyed.

4. We gave them food when they were hungry, and they were always grateful to us.

5. Each of the sailors received a large reward from the state.

6. They declared that they were grateful to us for what we had done.

7. They promised to go away if we gave them money.

8. When one of the two orators had spoken thus, the other replied as follows.

9. They reached such a degree of cowardice that they were afraid even of these barbarians.

10. Tell me who gave you the present which you value most highly.

11. Of these Greeks the former was the wiser, the latter the more successful.

12. As the night was dark the soldiers were wounding one another.

PREPOSITIONS

[*A table of Prose usages of Prepositions is given in the Appendix,* page 233.]

Exercise 123.

After this.

On account of this.

In addition to this.

To fight on horseback.

For the sake of money.

Down from the mountain.

According to law.

Contrary to law.

Along the river.

Without hope.

Every ten years.

On behalf of his son.

He spoke of his son.

He spoke against Nicias.

Up stream.

Down stream.

In the time of Solon.

He came with his friends.

In the presence of the king.

By means of a slave.

Day by day.

In our power.

With the help of the gods.

It was done by him.

The king and his followers.

They sailed towards Lemnos.

In the meantime.

They were drawn up four deep.

Exercise 124 [*A*].

1. If you value freedom highly you will never be subject to a tyrant.

2. As they were fighting on horseback they could easily overtake the fugitives.

3. They continued to fight all day long and did not stop till the evening.

4. It was reported that Philip was coming to attack us with as many as 20,000 men.

5. If they had acted contrary to law they would have been punished.

6. According to Pindar we ought to consider water the best of all things.

7. For many reasons I intend to help the Thebans, though they are waging war against my own country.

8. Whilst he was engaged in this he did not observe that the enemy had taken the city by storm.

9. For the most part philosophers discuss the origin of the world.

10. On this account they were compelled to be on friendly terms with the Athenians.[1]

11. I consider it of the utmost importance to remain friendly with Sparta.

---

[1] Dative alone.

Exercise 125 [*B*].

1. Except a few, all the Greeks resisted the Persians.

2. I will ask him to wait either instead of me or with me.

3. Those on the right wing were routed by this charge, but the hoplites on the left remained where they had been stationed.

4. It is in your power to confer a great benefit on your country.

5. If they march through our country they will destroy everything.

6. If they had made peace on better terms the peace would have lasted till now.

7. He has done, moreover, brave deeds on behalf of his native land.

8. After this Demosthenes often spoke against the friends of Aeschines.

9. If I were to become engaged on some other work I should not be able to finish this ; for which reason I shall not begin it, not even for your sake.

10. He set out for home at the same time as I did ; if he has not arrived, I fear something has happened.

11. They first marched along the river, and then, having crossed it by the bridge, encamped near the mountain.

Exercise 126 [*A*].

Meanwhile certain allies of the Syracusans, while on their way to Syracuse, were at the request of Nicias cut off by the Sikels. Had Nicias taken this step while Gylippus was on his march, the Athenians would perhaps have taken the city. Even now, 800 of these allies were slain, but 1500 reached Syracuse. Soon after this Demosthenes resolved to make a night attack upon the city. His men, in spite of having suffered so many hardships, were full of hope and confidence. They were now going to fight under a general who had won the highest reputation on account of his wisdom and courage, and they all believed that under his command they would take the city at last.

Exercise 127 [*B*].

In the spring of the following year Scipio set out with not less than 30,000 men for Carthage, which was distant only a few days' journey. He approached the town unobserved and fell unexpectedly upon the Punic garrison of about a thousand men, the fleet attacking from the side of [1] the sea, and the army at the same time from the mainland. Though it was not possible to hope for help, and though there were not enough men in the town to man the walls, Mago, who was in command of the garrison, did not lose heart, but armed the citizens and resisted valiantly. He even made a sortie, which however the Romans easily repulsed.

---

[1] from.

Exercise 128 [*A*].

REVISION.

The army being thus dispirited, Xenophon alone appeared to be of good courage, though he himself did not hope to see Greece again. For now that for a little time the barbarians had ceased from their attacks, the mountains which they saw in front terrified them. Xenophon therefore went about among the soldiers exhorting them. To the captains he said : 'The army chose you to be captains after the death of Clearchus, supposing that you were the bravest and most ready to suffer hardship of us all. If you now show yourselves disheartened, how shall I encourage the rest?' To the soldiers he spoke thus : 'If a man were to ask me, comrades, why you are so disheartened, I could not answer him ; nor would Cyrus have led you from Sardis to Babylon if he had known you were such men. You have passed through the greater dangers, the less remain. Yet, as if you were not the same men who defeated the Persians, you now shudder at mountains and wild beasts.'

Exercise 129 [*B*].

REVISION.

When all preparations had been made, Nicias was suddenly terrified by an eclipse of the moon. He sent men to consult the prophets, and declared that he would obey them in everything. According to Thucydides they replied that the army must wait for twenty-seven days, but other writers relate that Nicias himself increased the time. If this is true, who does not consider that Nicias, though he was the most pious of men, was guilty of the basest folly? For if the Athenians had set out without the knowledge of the Syracusans, both the fleet and the army would have been saved; whereas by waiting for so long a time they lost their only chance of escape.

Exercise 130 [*A*].

REVISION.

Three years later the Spartans, by making a truce for five years, allowed the Athenians to devote their attention to the war against Persia. Cimon eagerly seized[1] this opportunity. At home he was no longer powerful enough to oppose Pericles; but he hoped that at the head of a fleet he would be able not only to defeat the Persians but to enrich both his country and himself. If he had lived he would in all probability have accomplished his object[2]; but Thucydides tells us that, while he was blockading a city, Cimon died, and that the Athenians, compelled to abandon the siege from lack of food, won a victory both by sea and land over the Phoenicians and Cilicians.

---

[1] *i.e.* used.   [2] =what he was intending.

Exercise 131 [*B*].

REVISION.

In this year the war came to an end. They made peace on condition that the Athenians should restore the prisoners and all the cities taken in the war, and should receive back Amphipolis. If the Lacedaemonians had given up this city the Athenians would gladly have maintained the peace. But though the Lacedaemonians evacuated the town themselves, they refused to hand it over under plea that it was a free town; and when the Athenians complained the ephors replied: 'The Lacedaemonians are not in possession of Amphipolis. If the Athenians wish to possess it, let them reduce it themselves.' Within a short time the Athenians took Amphipolis by siege and treated the citizens cruelly; but knowing now that the Spartans would not abide by their agreement, they listened to Alcibiades when he advised them to create as many enemies as possible for Sparta in the Peloponnese.

Exercise 132 [*A*].

REVISION.

1. If the expedition had started at once they would have reached the town before the enemy.

2. The Athenians reduced this town though it was formerly in the hands of the Cilicians.

3. Peace was made on these conditions and both armies returned home.

4. I happened to be present when Demosthenes was speaking at Athens against Philip.

5. As if they had not heard what had happened, they continued their march towards Amphipolis.

6. Under these circumstances Xenophon resolved to march against the Carduchi and not to attempt to cross the river.

7. If we advance up the river we shall before long reach Babylon.

8. The Athenians made peace with the king on condition that the Ionian cities should be independent.

9. As far as I am concerned you are permitted to carry this message to the Thebans.

10. Accordingly the fleet weighed anchor and sailed towards Cyprus.

Exercise 133 [*B*].

REVISION.

1. If we were to keep our fleet strong, Athenians, we should never suffer defeat.

2. Had not the gates been betrayed by the guards we should be holding out still.

3. In this year the Athenians were very confident with regard to the war, as if they were never going to suffer another disaster.

4. If you sail round the island you will find a harbour.

5. The Athenians would not spare you now if you had been defeated, although you have fought in many battles on their behalf.

6. If a man advises the Athenians not to begin a war, he always appears to them a coward.

7. As having only just come from a foreign land, I admire everything that I see in Athens.

8. If you left behind about 400 men they would be sufficient to man the walls.

9. For the most part he finds pleasure in hunting.

10. He happened to have fallen ill, and moreover he was being constantly persecuted by Cleon and his friends.

INDEFINITE CONSTRUCTION

62. In English we make a sentence *indefinite* or *general* by altering the pronoun or conjunction. *E.g.* 'He said *what he thought*' is definite ; ' *Whatever he thought* he said ' is indefinite. In Greek this *indefiniteness* affects the mood.

In Primary time the Verb of an *indefinite* **clause is in the Subjunctive with ἄν ; in Historic time it is in the Optative without ἄν. The Negative is always μή.**

> *e.g.* ὅσα ἂν βούληται δώσω.
>
> *Whatever he wishes I will give.*
>
> εἴ τι μὴ βούλοιτο ἔχειν ἐδίδου.
>
> *Whatever he did not wish to keep he gave away.*
>
> ἐάν
> ὅταν } μάχωμαι, νικῶ.   *If ever I fight, I conquer.*
>
> εἰ
> ὁπότε } μαχοίμην, ἐνίκων.   *If ever I fought, I conquered.*

These Indefinite sentences in which *ἐάν* and *εἰ* are used in expressing *if ever, whenever, whatever*, etc., must be carefully distinguished from the Conditional sentences of Class B (pages 113, 114).

Exercise 134 [*A*].

1. You must follow your general wherever he leads you.
2. If ever they caught a stranger they put him to death.
3. Wherever I went I always found many friends.
4. Do not be afraid, but say whatever you wish.
5. If ever he did not speak the citizens were angry.

6. We will kill the traitors wherever we find them.

7. He ordered the soldiers to follow wherever the guides led them.

8. However these things turn out, you at least are innocent.

9. Whatever sort of message they bring, I shall rejoice to see them.

10. The general commanded his men to attack the enemy wherever they found them.

Exercise 135 [*B*].

1. Do whatever he orders you.

2. If ever a stranger comes to their land, they receive him kindly.

3. They ordered us to follow him wherever he led us.

4. Whatever hardships they suffered they never lost heart.

5. All whom you find send to me.

6. I know that men collect in large numbers wherever gold is found.

7. To whatever city he went he was admired.

8. Wherever he happened to be he always wrote a letter to me.

9. I shall send home any who seem to be fainthearted.

10. All who were not friends of Hippias were banished.

TEMPORAL CLAUSES

63. All clauses introduced by Conjunctions of time have their Verbs in the Indicative,[1] **unless they are Indefinite, in which case they follow the Indefinite construction.**

The commonest of such Conjunctions are ἐπειδή, *when, after,* ἐπειδὴ τάχιστα, *as soon as,* ἐξ οὗ, *since, after,* ἕως, *while, as long as,* ἕως, μέχρι, *until.*

'Until' is always indefinite when it refers to the Future.

e.g. ἔμεινα ἕως ἀφίκου.   *I waited till you came.*

μένε ἕως ἂν μάθῃς.   *Wait till you hear.*

ἡσύχαζον ἕως[2] οἱ πολέμιοι ἐπίοιεν.   *They waited for the enemy to charge.*

EXCEPTION—πρίν.

πρίν takes the Infinitive when the principal Verb is affirmative. Otherwise it follows the above rule.

This corresponds to a difference in the meaning of πρίν. With the Infinitive it can only be translated by *before.* With its other constructions it can be translated by either *before* or *until.*

Notice that, as in Indirect Statement, the subject of the Infinitive with πρίν, if it is the same as the subject of the principal verb, will be in the Nominative; and even if the subject is not expressed, a complement of the Infinitive will be in the Nominative.

---

[1] For the use of the Aorist in Temporal Clauses, see page 10, rule 8.

[2] Here 'until' is future relatively to the time of the principal verb.

e.g. πρὶν τοὺς πολεμίους ἐπελθεῖν ἀπέφυγον.   *They fled before the enemy charged.*

πρὶν ἀνὴρ γενέσθαι ἐτελεύτησεν·   *He died before he became a man.*

οὐκ ἄπειμι πρὶν ἂν σὺ ἔλθῃς.   *I shall not go till you come.*

οὐκ ἀπῆα πρὶν συ ἦλθες.   *I did not go until you came.*

N.B.—The above rule for πρίν will be sufficient at present.   But

(1) Sentences not actually negative were sometimes felt to involve negatives, and were then followed by the corresponding construction of πρίν.

(2) Wherever *before* in English cannot be changed to *until* without altering the sense it would be translated by πρίν with the Infinitive.   This will *sometimes* be the case after negatives.

e.g. οὐδὲ πρὶν ἡττηθῆναι ἐθάρρει.
Not even before being beaten had he any courage (*much less afterwards*).

where *until* would make nonsense.

Exercise 136 [A].

1. When Darius died Artaxerxes was made king.

2. While I was in Persia I learnt many strange things.

3. We shall continue to fight until we take the city.

4. Whenever there is an opportunity attack the enemy.

5. Before departing he gave the Athenians these instructions.

6. They did not dare to wage war on us till they had seized our generals.

7. After the cities had been destroyed, what happened?

8. He was called our friend till he captured Olynthus.

9. He kept quiet until he should have allies in Greece.

10. They did this till darkness came on.

Exercise 137 [B].

1. Whilst he was still speaking the messengers arrived.

2. Till I come let the treaty remain.

3. I am afraid the citizens will die of hunger before provisions are brought in.

4. When they had settled these matters they departed.

5. Whenever they came together they used to talk nonsense.

6. I dismissed the messengers before they had finished speaking.

7. After eating something they used to get up and proceed on their march.

8. Do not send for the doctor before you are ill.

9. Whilst he was in prison he saw his friends whenever he wished.

10. Since the time when I left Athens I have heard nothing about the war.

Exercise 138 [*A*].

1. Let us not try to storm the city until reinforcements arrive.

2. They continued to resist to the best of their ability until the general ordered them to throw away their arms.

3. From the time when I first arrived at Athens until you came, I did not cease to associate with Socrates.

4. You ought not to condemn these men before you hear what they have to say.

5. I always honoured him after hearing what great services he had rendered to Greece.

6. I all but killed him before I saw who he was.

7. I was not able to use the money until you wrote to me.

8. Whenever I see that man I wonder at his wisdom.

9. Xenophon ordered the soldiers to bring guides into the camp whenever they could find any.

10. They were all running in different directions until the orator came forward and told them not to be afraid.

Exercise 139 [B].

1. He was not willing to go until they drove him out by force.

2. Whenever he saw a man idling he rebuked him.

3. When the long walls had been built the Athenians ceased to fear the Spartans.

4. They kept the fleet in the harbour until the enemy's ships should sail away.

5. Think before you answer.

6. I shall not attempt the work until I know how to do it.

7. After the allies began to pay money instead of ships to the Athenians they were no longer free.

8. All the time that the city was being besieged, the inhabitants suffered terribly from lack of food.

9. Do not return until they summon you a second time.

10. They joined battle before they were ready.

11. They set out before getting their breakfast.

Exercise 140 [*A*].

Not long afterwards, when Herakles had nearly reached Mycenae, and was travelling along the sea-shore, Hera sent a great gnat that flew among the cattle, biting them till they all ran away in different directions. Several jumped into the sea, and Herakles jumped in after them and brought back all that he could catch, pulling some by the horns and driving others in front of him ; but the greater number swam out into the open sea and perished before he could overtake them. Then he tried to collect all those who had escaped into the forest, and continued to do this until he was worn out. All that he could recover he brought to Mycenae, and sacrificed them to Hera.

Exercise 141 [*A*].

If you continue, Athenians, to do as you are doing now, in a short time we shall be unable to withstand Philip either on land or on sea. You spend all the resources of the city on your own pleasure. If instead of that you were to build ships and pay soldiers with the same money, we should no longer have to fear Philip or any other foe. For our ancestors did not squander the resources of the city in time of peace; for which reason, whenever they were involved in a war they were ready. If while at peace they had thought nothing at all of war, they would never have won the glorious victories which you yourselves remember. But before war broke out they had prepared all their ships, their sailors, their supplies, and they would never spend a drachma for their pleasure until all these preparations had been made. Until you imitate them, your affairs will never prosper.

Exercise 142 [B].

After this Alcibiades became exceedingly depressed. Even before he knew that his enemies had resolved to kill him, be used to tell his secretary that the end of his life was at hand.[1] Once in a dream he saw himself lying on a funeral pyre and the people standing around to set it on fire. The very night after he had this dream he was awakened by a loud uproar, and saw that about fifty or sixty Persians had come while he was asleep, and were now setting fire to the house. Before they had finished their work, he wrapped a cloak round his head, that he might not be choked by the smoke, and ran out with a sword in his hand. As soon as he got out of the burning house he fell upon the Persians and put them to flight. They dared not fight him hand to hand, but some of them standing at a distance shot at him with arrows until at last he fell. Such was the end of Alcibiades.

---

[1] 'In a short time he is about to die.'

Exercise 143 [B].

Immediately after they had started they were delayed by adverse winds, and put into the bay of Pylos until the wind should cease. Before starting, Demosthenes had proposed to the Athenians to fortify some place in Laconian territory; and now that the opportunity had come, he begged the other generals, when they themselves sailed on to Sicily, to leave him in command of even a few hoplites at Pylos. While the whole fleet was still present, the sailors and marines built a small fort; when the rest departed, Demosthenes, with a few hoplites, was left behind to defend it. As soon as the news reached Sparta, a force was sent to take Pylos; but the fort was already too strong to be taken easily.

VERBS OF PREVENTING, ETC.

64. Verbs of 'Preventing,' 'Hindering,' 'Forbidding,' Denying,' in Greek may take—

(a) The Simple Infinitive.

(b) The Infinitive with μή.[1]

e.g. κωλύει αὐτοὺς τοῦτο ποιεῖν ⎤ *He prevents them*
εἴργει αὐτοὺς μὴ τοῦτο ποιεῖν ⎦ *from doing this.*

When the verb of *Preventing*, etc., is itself negatived (or is a question expecting the answer *no*), the double negative μὴ οὐ is generally used with the Infinitive.

e.g. οὐκ εἴργει αὐτοὺς μὴ οὐ τοῦτο ποιεῖν.
He does not prevent them from doing this.
τί ἐμποδὼν μὴ οὐκ ἀποθανεῖν ;
What is to prevent their being killed ?

[Here τί ἐμποδών is equivalent to οὐδὲν ἐμποδών.]

But κωλύω is not usually followed by a negative, even when negatived itself.

Exercise 144 [*A*].

1. Nothing will prevent their paying the penalty for their cowardice.

2. We cannot prevent his learning what we have done.

3. Xenophon tried to prevent his men lingering.

4. The Spartans could not prevent Pausanias from going whithersoever he wished.

5. What is to prevent our being deceived by Philip again ?

---

[1] Verbs of *Hindering, Preventing*, are often followed by the Genitive of the Infinitive—*e.g.* εἴργει αὐτοὺς τοῦ [μὴ] τοῦτο ποιεῖν.

6. I refrained from questioning him for fear he might deny that he had done this.

7. They were not hindered from hunting wherever they chose.

8. They did their best to prevent the expedition from starting.

9. They did not forbid his conversing with his friends, though he was in prison.

10. There is nothing to delay the citizens from voting at once.

11. I did not deny that I made a mistake.

Exercise 145 [B].

1. Did you not forbid the hoplites to cross the river?

2. This winter interrupted hostilities between the Athenians and Spartans.

3. There is nothing to prevent the exiles returning.

4. They were hindered by fear from accusing Alcibiades.

5. I forbade the people to send you into exile.

6. Let none ever deny that we served our State to the best of our ability.

7. It is to the advantage of all of us to prevent the strangers from suffering harm.

8. If they remain in our city nothing can prevent their voting in the Assembly.

9. The fact of not having a good harbour prevented the Spartans from being strong at sea.

10. Love of their country saved the Greeks from being worsted by the Persians.

SUMMARY OF THE USES
OF THE NEGATIVES *οὐ* AND *μή*

65. *οὐ* **negatives statements,** *μή* **negatives ideas and sentences that do not involve statements,** such as prohibitions, the protasis of a conditional sentence, etc. Therefore

οὐ is used in—	*μή* is used in—
Statements, direct and indirect (in the Ind., Opt., or Inf.).	All commands, exhortations, and wishes.
Direct questions that expect the answer '*yes*'; and in ordinary indirect questions.	Direct questions that expect the answer '*no*'; and in all deliberative questions.
Definite relative and temporal clauses.	All indefinite clauses.
Consecutive clauses with Indicative.	Consecutive clauses with Infinitive.
	Final clauses (with Subj., Opt., or Fut. Ind.).
	All conditions.
The Participle when it involves a statement.	The Participle with Conditional or Generic force. [See below, 66.]
The Infinitive in Indirect Statement.[1]	The Infinitive except in Indirect Statement.

---

[1] But see page 50 for *μή* used after verbs like *hope, promise, swear.*

66. *μή* used generically, *i.e.* in indicating a class.

μή is used both with the Indicative and with the Participle when we are describing a *class* and not any specific individuals.

> *e.g.* διδάξω σε ἃ μὴ οἶσθα.
>
> *I will teach you such things as you do not know.*
>
> διδάξω σε [ταῦτα] ἃ οὐκ οἶσθα.
>
> *I will teach you these things which you do not know.*

The first of these sentences avoids assertion (cf. in Latin *qui* with the *Subjunctive*); the second makes an assertion (Latin *qui* with the *Indicative*).

Compare also—

> οὗτοι οἱ οὐδὲν εἰδότες.
>
> *These men who know nothing.*
>
> οἱ μηδὲν εἰδότες.
>
> *Men who know nothing, the ignorant.*

67. Double Negatives—

1. The uses of the double negative *μὴ οὐ* are explained in Rule 43 (page 98) and Rule 64 (page 160).

2. *οὐ μή* with the Aorist Subjunctive (and sometimes with the Future Indicative) expresses an emphatic negative statement.[1]

> *e.g.* οὐ μὴ τοῦτο γένηται (or γενήσεται).
>
> *This certainly will not happen.*

---

[1] The use of *οὐ μή* with the 2nd Person of the Future Indicative to express a strong prohibition is entirely poetical.

Exercise 146 [*A*].

1. The captains were condemned on the ground that they had not tried to save the sailors.

2. They marched with all speed, so that no one was captured by the enemy.

3. They advanced slowly so as not to arrive before morning.

4. Not to speak is often worse than to speak rashly.

5. I was aware that this did not happen in our time.

6. Whenever the general was not present in person the army fared badly.

7. Though he was not a soldier himself he was able to lead an army when it was necessary.

8. When the ships did not return, the citizens began to despair.

9. I could not deny that I myself promised to be present.

10. Did you not hate this man although he had done you no wrong?

11. If they had not arrived at the critical moment the whole army would have been destroyed.

12. They will do you no harm unless you provoke them.

13. Whoever does not obey the laws is punished.

14. Let all who are unwilling to fight remain in the camp.

Exercise 147 [*B*].

1. Do not suppose that he is not trustworthy.

2. Disobedience is most perilous in an army.

3. Not having strength any more to go on, he rested.

4. Though the army had not been victorious, those who had not been killed in battle got safe home.

5. After this the Athenians no longer forbade his returning home.

6. I am afraid you do not yet believe me.

7. I should not allow you unless you first explained why you wish to take vengeance on him.

8. It is (the mark) of a shameless man not to love his father.

9. You are not skilled in this art, are you?

10. You shall certainly suffer nothing so far as I am concerned.

11. He turned away without answering anything, as if he had not heard clearly what I said

12. He made many mistakes on account of his never having been in command of an army before.

13. Those who do not speak well are not honoured at Athens.

14. Whatever you do not know now you will soon learn.

Exercise 148 [A].

REVISION.

There was nothing now to save [1] the whole force from destruction. The fact that Nicias had prevented the army from setting out, while there was still hope of escape, had given fresh confidence to the enemy and filled the Greek soldiers with rage and despair. [2] At this crisis [3] Nicias did his best to cheer and encourage the men, though he was well aware that no one was to blame but himself. He implored them not to despair, and asserted that for his own part he did not believe that the Syracusans could prevent their reaching the coast even if they endured many hardships on the march. But in reality he hardly hoped to persuade any one by such words; and though all were ready to do whatever he ordered, there probably was not a man who did not know that their case was hopeless.

---

[1] Use ἐμποδών.

[2] Say ‘knowing that Nicias . . ., the enemy were the more con fident and the Greeks more enraged, etc.’

[3] ‘The danger being so great.’

Exercise 149 [*A*].

REVISION.

In later times the story was told that Themistocles, after undergoing many difficulties and dangers, came to Ephesus, and from this place wrote as follows to the king: 'I, an Athenian, have come to thee—the man who did most harm to the Persians while I was compelled to resist thy father, but who also did him most good by withholding the Greeks from destroying the bridge over the Hellespont while he was journeying from Attica to Asia. Never would I have injured him, willingly at least; and now I am here, able to do thee much good, but persecuted by the Greeks on account of my goodwill to thee. I pray thee therefore to prevent thy subjects from harming me, and to suffer me to remain here until I am able to tell thee more clearly in what way thou mayest best take vengeance on thine enemies.' After seeing the king he continued to live near the coast, but did nothing to fulfil his promise, until at length he died a voluntary death so as not to be convicted of having made a vain boast.

Exercise 150 [*B*].

REVISION.

The Senate had previously decided not to release for ransom, as was usual, the prisoners taken by Phanosthenes, but to put them to death, on the ground that they were not enemies, but had rebelled against their mother city ; for they came from Thurii, an Athenian colony. But this decree could not be carried out unless ratified by the Assembly. When, therefore, the Assembly was held, an orator named Eumedes urged the people to show the Thurians no pity.[1] 'When the Melians revolted, Athenians, you put all their men to death, though they were not your kinsmen, nor even your allies. What shall prevent you from inflicting the same punishment upon the Thurians, who have committed a far worse crime ?'

---

[1] Spare.

Exercise 151 [*B*].

REVISION.

The Assembly was prevented from voting immediately by a certain citizen who reminded them that it was not according to the law to condemn even enemies unheard.[1] The prisoners were therefore brought in, and among them Dorieus of Rhodes, a man of magnificent stature,[2] who was known throughout Greece especially as having been thrice victorious in the pancratium at Olympia. And as this man came forward the people could not refrain from applauding him; and not allowing Eumedes to say another word, they voted that Dorieus should not be restrained from going whithersoever he wished, and, if he did not wish to depart, that he might remain at Athens as the guest of the people. Had Dorieus not been present, nothing would have saved the prisoners from being put to death the same day.

---

[1] 'Not having defended themselves' (ἀπολογέομαι).

[2] Say *in stature* (accus. of respect).

68. SUBJUNCTIVE AND OPTATIVE

SUMMARY OF USES

Subjunctive.	Optative.

INDEPENDENT.

(a) Exhortations (1st Person).

(b) Prohibitions (2nd Person Aorist).

(c) Deliberative questions.

(a) Wishes referring to the future.

(b) To make a modified statement or command—the sentence resembling the Apodosis of Conditionals *B* (2) ἴσως ἄν τις εἴ-ποι . . ., *Perhaps some one might say* . . .

DEPENDENT.

(a) Final sentences after Primary or Historic [1] tense.

(b) With verbs of *fearing* after Primary or Historic [1] tense.

(c) Conditional sentences with ἐάν [Class *B* (1)].

(d) Indefinite Relative and Temporal sentences with ἄν (Primary and sometimes Historic [1]).

(a) Final sentences after Historic tense.

(b) With verbs of *fearing* after Historic tense.

(c) Conditional sentences with εἰ in Protasis and ἄν in Apodosis [Class *B* (2)].

(d) Indefinite Relative and Temporal sentences (Historic).

(e) Indirect Statements after Historic tense.

(f) Indirect Questions after Historic tense.

---

[1] In (a), (b), (d) the Subjunctive is frequently used instead of the Optative by the Graphic Construction, and in (c) where the Conditional sentence is in Oratio Obliqua.

Similarly in (e) and (f) the Indicative is frequently used instead of the Optative.

Exercise 152 [*A*].

1. When are we to start?
2. We should see better there.
3. I was afraid they would rob us of our money.
4. Choose men to command this expedition.
5. We ascertained what they accused him of.
6. Do not leave this gate unguarded.
7. Whenever he is wronged, he takes vengeance on the man who has wronged him.
8. May you meet with success, if you march with Cyrus.
9. He would show himself more prudent, if he stayed at home.
10. Let us make haste, if we wish to bring this news before others.

Exercise 153 [*B*].

1. Why he does not choose an experienced man to finish the work, I cannot understand.
2. He called to him all whom he knew to be trustworthy.
3. Do you wish me to be ready to-day?
4. The army was drawn up in this manner to repulse cavalry.
5. He asked whether the general would arrive that day.
6. May you accomplish your task easily!
7. Do not go away without accomplishing anything.
8. I should be ashamed, judges, if I gained your pity by weeping.
9. If ever I deserve punishment, I am willing to endure it.
10. Whatever crimes he committed, he was never condemned.

Exercise 154 [*A*].

When Laodamas, King of Thebes, heard that the Epigoni were coming to avenge their fathers, he armed the citizens and marched out to meet them, and a battle took place [1] in front of the city gates. The Epigoni fought the more bravely because they remembered their fathers; and though the Thebans held their ground steadily at first, they lost heart after their king had been slain by Alcmaeon, and fled for refuge to the city. The Epigoni encamped before Thebes, saying that they would not raise the siege until they had taken the city; and meanwhile the Thebans held counsel as to how they could best save themselves. At last, at the advice of the prophet Tiresias, they resolved to leave the city unobserved by the enemy, taking with them all the possessions they could carry. They accomplished this while the Epigoni were feasting and rejoicing after the battle, and [2] the whole city was deserted before any of the enemy perceived what was happening.

---

[1] Say ' they fought.'

[2] Use ὥστε with Indicative.

Exercise 155 [*B*].

They determined to retreat, fearing that, if they marched further into the desert, they would suffer even worse from want of food.   Three thousand had been slain in the battle, but far more perished on the return march.   So hard pressed were they that they left behind the sick and the baggage in a certain town which had a small garrison.   These were besieged the whole winter, and were only rescued in the following year, when, being scarcely able to defend themselves longer, they were on the point of surrendering. Xerxes equipped another expedition, but before he set out ambassadors arrived from the Scythians to make peace. They agreed to give hostages and not to invade Persian territory, but to become allies of the Persians.   Thus the war ended.

Exercise 156 [*A*].

Nicias had drawn up the Athenians on the right wing and the Sicilian allies on the left, where, on account of the hill, they were not likely to share in the contest; for he greatly feared that if the Athenians were worsted the Sicilians would desert to the enemy. But before the battle began he addressed the Athenians as follows:—'Men of Athens, you perceive for yourselves in what danger we lie, and I know that I myself am responsible for it. But let all of you recall to mind the great deeds of our ancestors who put to flight the Persians at Marathon. Would that Miltiades were here to lead us to-day! But so far as I am able I shall do what becomes a general, and I believe the gods will be on our side.'

Exercise 157 [*B*].

What would have happened if Alexander, when at the height of his power, had invaded Italy? According to a Roman writer the Romans would have been able to get the upper hand at last, even if they had lost some battles. They would at any rate have been fighting at home, with ample provisions and allies to help them, whereas Alexander, if he had lost many men, would have been compelled to wait a long time before receiving reinforcements. Moreover, the Romans had shown[1] in their wars against Pyrrhus and Hannibal that in spite of frequent defeats[2] they never lost heart; and though they had no general competent to defeat Alexander in a battle, yet their soldiers were the best in the world, inasmuch as they were all free citizens fighting for their own lives and liberty.

---

[1] use str. aor. pass. of φαίνομαι.
[2] though often conquered.

WISHES IN PRESENT AND PAST TIME

69. **I. Wishes for the Future** are always expressed by the Optative [p. 78].

II. Wishes for the Present and Past (being necessarily unfulfilled) are expressed by εἴθε, εἰ γάρ with the Past tenses of the Indicative, like the unfulfilled conditions of Class A (2) [p. 112]. The Imperfect is used for Present time or Past continuous time, the Aorist for Past 'momentary' time.

But they may also be expressed by ὤφελον, -ες, -ε, etc. (with or without εἴθε, εἰ γάρ) followed by the Infinitive.

ὤφελον = 'ought,' is an Aorist of ὀφείλω, *to owe.*

In all wishes the Negative is μή.

> *e.g.* εἰ γὰρ αὐτοὺς εἶδες.
>> *O if you had seen them!   O that you had seen them !*
>> εἰ γὰρ τοσαύτην δύναμιν εἶχον·
>> *Would that I had so great power.*[1]

Or the same sentences may be expressed by
> [εἴθ'] ὤφελές με ἰδεῖν.[2]
> [εἰ γὰρ] ὤφελον τοσαύτην δύναμιν ἔχειν.

---

[1] Or, *Would that I had been in possession of such power* (in the past).
[2] Literally, *You ought to have seen me.*

Exercise 158 [*A*].

1. Would that I had died before seeing our city subdued !
2. May you never suffer such evils as you have inflicted on others !
3. Would that Miltiades were still our general !
4. Soldiers, may you reap the fruits of victory.
5. O that I had never been elected general !
6. Would that we might reach the harbour before the storm falls upon us !
7. The Athenians should never have sent an expedition against Syracuse.
8. May you never meet the man who betrayed your father !
9. Would that we had reached the city first !
10. Demosthenes should still have been alive to encourage us in the war.

Exercise 159 [*B*].

1. Would that I had lived in the time of Pericles !
2. Would that Jason and his companions had never set out !
3. O that you may be successful in this contest !
4. Would that Miltiades were here to lead us !
5. O that I had perished on that day !
6. Never may you learn who you are !
7. Would that I had died for thee, my son !
8. Would that we Greeks were marching on Susa and not on Thebes !
9. How I would that the son were like his father !
10. Heaven grant we may never behold such deeds done in Athens.

CONDITIONAL SENTENCES
IN ORATIO OBLIQUA

70. 1. The Protasis follows the rule for subordinate clauses in Oratio Obliqua already given on p. 84. If the Subjunctive of the Direct becomes Optative, of course ἐάν is changed to εἰ.

2. The Apodosis.

    (*a*) If the construction with ὅτι or ὡς be used, the rule on p. 48 is followed.

    (*b*) If the Infinitive (or Participle) construction be used, this will be in the same tense as the Indicative or Optative of the Direct speech.[1]

Whether (*a*) or (*b*) be used, the particle ἄν, if used in the Direct speech, must be retained in the Indirect.

EXAMPLES.

I. Using the Infinitive construction.

    A. 1. εἰ ἐβρόντησε, καὶ ἤστραψεν.

        ἔφη, εἰ ἐβρόντησε, καὶ ἀστράψαι.

        He said that if it (had) thundered it (had) also lightened.

    A. 2. εἰ ἥμαρτον, ἀπέθανον ἄν.

        ἔφη, εἰ ἥμαρτεν ἀποθανεῖν ἄν.

        He said that if he had made a mistake he would have been put to death.

---

[1] Including the Imperfect with the Present.

B. 1. $\left.\begin{array}{l} εἰ\ ζητήσεις \\ ἐὰν\ ζητήσῃς \end{array}\right\}$ εὑρήσεις.

$ἔφη\ αὐτὸν \left\{\begin{array}{l} εἰ\ ζητήσοι \\ ἐὰν\ ζητήσῃ \end{array}\right\}$ εὑρήσειν.

He said that if he sought he would find.

B. 2. εἰ ζητοίης, εὕροις ἄν.

ἔφη αὐτὸν εἰ ζητοίη εὑρεῖν ἄν.

He said that if he sought he would find.

II. Using the ὅτι construction.

A. 1. εἶπεν ὅτι εἰ ἐβρόντησε καὶ $\left\{\begin{array}{l} ἤστραψεν. \\ ἀστράψειε. \end{array}\right\}$

A. 2. εἶπεν ὅτι εἰ ἥμαρτεν ἀπέθανεν ἄν.

B. 1. εἶπεν ὅτι $\left\{\begin{array}{l} εἰ\ ζητοίη\ εὑρήσοι. \\ ἐὰν\ ζητῇ\ εὑρί\ σει. \end{array}\right\}$

B. 2. εἶπεν ὅτι εἰ ζητοίη εὕροι ἄν.

Exercise 160 [*A*].

1. I am sure that if we had drawn up the army more skilfully we should have won the battle.

2. He promised that he would not offend again if they dismissed him.

3. He said that if a man is ignorant he is happy.

4. He promised to meet me if I told him when I should arrive.

5. They supposed that if they gave up the prisoners the Spartans would restore Amphipolis.

6. I hoped to have had my share in this contest if I had not been prevented from being present.

7. They replied that they would have obeyed the king if they were his subjects.

8. The general defended himself by saying that if reinforcements had come, as the Athenians had promised, he would not have surrendered the town.

9. I know Peisistratus would not allow these things if he were tyrant of Athens.

10. They thought that if Cleon captured the Spartans in Sphacteria he would benefit Athens more than Nicias.

Exercise 161 [B].

1. I believe we should have conquered if he had had another general.

2. They promised to return if the war ceased.

3. I was afraid they would be badly treated if they became subject to the Persians.

4. I believe he would still have been alive if he had not suffered such misfortunes.

5. It was plain that they would perish if we did not go to their help.

6. They replied that they would have given back the money if there had been any need.

7. I am sure they could have saved the city if they had arrived in time.

8. It was evident that they intended to attack us if we crossed the river.

9. We should have attacked them at once if they had come down from the mountain.

10. They swore to reduce the city by famine if they were not able to take it by force.

Exercise 162 [A].

The law ordains, Athenians, that if any person has injured the people of Athens, he shall in the first place be imprisoned and tried by the people; and then if he be convicted he shall be put to death and his goods shall be confiscated. Why, then, are you in such vehement haste? Do you suppose that if you put off voting till to-morrow this law will be previously annulled? Ought you not rather to fear that, if by any chance in your anger you were to put an innocent man to death, you would repent too late? Would that you, Athenians, could not remember any such deeds done in the past! I think indeed that you would do more justly if you honoured these men with crowns; but at least if you delay your decision till to-morrow, it will still be possible for you to put the generals to death in whatever way you please.

Exercise 163 [*A*].

Cleon declared that if only the Athenians made him general he would capture Sphacteria in twenty days, and bring the Spartans as prisoners to Athens. He asserted that if the generals who were then in command had endeavoured to serve the interests of the state to the best of their ability, the island would have been captured long before. 'Send me,' he said, 'and you will never repent it.' To many it seemed that he had spoken without really wishing to be taken at his word.[1] But however that may be, the Athenian people, who were greatly dissatisfied with the present condition of affairs, elected him general at once. If they had reflected longer they would probably not have done this; but at any rate Cleon performed his promise, and returned to Athens victorious.

---

[1] to persuade them.

Exercise 164 [*B*].

The soldiers, who for a long time had evidently been discontented, at length declared that they would no longer obey their officers unless they were informed where they were going. They said that they would never have started if the general had not promised to tell them this as soon as they passed their own frontiers. Thereupon the general replied that what they said was true, but that it was not now expedient for them to learn all his plans, lest they should by some chance be divulged to the enemy. If they trusted him they would not repent it. Moreover, he pointed out how foolish they would be if they gave up their hopes of fame and riches because they were unwilling to wait until he thought good to explain everything to them.

Exercise 165 [B].

Zenophon in answer said, 'Callias, if Tissaphernes so pleased, Clearchus and all the generals would be seized and slain before we could go to their help.' While he was yet speaking they heard an outcry and disturbance in the camp, and rushing out to ascertain the cause, they met a certain Arcadian captain badly wounded, who, as he ran towards them, cried out that Clearchus was dead and the other generals had been seized. Immediately the Greeks seized their arms, fearing that the whole Persian army would be upon them. But the king was aware that the Greek hoplites were much better than his own horsemen, and had resolved not to employ force if he could effect anything by stratagem.

SUMMARY OF THE USES
OF THE INFINITIVE

71. I. With the Article.—When declined with the Article
the Infinitive may be treated exactly as a Noun, may stand
as the subject or object of a sentence, and may be governed
by Prepositions.   But as being still a verb it may also govern
an object and have a subject, ordinarily in the Accusative,
but in the Nominative if it is the same as the subject of the
Principal verb.   The Negative is always μή.

> *e.g.* ἐπέσχον τὸ τοῖς Ἀθηναίοις ἐπιχειρεῖν.
> *They put off attacking the Athenians.*
>
> ἐπαύσαντο $\begin{cases} τοῦ\ μάχεσθαι. \\ τῆς\ μάχης. \end{cases}$
> *They ceased fighting.*
>
> περὶ τοῦ τιμωρεῖσθαι Φίλιππον.
> *With regard to punishing Philip.*
>
> διὰ τὸ ξένος εἶναι οὐκ ἠδικήθη.
> *On account of his being a stranger he was not harmed.*
>
> ἐκ τοῦ μὴ δημηγορεῖν ἐνίους.
> *In consequence of some men's not speaking in public.*

For the use of this Infinitive after *prevent*, etc., see note,
p. 160.

The Present and Aorist of the Infinitive with the Article
do not retain any difference of *time*, but the difference between
'continued' and 'momentary' action as explained in Rule 41,
p. 92.

II. Without the Article.

1. In Indirect Statement.   See p. 50.

In this use of the Infinitive (and in this only) all the tenses retain their proper *time* distinctions as in the Indicative. It is only in this use that the negative is *οὐ*.

2. In Indirect Command.   See p. 82.

3. After Verbs of Preventing, etc.   See p. 160.

4. In Consecutives with ὥστε.   See p. 100.

5. After πρίν.   See p. 150.

6. The Prolative and Object Infinitives are as widely extended in Greek as in English ; and in the classes of verbs which take these Infinitives the two languages almost exactly correspond. *E.g.* Besides those that are included in the above classes such verbs as *compel, teach, cause, attempt,* etc.

7. So also **after Adjectives** expressing *ability, fitness,* etc.

> *e.g.* δεινὸς λέγειν, *skilled in speaking.*
> ἄξιος τιμᾶσθαι, *worthy to be honoured.*

8. An Infinitive of Purpose is possible in Greek after words like *choose* and *appoint, give* and *take, send* and *bring.*

> *e.g.* δέκα τῶν νεῶν προὔπεμψαν κηρῦξαι, etc.
> *They sent ten of the ships to proclaim,* etc.
> τὴν πόλιν φυλάττειν αὐτοῖς παρέδωκαν.
> *They delivered the city to them to guard.*

Exercise 166 [A].

1. We were all indignant at these things being concealed.

2. Ambassadors were sent to forbid the building of the walls.

3. No one was now able to prevent Philip from reducing Olynthus.

4. Though I did not know him myself, I have always heard that he was a most clever speaker.

5. I am not in a position to speak because I was not present myself.

6. He does not deny that he took part in the war.

7. We prevented him from returning before the end of the war.

8. They forbade him to come though he was ready to help them.

9. I will not deny that I did not arrive in time.

10. We were greatly annoyed at their not sending for us before.

11. We gave them these ships to use as they wished.

12. They promised to give back the hostages on condition that the Thebans did not break the truce.

Exercise 167 [*B*].

1. They entrusted to us these children to bring up.

2. We were allowed to come back from exile on condition that we should take no part in politics.

3. He was too generous a man to take vengeance on his enemy.

4. He was banished from Athens on account of his being himself convicted of treachery.

5. They handed over the city to the mercenaries to guard.

6. He never tried to prevent his son from doing whatever he wished.

7. So noble did the captive general appear that no one spoke or applauded as he rode through the city.

8. A great storm arose and caused all the ships to seek refuge in the harbour.

9. No one ever denied that we ought not to have given up the city.

10. The Ephors met to discuss the question of expelling Alcibiades from their country.

11. The general issued an order that the soldiers must not scatter to seek provisions.

12. I consider that Cleon is not worthy to be appointed general.

Exercise 168 [*A*].

REVISION.

Meanwhile the king, having taken up his position, as has been said, in the centre, and seeing no one coming against him, advanced as if to attack the Greeks on their flank. Cyrus, seeing this, charged at full speed with his six hundred, and broke the line in front of the king. The troopers were scattered in the ardour of pursuit,[1] and Cyrus was left alone with a handful of men. Even so all would have been well, if he had not suddenly caught sight of his brother. But on perceiving him in the throng, he cried out, 'There is the man!' and advanced furiously against him. The two brothers engaged at once in a hand-to-hand struggle. But Cyrus and his followers were too few to be victorious. Before long they were hurled to the ground, and Cyrus himself with eight others was slain.

---

[1] pursuing with great eagerness.

Exercise 169 [*B*].

REVISION.

In the spring this vast army began its march from Susa, with Xerxes himself in command. At first they advanced slowly; but when the king perceived that the Scythians constantly retreated before him he determined to send forward the cavalry as fast as possible, with orders not to join battle with the enemy but to check their retreat in every way. On the third day, however, this force was caught in an ambush and cut to pieces[1] by the enemy. Encouraged by this success the barbarians waited for Xerxes, where he had to cross a river. On their arrival the Persians encamped one night in the presence of the enemy, but on the next day arrayed their line of battle, the archers being stationed on the right, all the other light-armed troops on the left, and the hoplites occupying the centre. They repelled frequent charges of the enemy, but could not follow them when they retired, so that they gained neither glory nor booty by the battle.

---

[1] destroyed.

Exercise 170 [*A*].

REVISION.

If our ancestors, Athenians, when at war with the Persians, had done as you are doing now, Greece would never have become free, and we should be the subjects of some satrap. The story is told that, when the king sent to demand earth and water from the Athenians, the heralds were thrown into a well. For the Athenians in those days preferred to fight the Persians before negotiating with them. But you are not willing to do anything in defence of Athens till Philip comes to your very gates. Do not indeed believe Aeschines and his friends, who say that Philip is your friend? What kind of a friend, forsooth, is he? Have you not before now convicted him of trying to deceive you, especially as regards Amphipolis? And if now you make an agreement with him that he shall hand over Olynthus to you, all Greece will laugh you to scorn—nay, in a short time you will be a laughing-stock to yourselves.

Exercise 171 [*B*].

REVISION

It would be reasonable, Athenians, if you were to despatch against Philip all the forces of the city. But if you decide not to do this,—since you regard it, I believe, as too great a burden to serve abroad yourselves—at least attach a sufficient body of Athenians to whatever force of mercenaries you think enough for the war ; and secondly, let the whole force spend both winter and summer near the Macedonian coast, that it may be ready to go to the rescue wherever Philip makes an attack. And now dismiss these matters for the moment, and let me speak to you, Athenians, words that are unpleasant perhaps, but very necessary in this crisis. You yourselves often show how proud you are of your ancestors' deeds ; for whenever one speaks of them even briefly, you applaud so that the sailors in the Piraeus hear the noise. But reflect and ask one another how it was that your ancestors became famed throughout the world. It was by doing things of which you do nothing. They risked their homes for Greece—you will not risk the price of your theatre-tickets.[1] They went to the ends of the world themselves—you sit slothfully at home and send hired barbarians to do your work. To what a depth of shame has the city of Themistocles fallen !

---

[1] τὸ θεωρεῖν.

Exercise 172 [A].

REVISION.

It became now almost evident that the city would not be taken by direct assault. It was therefore resolved to reduce it by famine. Still in the course of the winter the immense army outside the walls were as great sufferers as the population within. The soldiers fell in great numbers owing to the intense [1] cold and insufficient food. For, as usual in such sieges, [2] these deaths far outnumbered those inflicted by the enemy's hand. The sufferings inside the city increased daily, [3] the people receiving only enough food to support life. With the approach of spring there was danger that supplies would be entirely cut off; and they scarcely hoped the general would be able to organise a fleet before the city fell.

Exercise 173 [B].

REVISION.

The Athenians now had very few ships left. These they drew up on the shore, and having made a small fort intended to defend themselves as brave men should. But few though they were, and badly armed and in want of food, the enemy shrank from attacking them, knowing the extraordinary courage which the Athenians always showed in adversity. Indeed they promised through a herald to make terms on condition the Athenians would immediately evacuate the island. But they replied that they could not retire without orders from home.

---

[1] terrible.   [2] as often befalls besiegers.
[3] Make 'those within the city' the subject.

Exercise 174 [*A*].

REVISION.

The king's army[1] was encamped for 120 days near Bristol;[1] for there more than anywhere else Fairfax[1] had received assistance. At first they bivouacked on the heights above the town, expecting to take it with one assault. But after they had thrice attempted to enter it at a point where, even at a distance, they perceived the wall to be weak, and had each time been prevented by the resolute resistance of the citizens,[2] they were obliged to make a camp in the low and marshy ground by the harbour, and wait until the citizens should be brought to terms by famine. To hasten this, they began to build a single wall round the city, but they could not guard it properly on the side of the river; and in consequence merchant ships sailed boldly into the harbour, and brought provisions for the garrison.

---

[1] Let the army be that of Nicias before Syracuse, and use *Hermocrates* for Fairfax.

[2] by the citizens resolutely resisting.

Exercise 175 [*B*].

REVISION.

This disaster in Egypt, by which more than 10,000 Athenians had perished, occasioned a great outburst of grief in the city;[1] for there was scarcely a single family which had not a son or a brother slain.[2] It would not have been strange if the citizens had despaired of their Egyptian schemes.[3] Yet on the very day which followed the receipt of the news, it was carried in the Assembly that a new expedition should be fitted out. But this expedition never landed in Egypt. For Cimon, who was placed in command, lingered a long time round Cyprus in order to defend the Greek cities there against the Phoenician fleet. On the day of the battle he was too ill to go on board, but he addressed the men before they embarked. He died in a manner worthy of the son of Miltiades, at the very moment when his victorious fleet put back to the shore.

---

[1] brought the utmost grief upon the city.
[2] from which either a son or a brother had not perished.
[3] Use πράγματα.

SPECIAL VOCABULARIES

N.B.—In the following Vocabularies genders are given (except where the meaning makes it unnecessary) and the genitives of all nouns, except regular nouns of the first and second Declensions. Principal Parts of Irregular Verbs are given in the Appendix, p. 223.

Exercise 1.

Greece, Ἑλλάς, -άδος, *f.*
Greeks, Ἕλληνες
always, ἀεί
brave, ἀνδρεῖος ; *Adv.* ἀνδρείως
courage, ἀνδρεία, *f.*
formerly, πάλαι
free, ἐλεύθερος
freedom, ἐλευθερία, *f.*
free (*Verb*), ἐλευθερόω
honour, τιμάω
hope, ἐλπίς, -ίδος, *f.*
give, δίδωμι
true, ἀληθής, -ές
often, πολλάκις
strange, δεινός
speak, λέγω
difficult, χαλεπός
difficulties, τὰ χαλεπά
think, νομίζω
base, αἰσχρός
rich, πλούσιος
many, πολλοί (πολύς, πολλή, πολύ)
have, ἔχω
harm, βλάπτω, *Acc.*
men of the present day, οἱ νῦν
here, ἐνθάδε
believe, obey, πείθομαι, *Dat.*
lie, ψεύδομαι
friend, φίλος

Exercise 2.

wise, σοφός
wisdom, σοφία, *f.*
be willing, wish, ἐθέλω, βούλομαι
well, εὖ
ship, ναῦς, νεώς, *f.*
safe, ἀσφαλής, -ές
harbour, λιμήν, -ένος, *m.*
admire, wonder at, θαυμάζω
become, γίγνομαι
slave, δοῦλος, -ου
slavery, δουλεία, *f.*
the men of old, οἱ πάλαι
barbarian, βάρβαρος

Exercise 3.

soldier, στρατιώτης, -ου
army, στράτευμα, -ατος, *n.* ;
    στρατός, *m.*
Athenian, Ἀθηναῖος
die, ἀποθνήσκω
city, πόλις, -εως, *f.* ; ἄστυ, -εως, *n.*
fight, μάχομαι
fly, φεύγω
escape, ἐκφεύγω
lie, ψεύδομαι
come, ἔρχομαι.   (See p. 230)
stand, ἕστηκα (*Perf.* of ἵστημι)
street, ὁδός, -οῦ, *f*

197

herald, κῆρυξ, -υκος
loud, μέγας, μεγάλη, μέγα
voice, φωνή, f.
noble, ἀγαθός, γενναῖος
destroy, ἀπόλλυμι (In *Middle*=
perish)
wall, τεῖχος, -ους, n
make, ποιέω
just, lately, ἄρτι
bring, φέρω
    out, ἐκφέρω
be sick, νοσέω
in, ἐν, *Dat.*
into, εἰς, *Acc.*
from, ἀπό, ἐκ, *Gen.*
woman, wife, γυνή, -αικός
graceful, χαρίεις, -εσσα, -εν
hand, χείρ, -ος, f.
send, πέμπω
    back, ἀποπέμπω

Exercise 4.

for, on behalf of, ὑπέρ, *Gen.*
worthy, ἄξιος
king, βασιλεύς, -έως, m.
lion, λέων, -οντος, m.
tooth, ὀδούς, -όντος, m.
sharp, ὀξύς, -εῖα, -ύ
father, πατήρ, -τρός
son, υἱός
citizen, πολίτης, -ου, m.
money, χρήματα, -ων, n. pl.
general, στρατηγός, m.
country, native land, πατρίς, -ίδος,
f.

Exercise 5.

hero, ἥρως, -ωος, m.
poor, πένης, -ητος
easy, ῥάδιος
battle, μάχη, f.

leader, ἡγεμών, -όνος, m.
destroy, διαφθείρω, ἀπόλλυμι
save, σώζω
rather than, μᾶλλον ἤ
orator, ῥήτωρ, -ορος, m.

Exercise 6.

conquer, νικάω
strong, ἰσχυρός
wild beast, θηρίον, n.
victory, νίκη, f.
enemy, πολέμιος, or pl. πολέμιοι
sail, πλέω
never, οὐδέποτε
arrive, ἀφικνέομαι
kill, ἀποκτείνω
betray, προδίδωμι
wrong, κακός

Exercise 7.

living creature, ζῷον, n.
beautiful, καλός
small, μικρός
tree, δένδρον, n.
flower, ἄνθος, -ους, n.
grow, αὐξάνομαι
island, νῆσος, -ου, f.
be killed, ἀποθνήσκω
by (of *agent*), ὑπό, *Gen.*
gold, χρυσός, m.
silver, ἄργυρος, m.
market, ἀγορά, f.
missile, dart, βέλος, -ους, n
throw, shoot, βάλλω
friend, φίλος, m.
present, gift, δῶρον, n.
child, παῖς, παιδός, m., f.
dear, φίλος
corn, σῖτος, m.
wine, οἶνος, m.
useful, χρήσιμος

Nicias, Νικίας, -ου
Demosthenes, Δημοσθένης, -ους
Callias, Καλλίας, -ου

Exercise 8.

take, αἱρέω
Persian, Πέρσης, -ου
brother, ἀδελφός, -οῦ

Exercise 9.

remain, μένω
dead, I am dead, τέθνηκα
day, ἡμέρα, f.
all, πᾶς, πᾶσα, πᾶν

Exercise 10.

attack, ἐπιτίθεμαι, Dat. προσβάλλω, Dat. [The latter may
be used in the Passive]
march, πορεύομαι [Aorist, ἐπο-
ρεύθην]
be in distress, difficulties, ἀπορέω
order, command, κελεύω
camp, στρατόπεδον, n.
await, δέχομαι
cross, διαβαίνω
river, ποταμός, m.
hear, ἀκούω, Gen. of person, Acc.
of thing heard
see, ὁράω   [p. 230]
enter, εἰσέρχομαι εἰς, Acc. (See
ask (a question), ἐρωτάω
answer, ἀποκρίνομαι
town, ἄστυ, -εως, n.
catch, καταλαμβάνω

Exercise 11.

sail out of, ἐκπλέω ἐκ, Gen.
encamp, στρατοπεδεύομαι
to, towards, πρός, Acc.
take, λαμβάνω, αἱρέω ; to be taken,
also ἁλίσκομαι

Exercise 12.

choose, αἱρέομαι
sell, ἀποδίδομαι
house, οἶκος, m., οἰκία, f.
Alcibiades, 'Αλκιβιάδης, -ου
win, φέρομαι
prize, ἄθλον, n.
finish (transitive), put an end to,
παύω
finish (intransitive), desist from,
cease from, παύομαι, Gen.
Socrates, Σωκράτης, -ους
teach, διδάσκω
sun, ἥλιος, m.
appear, φαίνομαι [Aorist, ἐφάνην]
show, ἀποδείκνυμι
resist, ἀμύνομαι
set free, λύω
ransom, λύομαι
capture, αἱρέω

Exercise 13.

storm, χειμών, -ῶνος, m.
quickly, ταχέως
sailor, ναύτης, -ου, m.
fish, ἰχθύς, -ύος, m.
defend, ἀμύνω, Dat. of person
defended, Acc. of person against
whom the defence is made
games, ἀγῶνες (pl. of ἀγών contest),
m.
keep safe, σῴζομαι
give back, ἀποδίδωμι
judge, κριτής, -οῦ, m.

Exercise 14.

book, βίβλος, -ου, f.
bury, θάπτω

Exercise 15.

increase (transitive), αὐξάνω
country, χώρα, f.

bring back, κομίζομαι
beat (defeat), νικάω

Exercise 16.

besiege, πολιορκέω
with all his forces, πανστρατίᾳ
stone, λίθος, m.
when, ἐπεί
wound, τραυματίζω
already, ἤδη
open, ἀνοίγνυμι
gate, πύλη, f.
skill, τέχνη, f.
bridge, γέφυρα, f.
messenger, ἄγγελος, m.
send, πέμπω

Exercise 17.

pelt, βάλλω
traitor, προδότης, -ου, m.
arrow, τόξευμα, -ατος, n.
break, λύω
great, μέγας, μεγάλη, μέγα

Exercise 18.

Athens, Ἀθῆναι, f. pl.
to Athens, Ἀθήναζε
from Athens, Ἀθήνηθεν
at Athens, Ἀθήνησι
Hellespont, Ἑλλήσποντος, m.
home, homewards, οἴκαδε
home, at home, οἴκοι
from home, οἴκοθεν
Thebes, Θῆβαι, f. pl.
Thebans, Θηβαῖοι
announce, ἀγγέλλω
Spartans, Λακεδαιμόνιοι
remain, μένω
the general and his followers,
    οἱ ἀμφὶ τὸν στρατηγόν
at Marathon, Μαραθῶνι, f.
greatly, πολύ

Exercise 19.

mainland, ἤπειρος, -ου, f.
Plataea, Πλαταιαί, f. pl.
Cyrus, Κῦρος
Sardis, Σάρδεις, f. pl. (like πόλις)
against, ἐπί, Acc.
Sparta, Σπάρτη, f.

Exercise 20.

night, νύξ, -κτός, f.
set out, start, αἴρω, ἀφορμάομαι
    [Aorist, ἀφωρμήθην]
dawn, morning, ἕως, ἕω, f.
at dawn, daybreak, ἅμ' ἡμέρᾳ,
    ἅμα τῇ ἕῳ
evening, ἑσπέρα, f.
towards evening, πρὸς ἑσπέραν
sleep, καθεύδω
stade (i.e. a furlong), στάδιον, n.
    [pl. στάδια or στάδιοι]
foot, πούς, ποδός, m.
run, τρέχω
parasang (a Persian measure of
    distance, nearly 4 miles), παρα-
    σάγγης, -ου, m.
to be distant from, ἀπέχω, with
    Gen. or with ἀπό and Gen.
early, πρώ
late, ὀψέ
winter, χειμών, -ῶνος, m.
long (of time), μακρός or πολύς
time, χρόνος, m.
year, ἔτος, -ους, n., or ἐνιαυτός, m.
height, ὕψος, -ους, n.
breadth, εὖρος, -ους, n.
length, μῆκος, -ους, n.
spear, αἰχμή, f.

Exercise 21.

on the following day, τῇ ὑστεραίᾳ
    (ἡμέρᾳ)
summer, θέρος, -ους, n.
by land, κατὰ γῆν

by sea, **κατὰ θάλασσαν**
rule, **ἄρχω**
month, **μήν, μηνός,** *m.*
enter, **εἰσέρχομαι εἰς,** *Acc.*
(See p. 230)
my, **ὁ ἐμός**
spring, **ἔαρ, ἦρος,** *n.*
another, **ἄλλος**
take place, happen, **γίγνομαι**
meadow, **λειμών, -ῶνος,** *m.*

Exercise 22.

much, **πολύς**
send out, **ἐκπέμπω**
force, **βία,** *f.*
powerful, **δυνατός**
life, **βίος,** *m.*

Exercise 23.

clever, **δεινός**
power, **δύναμις, -εως,** *f.* ;
κράτος, -ους, *n.*
faster, **θᾶσσον** (*comp.* of **ταχέως**)
glory, **κλέος, -ους,** *n.* ; **δόξα,** *f.*
Xenophon, **Ξενοφῶν, -ῶντος**
book, **βίβλος, -ου,** *f.*
write, **γράφω** or **συγγράφω**
Thucydides, **Θουκυδίδης, -ου**
broad, **εὐρύς, -εῖα, -ύ**
ditch, **τάφρος, -ου,** *f.*
Aristides, **Ἀριστείδης, -ου**
just, **δίκαιος**

Exercise 24.

disgraceful, **αἰσχρός**
weapon (missile), **βέλος, -ους,** *n.*
brother, **ἀδελφός**
attack, charge, **ἐπέρχομαι.**
(See p. 230)

Exercise 25.

hoplite, heavy armed soldier,
ὁπλίτης, -ου, *m.*

Persians, **οἱ Μῆδοι** or **οἱ Πέρσαι**
barbarian, **βάρβαρος,** *m.*
money, **ἀργύριον,** *n.*
(possessions), **χρήματα, -ων,**
n. pl.
less (*Adv.*), **ἧσσον**

Exercise 26.

enslave, **καταδουλόω**
Plataeans, **Πλαταιῆς, -έων**
(like *pl.* of **βασιλεύς**)
at once, immediately, **εὐθύς**
Jason, **Ἰάσων, -ονος**

Exercise 27.

Thermopylae, **Θερμοπύλαι, -ῶν,** *f.*
pl.
Ephialtes, **Ἐφιάλτης, -ου**
leave, leave behind, **λείπω, κατα-**
λείπω
again, **αὖθις, πάλιν**
greatly, very much, **σφόδρα, πολύ**
pleasant, sweet, **ἡδύς, -εῖα, -ύ**
seize, **συλλαμβάνω**

Exercise 28.

carry, **φέρω**
food, **σῖτος,** *m.* (*pl.* **τὰ σῖτα**)
condemn, **κατακρίνω**
after (*Prep.*), **μετά,** *Acc.*
come home, **κατέρχομαι**
honour, glory, **δόξα,** *f.*

Exercise 29.

evil tidings, **τὰ κακά**
Persia, **ἡ Περσική**
journey, **ὁδός, -οῦ,** *f.*
ask, request, **αἰτέω**
Archimedes, **Ἀρχιμήδης**

lead, ἄγω

leave, depart from, ἀπέρχομαι ἐκ, Gen.

Exercise 30.

to be in command of, ἡγεμονεύω, Gen.

few, ὀλίγοι

despise, καταφρονέω, Gen.

return, ἐπανέρχομαι

put to death, ἀποκτείνω. For Passive use ἀποθνήσκω

Exercise 31.

rout, put to flight, τρέπω

cavalry, ἱππῆς, -έων, m. pl. (like βασιλεύς)

retreat, ἀναχωρέω

allow, ἐάω

no one, nobody, οὐδείς

already, ἤδη

am able, δύναμαι

reach, arrive at, προσέρχομαι πρός, Acc. ἀφικνέομαι πρός, Acc.

Exercise 32.

set sail, weigh anchor, αἴρω

to be away, ἄπειμι

compel, ἀναγκάζω

Socrates, Σωκράτης, -ους

ready, ἑτοῖμος

ask questions, ἐρωτάω. [For Aorist, ἠρόμην from ἔρομαι may be used]

Exercise 33.

same, ὁ αὐτός

master, δεσπότης
    teacher, διδάσκαλος

dangerous, δεινός, m.

reward, μισθός, m.

consider, think, νομίζω

Exercise 34.

pleasing, ἡδύς, -εῖα, -ύ

receive, take, λαμβάνω, δέχομαι

to (of persons), ὡς, Acc.

Exercise 35.

love, φιλέω

good, ἀγαθός

some . . . others, οἱ μὲν . . . οἱ δέ

horse, ἵππος

be victorious, νικάω

go away, ἀπέρχομαι

go out, ἐξέρχομαι. (See p. 230)

sword, ξίφος, -ους, n.

Exercise 36.

report, ἀγγέλλω

punishment, ζημία, f.

willing, willingly, ἑκών, -οῦσα, -όν

Exercise 37.

towards, in the direction of, ἐπί, Gen.

Lemnos, Λῆμνος, -ου, f.

however, μέντοι (second word)

be persuaded, use πείθομαι (Passive of πείθω) with Dat.

the rest, οἱ ἄλλοι

defend, φυλάσσω

property, κτήματα, χρήματα, n. pl.

Exercise 38.

Mytilene, Μυτιλήνη, f.

especially, most of all, μάλιστα, Adv. from μάλα

Lesbian, Λέσβιος

accomplish, πράσσω, ἐκπράσσω

retreat, ἀναχωρέω

place, τόπος, m. ; χωρίον, n.

first, *Adv.*, πρῶτον
water, ὕδωρ, -ατος, *n.*
where, *Rel. Adv.*, οὖ, ὅπου
begin, ἄρχομαι
suffer terribly, δεινὰ πάσχειν (*Lit.*
  suffer terrible things)
provisions, ἐπιτήδεια, *n. pl.*
bring, κομίζω
it seems good, δοκεῖ, *Dat.*
following, next, ἐπιγιγνόμενος

Exercise 39.

at the approach of spring, ἅμα τῷ
  ἦρι
baggage, σκεύη, *n. pl.*, from σκεῦος,
  -ους
leave behind, καταλείπω
cross (a mountain), ὑπερβαίνω
go down, καταβαίνω
mountain, ὄρος, -ους, *n.*
plain, πεδίον, *n.*
await, προσδέχομαι
infantry, πεζοί (from πεζός, a foot-
  soldier)

Exercise 40.

Persians, Μῆδοι
Marathon, Μαραθών, -ῶνος, *f.*
reach, ἀφικνέομαι πρός, εἰς, *Acc.*
draw up, array, τάσσω
be general, στρατηγέω
Miltiades, Μιλτιάδης, -ου
be about, μέλλω (*Inf. Future*)
state, πόλις, -εως, *f.*
be grateful, χάριν οἶδα, χάριν
  ἔχω, *Dat.*
help, come to help, βοηθέω, *Dat.*
ready, ἑτοῖμος (with *Inf.*)
it is possible, ἔξεστι
host, πλῆθος, -ους, *n.*
fall upon, attack, ἐμπίπτω, *Dat.*
disembark, ἀποβαίνω ἐκ, *Gen.*

fear, φοβέομαι ; *Aorist*, in *Middle*
  sense, ἐφοβήθην
attack, προσβολή, *f.*

Exercise 41.

say, tell, φημί ; *Past* ἔφην.
  [Followed by *Acc.* and *Inf.*]
    λέγω ; *Aorist*, εἶπον. [Gener-
    ally followed by ὡς or ὅτι]
say that . . . not, οὐ φημί, λέγω
  ὅτι οὐ
answer, ἀποκρίνομαι [ὅτι], ὑπολαμβάνω
report, ἀγγέλλω, ἀπαγγέλλω
confess, admit, ὁμολογέω
promise, ὑπισχνέομαι
hope, ἐλπίζω
swear, ὄμνυμι
threaten, ἀπειλέω
think, νομίζω, οἴομαι
know, οἶδα
perceive, αἰσθάνομαι
hear, ἀκούω
ascertain, πυνθάνομαι
approach, προσέρχομαι
marsh, λίμνη, *f.*
fall, πίπτω
  down, καταπίπτω
encamp, αὐλίζομαι, στρατοπεδεύομαι
fortify, τειχίζω
Demosthenes, Δημοσθένης, -ους
Philip, Φίλιππος
be able, δύναμαι
be present, πάρειμι

Exercise 43.

scout, κατάσκοπος, *m.*
Aeneas, Αἰνείας, -ου
right, δίκαιος
Thermopylae, Θερμοπύλαι, -ῶν, *f.*
deed, ἔργον

Exercise 44.

burn (*intransitive*), καίομαι
(*Middle* of καίω)
assert (with idea of pretence), φάσκω
bring to, προσφέρω πρός, *Acc.*
prisoner of war, αἰχμάλωτος
do wrong, ἀδικέω
soul, ψυχή, *f.*
immortal, ἀθάνατος, -ον
once, once upon a time. ποτέ (*enclitic*)

Exercise 45.

after this, μετὰ ταῦτα, ἐκ τούτων
believe, πείθομαι
despair, be despondent, ἀθυμέω
speedily, ταχέως, διὰ τάχους
whole, πᾶς
news, τὰ ἀγγελθέντα

Exercise 46.

advance, προχωρέω
Attica, ἡ Ἀττική
chief men, οἱ πρῶτοι (τῆς πόλεως)
senate, βουλή, *f.*
Acropolis, ἀκρόπολις, *f.*
advise, πείθω
the majority, οἱ πολλοί
determine, use δοκεῖ (*impers.*), *Dat.*
embark, ἐμβαίνειν εἰς, *Acc.*
in safety, ἐν ἀσφαλεῖ
wooden, ξύλινος (*Adj.* formed from ξύλον, wood)
god, θεός, *m.*
take refuge in, καταφεύγω εἰς

Exercise 47.

assist, help, ὠφελέω, *Acc.*
plainly, clearly, σαφῶς

destroy, overthrow (a city), καθαιρέω
finish, end, τελευτάω (also used *intransitively*)
punish, κολάζω
set sail, αἴρω

Exercise 48.

Conon, Κόνων, -ωνος
be taken, ἁλίσκομαι
invade, εἰσβάλλω εἰς

Exercise 50.

try, πειράομαι
field, ἀγρός, *m.*

Exercise 51.

meadow, λειμών, -ῶνος, *m.*
thither, ἐκεῖσε
boy, παῖς, -δός
speak to, converse with, διαλέγομαι, *Dat.*
escape, ἐκφεύγω

Exercise 52.

way, ὁδός, -οῦ, *f.*
find, εὑρίσκω
how (with *Adjs.* and *Advs.*), ὡς
I am come, ἥκω
wonder, θαυμάζω

Exercise 53.

lead (of a road), φέρω
learn, μανθάνω
train, παιδεύω
enemy (often *private* enemy), ἐχθρός
here, ἐνθάδε
there, ἐκεῖ

Exercise 54.

why ? τί; διὰ τί;
no longer, οὐκέτι
friendly, εὔνους, -ουν
seem, δοκέω, φαίνομαι
come to the help of, βοηθέω. Dat.

Exercise 55.

be in, ἔνειμι
archer, τοξότης, -ου, m.
so great, τοσοῦτος, -αύτη, -οῦτον
danger, κίνδυνος
find out, ascertain, γιγνώσκω

Exercise 56.

ambassadors, πρέσβεις, -εων
fruit, καρπός, m.
gather, συγκομίζομαι
tree, δένδρον
twice a year, δὶς τοῦ ἐνιαυτοῦ
inhabit, ἐνοικέω
inhabitants, οἱ ἐνοικοῦντες,
    οἱ ἔνοικοι
kindly, graciously, ἠπίως, εὐμενῶς
pass through, διαβαίνω, Acc.
suffer harm, κακὸν πάσχω
strange, foreign, βάρβαρος, -ον
understand, συνίημι
people, δῆμος

Exercise 57.

independent, αὐτόνομος, -ον
permit, ἐάω
therefore, οὖν (2nd word)
revolt, ἀφίσταμαι (also the in-
    transitive tenses of ἀφίστημι in
    the Active)
few, ὀλίγοι
rule, ἀρχή, f.
hither, δεῦρο

become enraged, ὀργίζομαι
soon, δι' ὀλίγου, τάχα

Exercise 58.

assemble, συνέρχομαι (followed by
    εἰς or πρός with Acc.)
shore, αἰγιαλός, m.
Colchis, Κολχίς, -ίδος, f.
seek, ζητέω
golden, χρύσους, -η, -ουν
come down (esp. towards the sea)
    κατέρχομαι
send for, μεταπέμπομαι, Acc.
ox, βοῦς, βοός
skin, ἀσκός, m.
come on, ensue, ἐπιγίγνομαι
still, yet, ἔτι
pirate, robber, λῃστής, -οῦ
day before, προτεραία (ἡμέρα)

Exercise 59.

return (esp. from exile), κατέρχο-
    μαι. (See p. 230)
stranger, guest, ξένος, m.
Jason, Ἰάσων, -ονος
Medea, Μήδεια
young, νέος
not yet, οὔπω
pursue, διώκω
near, ἐγγύς, Adv.
be at a loss, ἀπορέω
limb, μέλος, -ους, n.
throw, cast, βάλλω, ῥίπτω
stop, hinder, κωλύω
only (Adj.), μόνος
approach, draw near, προσέρ-
    χομαι
thus (referring to what goes be-
    fore), οὕτως; (referring to what
    follows), ὧδε

Exercise 60.

need, δέομαι
condemn, καταγιγνώσκω
cowardice, κακία, f.
accuse, αἰτιάομαι
hear, ἀκούω, Gen. of person,
Acc. of thing
sing, ᾄδω
noise, ψόφος, m.
remember, μέμνημαι (from μιμνή-
σκω)
ancestor, πρόγονος
folly, μωρία, ἄνοια, f.
separate, ἀπαλλάσσω
forget, ἐπιλανθάνομαι

Exercise 61.

message, ἀγγελία, f.
touch, ἅπτομαι
money (i.e. coined money), ἀργύριον
begin, ἄρχομαι
assistance, βοήθεια, f.
buy, ὠνέομαι [Aorist, ἐπριάμην]
drachma, δραχμή, f.
share, μετέχω
admire, θαυμάζω, Acc. of person,
Gen. of cause
pity, οἰκτίρω, Acc. of person,
Gen. of cause
be grateful, χάριν ἔχω or χάριν οἶδα, Dat. of person, Gen. of cause
Cleon, Κλέων, -ωνος
give a share of, μεταδίδωμαι, Dat.
of person, Gen. of thing shared
envy, ζηλόω, Acc. of person,
Gen. of cause
leisure, σχολή, f.

Exercise 62.

help, go to the help of, βοηθέω, Dat.
allies, σύμμαχοι
it is expedient, συμφέρει, Dat.
obey, πείθομαι, Dat.

it is possible, ἔξεστι, Dat. [Often
used to translate may or be al-
lowed]
it seems good, δοκεῖ, Dat. [Often
used to translate they determined, etc., ἔδοξεν αὐτοῖς]
infantry, πεζός, m.
by force, βίᾳ
Apollo, Ἀπόλλων, -ωνος, m.
follow, ἕπομαι, Dat.
fight (against), μάχομαι, Dat.
temple, νεώς, -ώ, m.
Delos, Δῆλος, -ου, f.

Exercise 63.

most, the majority, οἱ πολλοί
use, χράομαι, Dat.
help, βοήθεια, f.
birth, race, γένος, -ους, n.
try, πειράομαι
often, many times, πολλάκις
good fortune, εὐτυχία, f.
before, formerly, πρότερον, τὸ
πρίν

Exercise 64.

live, dwell, οἰκέω
meet, ἐντυγχάνω, Dat.
conceal, hide, κρύπτω, double Acc.
broad, εὐρύς, -εῖα, -ύ ; but here use
the Adverbial Accusative, εὖρος,
in breadth
in no respect, not at all, οὐδέν
music, ἡ μουσική
a certain, τις (enclitic)

Exercise 65.

speak evil of, κακῶς⎫λέγω, Acc.
κακὰ ⎭
speak well of, εὖ λέγω, Acc.
injure, κακῶς⎫δράω, ποιέω, Acc.
κακὰ ⎭
do good to, εὖ ⎫
ἀγαθὰ⎭ποιέω, Acc.

rulers, οἱ ἄρχοντες, οἱ ἐν τέλει
Lysander, Λύσανδρος
name, ὄνομα, -ατος, n.
in other respects, τὰ ἄλλα
be pleased with, ἥδομαι, Dat.
feel pain, ἀλγέω

Exercise 66.

law, νόμος, m.
Mycenae, Μυκῆναι, -ῶν
overcome, get the better of, περι-
    γίγνομαι, Gen.
conquer, νικάω, Acc. ; κρατέω,
    Gen.
be in possession of, κρατέω
Thracian, Θρᾷξ, -ακός
be fitting, πρέπει (impers.), Dat.
word, λόγος, m.
be superior to, διαφέρω, Gen.

Exercise 67.

parent, γονεύς, -έως
fortunate, εὐτυχής, -ές
find out, ascertain, πυνθάνομαι
deceive, ἐξαπατάω
tyrant, τύραννος, m.

Exercise 68.

never, οὐδέποτε, μηδέποτ·
miserably, ἀθλίως
speak truth, ἀληθεύω
foolish, μῶρος, ἀνόητος

Exercise 69.

again, αὖθις, πάλιν
flower, ἄνθος, -ους, n.

Exercise 70.

desire, ἐπιθυμέω, Gen.
riches, πλοῦτος, m.
yield, hand over, παραδίδωμι

Exercise 71.

advise, παραινέω, Dat.
set free, let go, ἀφίημι
make peace, σπονδὰς ποιέομαι·
warn, νουθετέω
Olynthus, Ὄλυνθος, -ου, f.
    territory of, ἡ Ὀλυνθιακή
induce, πείθω
despise, ὀλιγωρέω, καταφρονέω,
    Gen.
exhort, παρακελεύομαι, Dat.
Themistocles, Θεμιστοκλῆς, -έους
beg, entreat, παραιτέομαι
spare, φείδομαι, Gen.
innocent, ἀναίτιος, -ον
resist, ἀμύνομαι, Acc. ; ἀνθίσταμαι,
    Dat.

Exercise 72.

charge, ἔπειμι, Dat.
able, οἷός τε
they were able, οἷοί τε ἦσαν, etc.
youth, νεανίας, -ου, m.
foreign lands, ἡ βάρβαρος [χώρα]
with difficulty, hardly, σχολῇ
treaty, σπονδαί, f. pl.
break (treaty), λύω
make treaty with, σπονδὰς ποιεῖ-
    σθαι πρός, Acc.
authorities, magistrates, οἱ ἐν τέλει
remain, linger, διατρίβω
in vain, μάτην
journey, πορεύομαι
captive, αἰχμάλωτος

Exercise 73.

treat badly, κακὰ ποιέω,
    Acc. person
lead, guide, ἡγέομαι, Dat.
sophist, σοφιστής, -οῦ, m.

make a display of, ἐπιδείκνυμαι
read, ἀναγιγνώσκω
letter, ἐπιστολή, f.
prisoner (in prison), δεσμώτης, -ου,
   (of war), αἰχμάλωτος
pardon, συγγιγνώσκω, *Dat.*

Exercise 74.

half, ἥμισυς, -εια, -υ. (Use either
as ordinary *Adj.*, *e.g.* τὸ ἥμισυ
τεῖχος half the wall, or with
the noun in *Gen.*, but giving its
gender and number to ἥμισυς,
e.g. αἱ ἡμίσειαι τῶν νεῶν, half
the ships)
innocent, ἀναίτιος, -ον
arrest, συλλαμβάνω
believe, πιστεύω
upright, δίκαιος

Exercise 75.

Minyae, Μίνυαι, -ῶν, *m.*
make war upon, πόλεμον ἐπιφέρω,
   Dat.
every year, ὅσα ἔτη
give, provide, πορίζω
Hercules, Ἡρακλῆς, -έους
ear, οὖς, ὠτός, *n.*
nose, ῥίς, ῥινός, *f.* or *pl.* ῥῖνες
cut off, ἀποτέμνω
tribute, φόρος, *m.*
then (=next, afterwards, often
opposed to πρῶτον μέν), ἔπειτα
[δέ]
avenge, τιμωρέω, *Dat.* of person
avenged, *Acc.* of person on
whom vengeance is taken. *Middle*, τιμωρέομαι, I avenge myself
on, *Acc.*
swear, ὄμνυμι
raze, καθαιρέω

to the ground, utterly, κατ' ἄκρας
refuse, οὐκ ἐθέλω

Exercise 76.

Alcmaeon, Ἀλκμαίων, -ωνος
however, μέντοι (2nd word),
ὅμως (1st word)
Delphi, Δελφοί, -ῶν, *m.*
Pythia (Priestess of Apollo),
ἡ Πυθία
despair, ἀθυμέω, ἀθύμως ἔχω
Achelous (river), Ἀχελῷος, *m.*
sand, ψάμμος, -ου, *f.*
earth, γῆ, *f.*
bring down, καταφέρω
new, νέος
allow, ἐάω, *Acc.* ἐπιτρέπω, *Dat.*
live, dwell in, ἐνοικέω ἐν

Exercise 77.

feast, ἑορτή, *f.*
middle, μέσος (taking the *Predicative* position, *e.g.* μέση ἡ
νῆσος, the middle of the island)
Phineus, Φινεύς, -έως
hall, αὐλή, *f.*
at the head of, ἄγων
band, crowd, ὄχλος, *m.*
Perseus, Περσεύς, -έως
steal, κλέπτω
Andromeda, Ἀνδρομέδη
give in marriage, ἐκδίδωμι
adversary, opponent, ἐναντίος
equally, on equal terms, ἐξ ἴσου
at last, τέλος or τὸ τέλος
Gorgon, Γοργώ, -οῦς, *f.*
head, κεφαλή, *f.*
draw forth, uncover, ἐκκαλύπτω
display, ἀποδείκνυμι
made of stone, λίθινος. (Here use
with γίγνομαι)

Exercise 78.

Troy, Τροία, f.
Trojans, Τρῶες, -ων
at sunset, ἅμ' ἡλίῳ καταδύντι
Cyclops, Κύκλωψ, -ωπος
meet, ἐντυγχάνω, Dat.
Ulysses, Ὀδυσσεύς, -έως
what had befallen him = what he
had suffered
comrade, companion, ἑταῖρος, m.
alone, μόνος
cavern, σπήλαιον, n.
beg, entreat, παραιτέομαι
run the risk of, κινδυνεύω, with
Inf.
hunger, famine, λιμός, m.
shepherd, ποιμήν, -ένος, m.
Polyphemus, Πολύφημος
suppliant, ἱκέτης, -ου, m.

Exercise 79.

appoint, make, transitive tenses
of καθίστημι
be appointed, intransitive tenses
and Middle of καθίστημι
take bribes, δῶρα λαμβάνω
pay (tribute), φέρω
throw away, ῥίπτω
cause to revolt, transitive tenses
of ἀφίστημι (ἀπό)
revolt, intransitive tenses and
Middle of ἀφίστημι
for my part, τὸ ἐπ' ἐμέ
be angry, ὀργίζομαι, Dat., or δι'
ὀργῆς ἔχειν, Acc.
abandon, desert, ἀπολείπω
in public, publicly, δημοσίᾳ
privately, ἰδίᾳ
serve, ὠφελέω
the state, ἡ πόλις or τὸ κοινόν
to the best of their ability, κατὰ
δύναμιν

reduce, subdue, καταστρέφομαι
punish (take vengeance on), τιμωρέομαι, Acc.
tribe, φῦλον, n.

Exercise 80.

Milesians, Μιλήσιοι
oppress, πιέζω
rank, τάξις, -εως, f.
former, πρίν, Adv.
plague, pestilence, λοιμός, m.
spring up, arise, γίγνομαι
delay, wait, ἐπέχω
reproach, ὀνειδίζω, Dat.
unfortunate, δυστυχής
duty, τὸ προσῆκον
Homer, Ὅμηρος
praise, ἐπαινέω, Acc.
Agamemnon, Ἀγαμέμνων, -ονος

Exercise 81.

continue, remain, διατελέω
(with Participle)
faithful, πιστός
peace, εἰρήνη, f.
voyage, πλοῦς, πλοῦ, m.

Exercise 82.

suddenly, ἐξαίφνης, ἄφνω
stand up, intransitive tenses and
Middle of ἀνίστημι
people, δῆμος, m.
loose, λύω

Exercise 83.

use all means, πάντι τρόπῳ χράομαι
you must, δεῖ σε with Inf.
Brasidas, Βρασίδας, -ου
call, summon, καλέω, προσκαλέω,
μεταπέμπομαι

consult, ask the opinion of, συμβουλεύομαι, κοινόομαι, Dat.
on behalf of, ὑπέρ, Gen.
hasten (trans.), σπεύδω
make haste, hasten (intrans.), σπεύδω or Middle, ἐπείγομαι
return, ἐπανέρχομαι
trophy, τρόπαιον
set up, ἵστημι (transitive tenses)
bury, θάπτω
be, be sufficient, ὑπάρχω

Exercise 84.

watch, τηρέω
carefully, ἐπιμελῶς
poet, ποιητής, -οῦ, m.
write poetry, ποιέω
write a prose book, generally, συγγράφω
inform him of=announce to him, ἀγγέλλω
doctor, ἰατρός, m.
attend to, θεραπεύω
in all directions, everywhere, πανταχόσε
burn, burn up, κατακαίω
Spartan (one of the true Spartans), Σπαρτιάτης, -ου

Exercise 85.

Thrace, Θράκη, f.
dead, dead body, νεκρός
falsely, ψευδῶς
obtain, κτάομαι
powerful, δυνατός
for the future, again, τοῦ λοιποῦ

Exercise 86.

consult (the oracle), χράομαι, Dat.
satrap, σατράπης, -ου
trench, τάφρος, f.
discover, εὑρίσκω, μανθάνω

Exercise 87.

unexpectedly, ἀπροσδοκήτως, or use the Adj. ἀπροσδόκητος, -ον, which means both unexpected and not expecting, unaware
be punished, δίκας δίδωμι (Lat. poenas dare)
punish, exact penalty, δίκας λαμβάνω παρά (Lat. poenas sumere)
take care, φυλάσσομαι, ἐπιμελέομαι
write down, συγγράφω
prudent, σώφρων, φρόνιμος

Exercise 88.

lose, ἀπόλλυμι

Exercise 89.

sensible, prudent, wise, φρόνιμος
careless, lazy, ῥᾴθυμος
opportunity, καιρός, m.
let slip an opportunity, καιρὸν παρίημι
hardship, toil, πόνος, m.

Exercise 90.

bold, τολμηρός, θρασύς, -εῖα, -ύ
unwilling, against their will, ἄκων, -ουσα, -ον
hold out, ἀντέχω
dread, δέδοικα, or δέδια

Exercise 91.

closely, συνεχῶς
Olynthus, Ὄλυνθος, f.
choose, αἱρέομαι, ἐξαιρέομαι
weak, ἀσθενής
summon home (from exile), κατάγω
Syracusans, Συρακόσιοι
build, οἰκοδομέω
surround, περιέχω

spend, ἀναλίσκω
in the time of, ἐπί, Gen.
pay, μισθός, m.
provide, παρέχω, πορίζω

Exercise 92.
consult, κοινόομαι, Dat., συμβουλεύομαι, Dat.
rejoice, χαίρω
overthrow (subdue), καταστρέφομαι
empire, ἀρχή
honourable, καλός
be banished, ἐκπίπτω

Exercise 93.
Cretans, Κρῆτες, -ῶν
Poseidon, Ποσειδῶν, -ῶνος (Acc. Ποσειδῶ)
Minos, Μίνως, -ως or -ω
bull, ταῦρος, m.
sacrifice, θύω
wave, κῦμα, -ατος, n.
keep, κατέχω
mad, μανικός
forest, ὕλη, f.
keep one's word, τῇ πίστει ἐμμένειν (πίστις, -εως, pledge)
monster, θηρίον, n.

Exercise 94.
Eurystheus, Εὐρυσθεύς, -έως
rope, σχοινίον, n.
spear, αἰχμή, f.
roar, make a noise, βρυχάομαι
on (from) all sides, πανταχόθεν
approach, προσέρχομαι
impossible, ἀδύνατον
avoid, ὑπεξίσταμαι
firmly, βεβαίως
horn, κέρας, -ατος, n.
hold, κατέχω

after a short time, οὐ διὰ μακροῦ, δι' ὀλίγου
exhaust, κατατρίβω

Exercise 95.
win a victory, νικάω
wreck, ναυάγιον, n.
cling to, ἔχομαι, Gen.
officers, οἱ ἄρχοντες
harm, κακόν
to be put on trial, ἐς κρίσιν καταστῆναι
I defend myself, ἀπολογέομαι
listen to, ἀκροάομαι
the penalty, τὸ δίκας διδόναι

Exercise 96.
Cadmus, Κάδμος, m.
Cadmea, Καδμεία, f.
citadel, ἀκρόπολις, -εως, f.
name, ὀνομάζω
fortify, περιτειχίζω
Amphion, 'Αμφίων, -ωνος
compel, ἀναγκάζω
to be built round, περιβάλλεσθαι, Dat.
from all sides, πανταχόθεν

Exercise 97.
people (generally), οἱ ἄνθρωποι

Exercise 98.
to be ill, νοσέω

Exercise 99.
send forward, προπέμπω
forbid, οὐκ ἐάω
guilty, αἴτιος
acquit, ἀπολύω
return, ἐπανέρχομαι
how long? πόσον χρόνον;

last, διατελέω
unprepared, ἀπροσδόκητος

Exercise 101.

be ignorant, ἀγνοέω
be mistaken, ἁμαρτάνω

Exercise 102.

work, ἔργον
this is so, this is the case, ταῦτα
οὕτως ἔχει
dare, τολμάω

Exercise 103.

coward, cowardly, κακός, δειλός
plot against, ἐπιβουλεύω, Dat.

Exercise 104.

without our help, ἄνευ ἡμῶν
Potidaea, Ποτίδαια, f.
also, even, καί
such a thing, τὸ τοιοῦτο
Pydna, Πύδνη, f.
give advice, συμβουλεύω

Exercise 105.

unjust, ἄδικος, -ον
blame, μέμφομαι, Dat.
be well (of things), τὰ πράγματα
καλῶς ἔχει
letter, ἐπιστολή, f.
welcome, ἀσπάζομαι
be master of, κρατέω, Gen.

Exercise 106.

made the following proclamation =
announce these things, τάδε.
(See p. 133)
through, all round, περί, Acc.
Polynices, Πολυνείκης, -ους
Argives, Ἀργεῖοι

sister, ἀδελφή, f.
so greatly, τοσοῦτο(ν), Adv. Acc.
disobey, ἀπειθέω, Dat.
even if, καὶ ἐάν, καὶ εἰ
very, exceedingly, μάλα, σφόδρα
be angry, ἀγανακτέω
act rightly, ποιέω τὸ προσῆκον
be afraid, δέδοικα
guard, φύλαξ, -ακος
shut up (in prison), εἴργω

Exercise 107.

come forward (to speak), παρέρχομαι
Athenians—in a speech often, ὦ
ἄνδρες Ἀθηναῖοι (so, ἄνδρες
στρατιῶται, etc.)
increase, αὐξάνω, αὔξω
the present danger, τὸ αὐτίκα
δεινόν
as . . . as, οὕτως . . . ὡς
but as it is, νῦν δέ
be confident, θαρρέω
as strongly as possible, ὡς κράτιστα
forces, δύναμις, -εως, f.
collect, levy, ἀθροίζω
common, κοινός

Exercise 108.

trust, πιστεύω, Dat.
panic, φόβος, m.
garrison, φρουροί (from φρουρός,
a guard), φρούριον
call together, συγκαλέω
comrades (Voc.), ὦ ἄνδρες
disaster, συμφορά, f.
consider, deliberate, βουλεύομαι
be expedient, συμφέρει, Dat.
for the present, ἐν τῷ παρόντι
at the present moment, τὸ παραυ-
τίκα

take service, serve as a soldier, στρατεύω
be in want of, ἀπορέω, δέομαι, *Gen.*
the opportunity comes, παρέχει (*impers.*)

Exercise 109.
address, exhort, παρακελεύομαι, *Dat.*
perhaps, ἴσως
on the side of, μετά, *Gen.*
defend, ἀμύνομαι, *Dat.*
impious, ἀσεβής, -ές

Exercise 110.
happen, τυγχάνω
escape notice, λανθάνω, *Acc.*
just, δίκαιος
anticipate, φθάνω, *Acc.*
and that too, καὶ ταῦτα (*Adv. Acc.*)

Exercise 111.
run, τρέχω
blame, ἐν αἰτίᾳ ἔχω
judges, jurymen, δικασταί (from δικαστής, -οῦ)
dismiss, ἀφίημι
from (of persons), παρά
both, ἀμφότεροι οἱ . . .
splendid, καλός

Exercise 112.
be delighted, ἥδομαι, *Dat.*
treat, behave to, χράομαι, *Dat.*
threaten, ἀπειλέω, *Dat.*
carelessness, ἀμελεία, *f.*
strive for, ἐρίζω περί, *Gen.*
leadership, ἡγεμονία, *f.*
Cimon, Κίμων, -ωνος
Lemnos, Λῆμνος, -ου, *f.*
it is possible, πάρεστι

Exercise 113.
live, pass one's life, διάγω
be hated by, hateful to, ἀπεχθάνομαι, *Dat.*
the government, οἱ ἐν τέλει
Brasidas and his men, { οἱ ἀμφὶ / οἱ περὶ } τὸν Βρασίδαν
rejoice, χαίρω
shield, ἀσπίς, -ίδος, *f.*
preserve, σῴζομαι
cautiously, εὐλαβῶς
position (military), χωρίον, *n.*

Exercise 114.
pass (of time, as subject), διέρχομαι *or* use μετά, *Acc.*
Oedipus, Οἰδίπους, -οδος
Corinth, Κόρινθος, -ου, *f.*
oracle, χρηστήριον, *n.*
queen, βασίλεια
madness, infatuation, ἄτη, *f.*
marry (of man), γαμέω
      (of woman), γαμοῦμαι
herdsman, ποιμήν, -ένος
tie, bind, δέω
string, cord, σχοινίον, *n.*
old man, γέρων, -οντος, *m.*

Exercise 115.
Jocasta, Ἰοκάστη
bear, endure, ὑπομένω
room, θάλαμος, *m.*
thereupon, ἔπειτα, ἔνθα δή, ἐκ δὲ τούτων
daughter, θυγάτηρ, -τρός
wander, πλανάομαι
for the future, τὸ λοιπόν

Exercise 116.
I repent, μεταμέλει μοι
plunder, λεία, *f.*
resolve, use δοκεῖ
to be impossible, ἀδύνατον εἶναι

snow, χιών, -όνος, f.
halt, ἀναπαύομαι
it is to my advantage, λυσιτελεῖ
μοι, συμφέρει μοι
give up, surrender, παραδίδωμι
Themistocles, Θεμιστοκλῆς, -έους
equip, παρασκευάζομαι
fleet, ναυτικόν, n.

Exercise 117.
I have a part in, μέτεστί μοι with
Gen.
hold out, ἀνέχομαι
advise, παραινέω, Dat.
wrong, ἄδικος
Roman, 'Ρωμαῖος
I have an opportunity, παρέχει μοι

Exercise 118.
verbal adj. of δίδωμι, δοτέος; of
λαμβάνω, ληπτέος; of ἵστημι,
στατέος
give a share of, μεταδίδωμι; Gen.
of thing, Dat. of person
give in marriage, ἐκδίδωμι
undertake, ἀντιλαμβάνω, Gen.;
ἐπιχειρέω, Dat.
captain, λοχαγός, m.
pass the word along, proclaim,
παραγγέλλω
remove (trans.), μετανίστημι; (intrans.), intransitive tenses and
Middle of μετανίσμημι
Salamis, Σαλαμίς, -ῖνος, f.

Exercise 119.
fall into hands of, ὑποχείριος γίγνομαι, Dat.
clothes, clothing, ἐσθής, -ῆτος, f.
in time, at the right time, ἐς
καιρόν, ἐν καιρῷ
guest, ξένος

win, κτάομαι
bread, ἄρτοι, m. pl.

Exercise 120.
hate, μισέω
I have gone away, οἴχομαι
just, δίκαιος
unjust, ἄδικος
successful, εὐτυχής

Exercise 121.
reward, μισθὸν διδόναι, Dat.
capable of, ἱκανός, Inf.
to such a pitch of, ἐς τοσοῦτο, Gen.
boldness, daring, τόλμα
vote, ψηφίζομαι, Inf.
to go to war, πολεμέω
keep peace, remain at peace,
εἰρήνην ἄγω
before that, πρὸ τοῦ
obol, ὀβολός, m.
every day, day by day, καθ' ἡμέραν
at a run, δρόμῳ (from δρόμος, m.)
run forward, προθέω
wing (of army), κέρας, -ως, n.
simultaneously, ἅμα
survive, περιγίγνομαι
look at, προσβλέπω, Acc.
Aeschines, Αἰσχίνης, -ου
Hannibal, 'Αννίβας, -α
Alexander, 'Αλέξανδρος

Exercise 122.
esteem highly, περὶ πολλοῦ (πλείονος, πλείστου) ποιέομαι, Acc.
elder, πρεσβύτερος
be hungry, πεινάω
dark, σκοτεινός
wound, τραυματίζω, τιτρώσκω

Exercise 123.
stream, ῥοῦς (ῥόος), ῥοῦ, m.

Exercise 124.
overtake, καταλαμβάνω
intend, διανοέομαι
be engaged in, σπουδάζω περί,
Gen.
observe, αἰσθάνομαι
philosopher, φιλόσοφος, m.
origin, beginning, ἀρχή, f.
world (=universe), κόσμος, m.

Exercise 125.
on the right (wing), ἐπὶ δεξιᾷ
on the left (wing), ἐπ' ἀριστερᾷ
charge, προσβολή, f.
station, place, καθίστημι. For
Passive use Intransitive tenses
the present, τὸ νῦν
finish, ἐκτελέω

Exercise 126.
meanwhile, ἐν τούτῳ
cut off, intercept, ἀπολαμβάνω
Sikels, Σίκελοι
attack, προσβάλλω, Dat.
soon after this, οὐ διὰ πολλοῦ
full, πλέως, -α, -ων, Gen.
confidence, θάρσος, -ους, n.
win reputation for, δόξαν κτάομαι,
Gen.
wisdom, good sense, φρόνησις

Exercise 127.
Carthage, Καρχηδών, -όνος, f.
Carthaginian, Punic, Καρχηδόνιος
be distant, ἀπέχω
about (of numbers), μάλιστα, ὡς
army, land force, πεζός, m.
help, reinforcements, βοήθεια, f.
enough, ἱκανός, Inf. or ὥστε with
Inf.
man, πληρόω
be in command of, ἐφέστηκα

arm, καθοπλίζω
sortie, sally, ἐκδρομή
repulse, ἀποκρούομαι
Romans, Ῥωμαῖοι

Exercise 128.
be cheerful, of good courage, εὐθυμέω
for a little time, ὀλίγον χρόνον
in front, ἐκ τοῦ ἔμπροσθεν
terrify, φοβέω, ἐκπλήσσω
go about among, φοιτάω ἐν, Dat.
exhort, παρακελεύομαι, Dat.
Babylon, Βαβυλών, -ῶνος, f.
pass through, surmount, περιγίγνομαι, Gen.
rout, τρέπω
shudder at, ἀποκνέω, Acc.
wild beast, θήρ, θηρός, m., θηρίον, n.

Exercise 129.
prepare, παρασκευάζω
eclipse, ἔκλειψις, -εως, f.
moon, σελήνη, f.
prophet, μάντις, -εως, m.
wait, rest, ἀναπαύομαι
writer, historian, συγγραφεύς, -εως
relate, ἐξηγέομαι
pious, εὐσεβής, -ές
be guilty of, ὀφλισκάνω, Acc.
waste (time), διατρίβω
chance, opportunity, καιρός, m.

Exercise 130.
devote attention to, undertake
strenuously, ἅπτομαι, Gen.,
προσέχω, Dat.
eagerly, προθύμως
oppose, ἐναντιόομαι, Dat.
fleet, τὸ ναυτικόν, στόλος ναυτικός
enrich, πλουτίζω, Fut. πλουτιῶ

live on, survive, ἐπιβιόω, *Aorist*,
ἐπεβίων
probably, κατὰ τὸ εἰκός
lack, scarcity, ἔνδεια, ἀπορία, *f.*
raise, abandon, a siege, παύομαι
τῆς πολιορκίας
by land and sea, καὶ κατὰ γῆν καὶ
κατὰ θάλασσαν
Phoenicians, Φοίνικες, -ων
Cilicians, Κίλικες, -ων

Exercise 131.

make peace, σπένδομαι, σπονδὰς
ποιέομαι
restore, ἀποδίδωμι
receive back, ἀπολαμβάνω
Amphipolis, Ἀμφίπολις, -εως, *f.*
gladly, ἡδέως
maintain, abide by, ἐμμένω, *Dat.*
evacuate, ἐξέρχομαι ἐκ
complain, be vexed, δεινὸν
ποιέομαι
ephors, ἔφοροι
possess, κέκτημαι(*Perf.* of κτάομαι)
reduce, bring over to one's side,
προσάγομαι
take by siege, ἐκπολιορκέω
treat, χράομαι, *Dat.*
cruel, ὠμός
agreement, τὰ ῥητά
Peloponnese, Πελοπόννησος, -ου, *f.*
create, cause to be . . ., καθίστημι

Exercise 132.

expedition, στρατεία, *f.*
Carduchi, Κάρδουχοι
Ionian, Ἰόνιος
Cyprus, Κύπρος, -ου, *f.*
weigh anchor, αἴρω

Exercise 133.

keep, ἔχω
hunt, θηρεύω

Exercise 134.

whoever, ὅστις, εἴ τις
wherever, ὅπου (if *where = whither*,
ὅποι)
whenever, ὁπότε, εἴ ποτε
however, ὅπως
however many, ὅσοι
of whatever kind, ὁποῖος
turn out, ἀποβαίνω

Exercise 136.

when (*Temporal Conjunction*),
ἐπεί, ἐπειδή [1]
until, ἕως, μέχρι, πρίν
while, ἕως
before, πρίν
after, ἐπειδή, ἀφ' οὗ, ἐξ οὗ (χρόνου
understood)
Darius, Δαρεῖος, -ου
Artaxerxes, Ἀρταξέρξης, -ου
be made, appointed, *intransitive*
tenses of καθίστημι
Persia, ἡ Περσική
give instructions to, προστάσσω,
Dat.
seize, arrest, συλλαμβάνω
keep quiet, ἡσυχάζω, ἡσυχίαν ἔχω
darkness, σκότος, *m.*

Exercise 137.

bring in, εἰσφέρω, εἰσκομίζω
settle, διατίθεμαι
talk nonsense, φλυαρέω
get up, *intransitive* tenses and
Middle of ἀνίστημι

---

[1] ὅτε is a Relative and is not used except with an antecedent expressed or understood ; *e.g.* ἦν ποτε χρόνος ὅτε γίγαντες ἦσαν, there was a time when there were giants.

eat, ἐσθίω
prison, δεσμωτήριον, n.

Exercise 138.

storm, ${κατὰ κράτος \atop βίᾳ}$ αἱρέω
associate with, φοιτάω παρά, Acc.
all but, ὅσον οὐ
in different directions, ἄλλος
ἄλλοσε
run about, διαθέω

Exercise 139.

drive out, ἐκβάλλω
be idle, ῥᾳθυμέω
rebuke, ἐπιτιμάω, Dat.
think, ponder, φροντίζω
know how, οἶδα, ἐπίσταμαι, Inf.
pay, ἀποδίδωμι
all the time that, ὅσον χρόνον
a second time, τὸ δεύτερον
breakfast, ἄριστον, n.
get one's breakfast, ἀριστοποιέομαι
join battle with, μάχην συνάπτειν
πρός, Acc.
ἐς χεῖρας ἔρχομαι, Dat. (of
fighting at close quarters)

Exercise 140.

not long afterwards, οὐ πολλῷ
ὕστερον
nearly, σχεδόν
gnat, κώνωψ, -ωτος, m.
bite, δάκνω
cattle, κτήνη, -ῶν, n. pl., from
κτῆνος
fly, πέτομαι
leap into, εἰσάλλομαι εἰς, Acc.
(Aorist, εἰσηλάμην in Ind. but
Str. Aorist forms in other moods)
bring back, ἀπάνω

pull, ἐπισπάω
drive, ἐλαύνω
sea, open sea, πόντος, m.
swim, νέω
out, ἐκνέω
collect, ἀγείρω, συναγείρω
be tired, worn out, ἀποκάμνω
recover, ἀναλαμβάνω

Exercise 141.

resources, χρήματα, -ων, n.
spend, ἀναλίσκω, δαπανάω
pleasure, ἡδονή, f.
build (ships), κατασκευάζω
be involved in, intransitive tenses
and Middle of καθίστημι, followed by εἰς, Acc.
imitate, τὰ ὅμοια πράσσω, Dat.
prosper (of things), προχωρέω, or
Passive of κατορθόω

Exercise 142.

secretary, ἐπιστολεύς, -έως
once, ποτέ
in a dream, ὄναρ, Adv.
funeral pyre, πυρά, f.
lie, κεῖμαι
set on fire, ἅπτω
uproar, θόρυβος, m.
awaken, arouse, ἐγείρω
finish, complete, ἐξεργάζομαι
cloak, χλαῖνα, f.
wrap up, ἐγκαλύπτω (here Middle)
smoke, καπνός, m.
choke, ἀποπνίγω; Aorist Passive,
ἀπεπνίγην
at a distance, διὰ πολλοῦ
shoot with arrows at, τοξεύω,
Acc.
arrow, τόξευμα, -ατος, n.
die, end one's life, τελευτάω

Exercise 143.

delay (*trans.*), κωλύω
adverse, ἐναντίος
wind, ἄνεμος, *m.*
put in (of ships), προσέχω εἰς, *Acc.*
bay, κόλπος, *m.*
propose, συμβουλεύω, *Dat.*
Laconian territory, ἡ Λακωνική
the opportunity having come, παρασχόν, *Acc. Abs.*
marine, ἐπιβάτης, -ου
fort, τείχισμα
as soon as, ἐπεὶ τάχιστα
Pylos, Πύλος, *m.*

Exercise 144.

prevent, εἴργω, κωλύω
what prevents? nothing prevents, τί; οὐδὲν ἐμποδών ἐστιν
forbid, οὐκ ἐάω, ἀπαγορεύω; *Aorist*, ἀπεῖπον
deny, ἀπαρνέομαι
refrain, ἀπέχομαι
Pausanias, Παυσανίας, -ου
converse with, διαλέγομαι, *Dat.*
to the best of their power, κατὰ δύναμιν

Exercise 145.

winter, χειμών, -ῶνος, *m.*
exile, φυγάς, -άδος
be worsted, ἡσσάομαι
love of their country, say τὸ φιλοπόλεις εἶναι

Exercise 146.

captain (of ship), τριήραρχος, *m.*
slow, βραδύς, -εῖα, -ύ; *Adv.* βραδέως
rashly, ἀσκέπτως
hate, μισέω

provoke, παροξύνω
fare badly, κακῶς πράσσω
at the critical moment, εἰς καιρόν

Exercise 147.

trustworthy, πιστός
perilous, σφαλερός
have strength, ἰσχύω, *Inf.*
escape safely, get safe to, σῴζομαι εἰς [*Passive Aorist* in this sense]
shameless, ἀναιδής, -ές
skilful in, ἐπιστήμων, -ονος, *Gen.*
art, τέχνη, *f.*
turn away (*intrans.*), ἀποστρέφομαι; *Aorist*, ἀπεστράφην

Exercise 148.

cheer, θαρσύνω
encourage, παραμυθέομαι, *Dat.*
to blame, αἴτιος
in reality, τῷ ὄντι
there was not a man who . . . not, οὐδεὶς ὅστις οὐκ
be hopeless (of things), τὰ πράγματα ἀνελπίστως ἔχει

Exercise 149.

in later times, χρόνῳ ὕστερον
tell a story, μυθολογέω
undergo, *intransitive* tenses of ὑφίστημι, *Acc.*
Ephesus, Ἔφεσος, -ου, *f.*
of necessity, perforce, ἀνάγκῃ
willingly at least, ἑκὼν εἶναι
persecute, διώκω
good will, εὔνοια, *f.*
subjects, ὑπήκοοι, *m.*
take vengeance on, τιμωρέομαι, *Acc.*
fulfil a promise, ὑπόσχεσιν ἀποδίδωμι

die a voluntary death, commit suicide, βιάζεσθαι ἑαυτόν
vainly, μάτην
boast, κομπάζω
convict of, ἐλέγχω with *Participle*

Exercise 150.

decide previously (of the senate), προβουλεύω
decree, προβούλευμα
as was usual, κατὰ τὸ εἰωθός
release for ransom, ἀπολυτρόω
rebel, *intransitive* tenses of ἀφίστημι
colony, ἀποικία, *f.*
urge, πείθω
mother city, μητρόπολις, -εως, *f.*
carry out (a decree), περαίνω
ratify, κυρόω
hold a public assembly, ἐκκλησίαν ποιέω
Thurians, Θούριοι
kinsman, συγγενής, -οῦς
inflict punishment on, δίκην λαμβάνω παρά, *Gen.*

Exercise 151.

remind, ἀναμιμνήσκω
speak in defence of oneself, ἀπολογέομαι
Dorieus, Δωριεύς, -έως
Rhodian, 'Ρόδιος
stature, μέγεθος, -ους, *n.*
magnificent, εὐπρεπής
known, famous, γνώριμος
throughout, ἀνά, *Acc.*
especially, ἄλλως τε καί
Olympian games, τὰ 'Ολύμπια
pancratium, παγκράτιον, *n.*
be victorious in, νικάω, *Acc.*
restrain, ἀπέχω, κατέχω
applaud, ἀναθορυβέω

Exercise 152.

rob, ἀφαιρέομαι, *double Acc.*
accuse, αἰτιάομαι, *Acc.* of person, *Gen.* of crime
ἐγκαλέω, *Dat.* of person, *Acc.* of crime
unguarded, ἀφύλακτος, -ον, ἔρημος
make haste, σπεύδω

Exercise 153.

experienced, ἐπιστήμων, -ονος, ἔμπειρος
to-day, τήμερον, *Adv.*
on that day, αὐθήμερον, *Adv.*
task, ἔργον
without accomplishing one's purpose, without success, ἄπρακτος, -ον
be ashamed, αἰσχύνομαι
weep, κλαίω
pity, ἔλεος, *m.*
deserve, ἄξιός εἰμι, *Inf.*
endure (punishment), ὑπέχω

Exercise 154.

Epigoni, 'Επίγονοι, -ων
avenge, τιμωρέω, *Dat.* of person avenged, *Acc.* of person on whom vengeance is taken. In the *Middle* τιμωρέομαι *Acc.* = take vengeance on
hold one's ground, ἀνθίσταμαι
steadily, firmly, βεβαίως
raise the siege, intrans. tenses and *Middle* of ἀπανίστημι
at the advice of, use πείθω
Tiresias, Τειρεσίας, -ου
unobserved, secretly, λάθρᾳ (or use λανθάνω)
feast, εὐωχέομαι
desert, ἐρημόω

Exercise 155.

further, πορρωτέρω (from πόρρω)
desert, ἔρημος [as *Subst.* ἡ ἔρημος
(*sc.* χώρα)]
be hard pressd, πιέζομαι
surrender (*intrans.*), ἐνδίδωμι
on the point of, all but, ὅσον οὐκ
Scythians, Σκύθαι, -ῶν
agree, come to terms, συμβαίνω
(followed by ἐφ᾽ ᾧτε)
hostage, ὅμηρος, *m.*
invade, εἰσβάλλω εἰς

Exercise 156.

right, δεξιός
left, ἀριστερός, εὐώνυμος, -ον
hill, λόφος, *m.*
desert, αὐτομολέω
know, am conscious, σύνοιδα
ἐμαυτῷ
responsible, αἴτιος
so far as, ὅσον
be on one's side, fight for one,
συμμάχομαι, *Dat.*

Exercise 157.

Italy, Ἰταλία, *f.*
at the height, ἐν ἀκμῇ
power, ῥώμη
get the upper hand, περιγίγνομαι,
Gen.
sometimes, ἐνίοτε
ample, ἱκανός
Pyrrhus, Πύρρος, -ου

Exercise 158.

subdue, καταστρέφομαι
reap fruit, κομίζω τοὺς καρπούς
elect, αἱρέομαι, χειροτονέω

Exercise 159.

Pericles, Περικλῆς, -έους
contest, ἅμιλλα, *f.*
Susa, Σοῦσα, -ων, *n.*
like, ὅμοιος

Exercise 160

skilfully, ἐπιστημόνως
meet, ἀπαντάω, *Dat.*
contest, ἀγών, -ῶνος, *m.*

Exercise 161.

it is plain that, use personal construction—δῆλός εἰμι with *Participle*
be badly treated, κακῶς πάσχω

Exercise 162.

ordain, κελεύω
imprison, καταδέω
try, bring to trial, καθίστημι εἰς
κρίσιν (in *Passive* sense use *intransitive* tenses)
property is confiscated, τὰ κτήματα
δημόσια γίγνεται, ἐστί (lit. become public property)
be in vehement haste, λίαν ἐπείγομαι
put off, ἀναβάλλω
to-morrow, ἡ αὔριον (*sc.* ἡμέρα)
annul, καταλύω
too late, ὀψέ
repent, μεταμέλει (*impers.*), *Dat.*
in the past, ἐν τῷ παρελθόντι χρόνῳ
think, deem, ἀξιόω
crown, στέφανος, *m.*
at least, however that may be,
δ᾽ οὖν
decide, come to a decision, διακρίνομαι
way, manner, τρόπος

Exercise 163.

be dissatisfied with, χαλεπῶς φέρω, Acc.

present condition of affairs, τὰ παρόντα

reflect, φροντίζω, ἐνθυμέομαι

Exercise 164.

be discontented, δεινὸν ποιέομαι

officers (general word), οἱ ἄρχοντες

divulge, μηνύω

explain, ἐξηγέομαι

frontier, ὅρος, m.

Exercise 165.

in answer, ὑπολαβών

Tissaphernes, Τισσαφέρνης, -ους

outcry, κραυγή, f.

cause, αἰτία, f.

Arcadian, Ἀρκάς, -άδος

cry out, βοάω

be better than, διαφέρω, Gen.

stratagem, craft, δόλος, m.

Exercise 166.

clever at, δεινός, Inf.

be unable, not in a position to, οὐκ ἔχω, Inf. ; οὐχ οἷός τέ εἰμι, Inf.

Exercise 167.

bring up, τρέφω

politics, τὰ τῆς πόλεως πράγματα

generous, high-minded, ἐλευθέριος

convict of, ἐλέγχω, with Gen. or Participle

treachery, προδοσία, f.

mercenary, μισθοφόρος, m.

mercenary force, τὸ ξενικόν

ride, ἐλαύνω

discuss, settle, διακαρίνομαι περί, Gen.

scatter (trans.), διασκεδάννυμι; (intrans.), διασπείρομαι (or Passive of διασκεδάννυμι)

Exercise 168.

take up position, intransitive tenses of καθίστημι

centre, τὸ μέσον

on the flank, κατὰ κέρας

break (a line), παραρρήγνυμι

eagerness, ardour, σπουδή, f.

catch sight of, καθοράω

throng, ὄχλος, m.

furiously, recklessly, προπετῶς

hurl (from horse), κατακυλίνδω) (tenses as if from κατακυλίζω)

with eight others, say 'himself the ninth'

Exercise 169.

retreat before, ὑπεξέρχομαι, Acc.

ambush, ἐνέδρα, f.

be encouraged, θαρρέω

in the presence of, over against, ἐναντίον, Gen.

arrange a line of battle. παρατάσσομαι, ἀντιτάσσομαι

archer, τοξότης, -ου, m.

light-armed troops, πελτασταί (from πελταστής, -οῦ), ψιλοί

Exercise 170.

well, φρέαρ, -ατος, n.

prefer, προαιρέομαι

negotiate with, πράσσειν πρός, Acc.

forsooth, ἄρα, δῆτα

laugh to scorn, καταγελάω, Gen.

be a laughing-stock, καταγέλαστός εἰμι

nay, use μᾶλλον δέ

Exercise 171.

to be reasonable, εἰκὸς εἶναι
despatch, ἀποστέλλω
burdensome, ἐπαχθής, -ές
be abroad, away from home, ἀποδημέω
spend (of time), διάγω
attach, add, προστίθημι
be sufficient, ἀποχράω (Inf. ἀποχρῆν)
sea-coast, παραλία, f.
Macedonian, Μακεδονικός
summer, θέρος, -ους, n.
dismiss (from one's thoughts), ἐάω
for the moment, πρὸς τὸ παρόν
unpleasant, δυσχερής, -ές
necessary, ἐπιτήδειος
crisis, καιρός, m.
be proud of, σεμνύνομαι ἐπί,
  Dat.
briefly, διὰ βραχέων
famed, ἐπιφανής, -ές
world, use γῆ
risk, παραβάλλομαι
the ends of the world, τὰ ἔσχατα
  τῆς γῆς
be slothful, ῥᾳθυμέω
hire, μισθόομαι (Middle)
shame, αἰσχύνη

Exercise 172.

(direct) assault, προσβολή
immense (of number), ἀναρίθμητος
cold, ψῦχος, -ους, n.
befall, συμβαίνει (impers.), Dat.
support life, τὴν ἀναγκαῖον τροφὴν
  παρέχειν
be in danger, run risk of, κινδυνεύω, Inf.
deprive of, ἀποστερέω
organise, συσκευάζω

Exercise 173.

draw up, haul up, ἀνέλκω
badly, poorly, φαύλως
shrink from, ἀποκνέω, Inf.
be in adversity, δυστυχέω
those at home, οἱ οἴκοι

Exercise 174.

more than from any other place,
  εἰ καὶ ἄλλοθεν
height, ἄκρον, n.
with one assault, μιᾷ ὁρμῇ
bivouack, αὐλίζομαι
each time, ἑκάστοτε
resolutely, θαρραλέως
low-lying, πεδινός
marshy, λιμνώδης, -ές
bring to terms, ἀναγκάζειν περὶ
  ἀπαλλαγῆς πράσσειν
single, ἁπλοῦς, -ῆ, -οῦν
build a wall round the city, πόλιν
  ἀποτειχίζειν (τείχει)
properly, ἐπιεικῶς
merchant ship, ὁλκάς, -άδος, f.

Exercise 175.

Egypt, Αἴγυπτος, -ου, f.
grief, πένθος, -ους, n.
utmost, ἔσχατος
bring upon, ἐμβάλλω, Acc. of
  thing, Dat. of person
scarcely, μόλις
family, οἶκος
fit out, παρασκευάζω
battle by sea, ναυμαχία, f.
moment, καιρός
put back to shore, κατάγομαι (Passive of κατάγω = bring to shore)

APPENDIX I

PRINCIPAL PARTS OF VERBS—PROSE FORMS.

Where the parts of a Compound Verb are not given, they will be found under the Simple Verb.

Present.	Future.	Aorist.	Perf. Act.	Perf. Pass.	Aor. Pass.
ἀγγέλλω, announce	ἀγγελῶ	ἤγγειλα	ἤγγελκα	ἤγγελμαι	ἠγγέλθην
ἀγείρω, collect		ἤγειρα			ἠγέρθην
ἄγω, lead	ἄξω	ἤγαγον	ἦχα[1]	ἦγμαι	ἤχθην
αἱρέω, take	αἱρήσω	εἷλον	ᾕρηκα	ᾕρημαι	ᾑρέθην
αἴρω, raise, start	ἀρῶ	ἦρα	ἦρκα	ἦρμαι	ἤρθην
αἰσθάνομαι, perceive	αἰσθήσομαι	ᾐσθόμην		ᾔσθημαι	
αἰσχύνομαι, am ashamed	αἰσχυνοῦμαι				ᾐσχύνθην
ἀκούω, hear	ἀκούσομαι	ἤκουσα	ἀκήκοα		ἠκούσθην
ἁλίσκομαι, am caught	ἁλώσομαι	ἑάλων	ἑάλωκα		
ἅλλομαι, leap	ἁλοῦμαι	ἡλάμην [Strong Aor. in other moods.]			
ἁμαρτάνω, be mistaken	ἁμαρτήσομαι	ἥμαρτον	ἡμάρτηκα	ἡμάρτημαι	ἡμαρτήθην
ἀμύνω, defend	ἀμυνῶ	ἤμυνα			
ἀναλίσκω, spend	ἀναλώσω	ἀνήλωσα	ἀνήλωκα	ἀνήλωμαι	ἀνηλώθην
ἀνέχομαι, endure	ἀνέξομαι	ἠνεσχόμην			
ἀνοίγνυμι, open	ἀνοίξω	ἀνέῳξα		ἀνέῳγμαι	ἀνεῴχθην
ἀπαντάω, meet	ἀπαντήσομαι	ἀπήντησα	ἀπήντηκα		
ἀπεχθάνομαι, am hated	ἀπεχθήσομαι	ἀπηχθόμην		ἀπήχθημαι	
ἀποκρίνομαι, answer	ἀποκρινοῦμαι	ἀπεκρινάμην		ἀποκέκριμαι	
αὐλίζομαι, encamp		ηὐλισάμην			ηὐλίσθην

[1] Only in compounds συν- and προ-.

Present.	Future.	Aorist.	Perf. Act.	Perf. Pass.	Aor. Pass.
αὐξάνω, αὔξω, } increase	αὐξήσω	ηὔξησα	ηὔξηκα	ηὔξημαι	ηὐξήθην
ἀφικνέομαι, arrive	ἀφίξομαι	ἀφικόμην		ἀφῖγμαι	
βαίνω, go	βήσομαι	ἔβην [1]	βέβηκα		
βάλλω, throw	βαλῶ	ἔβαλον	βέβληκα	βέβλημαι	ἐβλήθην
βούλομαι, wish	βουλήσομαι			βεβούλημαι	ἐβουλήθην
γαμέω, marry [2]	γαμῶ	ἔγημα	γεγάμηκα	γεγάμημαι	
γίγνομαι, become	γενήσομαι	ἐγενόμην	γέγονα	γεγένημαι	
γιγνώσκω, ascertain	γνώσομαι	ἔγνων [3]	ἔγνωκα	ἔγνωσμαι	ἐγνώσθην
δάκνω, bite	δήξομαι	ἔδακον		δέδηγμαι	ἐδήχθην
δείκνυμι, show	δείξω	ἔδειξα	δέδειχα	δέδειγμαι	ἐδείχθην
δέχομαι, receive	δέξομαι	ἐδεξάμην		δέδεγμαι	
δέομαι, need, ask	δεήσομαι			δεδέημαι	ἐδεήθην
δεῖ, it is necessary	δεήσει	ἐδέησε			
δέω, want, lack	δεήσω	ἐδέησα			
δέω, bind	δήσω	ἔδησα	δέδεκα	δέδεμαι	ἐδεθην
διαλέγομαι, converse	διαλέξομαι			διείλεγμαι	διελέχθην
διαφθείρω, destroy	διαφθερῶ	διέφθειρα	διέφθαρκα	διέφθαρμαι	διεφθάρην
διδάσκω, teach	διδάξω	ἐδίδαξα	δεδίδαχα	δεδίδαγμαι	ἐδιδάχθην
δίδωμι, give	δώσω	ἔδωκα ἐδόμην	δέδωκα	δέδομαι	ἐδόθην
δοκέω, seem	δόξω	ἔδοξα		δέδοκται	
δύναμαι, can	δυνήσομαι			δεδύνημαι	ἐδυνήθην
δύω, dip, sink (tr.)	δύσω (tr.)	ἔδυσα (tr.) ἔδυν (intr.)	δέδυκα (intr.)	δέδυμαι	ἐδύθην
ἐάω, allow	ἐάσω	εἴασα	εἴακα	εἴαμαι	εἰάθην
ἐγείρω, arouse	ἐγερῶ	ἤγειρα	ἐγρήγορα (intr.)		ἠγέρθην
ἐθέλω, wish	ἐθελήσω	ἠθέλησα	ἠθέληκα		
εἴργω, imprison, prevent	εἴρξω	εἶρξα		εἶργμαι	εἴρχθην

---

[1] The moods are ἔβην, βῆθι, βῶ, βαίην, βῆναι, βάς.
[2] Act. γαμῶ γυναῖκα, duco uxorem; Mid. γαμοῦμαι ἀνδρί, nubo viro.
[3] The moods are ἔγνων, γνῶθι, γνῶ, γνοίην, γνῶναι, γνούς.

Present.	Future.	Aorist.	Perf. Act.	Perf. Pass.	Aor. Pass.
ἐκπλήσσω, terrify	ἐκπλήξω	ἐξέπληξα		ἐκπέπληγμαι	ἐξεπλάγην
ἐλαύνω, drive	ἐλῶ	ἤλασα	ἐλήλακα	ἐλήλαμαι	ἠλάθην
ἐλέγχω, convict	ἐλέγξω	ἤλεγξα		ἐλήλεγμαι	ἠλέγχθην
ἕλκω, drag	ἕλξω	εἵλκυσα	εἵλκυκα	εἵλκυσμαι	εἱλκύσθην
ἐναντιόομαι, oppose	ἐναντιώσομαι			ἠναντίωμαι	ἠναντιώθην
ἐπαινέω, praise	ἐπαινέσομαι	ἐπῄνεσα	ἐπῄνεκα		ἐπῃνέθην
ἐπιλανθάνομαι, forget	ἐπιλήσομαι	ἐπελαθόμην		ἐπιλέλησμαι	
ἐπίσταμαι, understand	ἐπιστήσομαι				ἠπιστήθην
ἕπομαι, follow	ἕψομαι	ἑσπόμην			
ἐρωτάω, ask, question	ἐρωτήσω / ἐρήσομαι	ἠρόμην	ἠρώτηκα	ἠρώτημαι	ἠρωτήθην
ἐργάζομαι, work	ἐργάσομαι	εἰργασάμην		εἴργασμαι	εἰργάσθην
ἔρχομαι, go, come [1]	εἶμι	ἦλθον	ἐλήλυθα		
ἐσθίω, eat	ἔδομαι	ἔφαγον			
εὐλαβοῦμαι, beware	εὐλαβήσομαι				ηὐλαβήθην
εὑρίσκω, find	εὑρήσω	ηὗρον	ηὕρηκα	ηὕρημαι	ηὑρέθην
ἔχω, have	ἕξω / σχήσω	ἔσχον	ἔσχηκα	-έσχημαι	
ζάω, live	βιώσομαι	ἐβίων	βεβίωκα		
ἥδομαι, rejoice, am pleased	ἡσθήσομαι				ἥσθην
ἥκω, am come	ἥξω				
θάπτω, bury	θάψω	ἔθαψα		τέθαμμαι	ἐτάφην
θαυμάζω, wonder (at)	θαυμάσομαι	ἐθαύμασα	τεθαύμακα	τεθαύμασμαι	ἐθαυμάσθην
-θνήσκω, die	θανοῦμαι	-έθανον	τέθνηκα		

[1] See p. 231.

Present.	Future.	Aorist.	Perf. Act.	Perf. Pass.	Aor. Pass.
ἵημι, send, let go	ἥσω	ἧκα εἵμην	εἷκα	εἷμαι	εἵθην
ἵστημι, place (tr.)	στήσω (tr.)	ἔστησα (tr.) ἔστην (intr.)	ἕστηκα (intr.)	ἕσταμαι	ἐστάθην
καίω, burn	καύσω	ἔκαυσα	κέκαυκα	κέκαυμαι	ἐκαύθην
καλέω, call	καλῶ	ἐκάλεσα	κέκληκα	κέκλημαι	ἐκλήθην
κάμνω, toil	καμοῦμαι	ἔκαμον	κέκμηκα		
καταγελάω, scorn, laugh at	καταγελάσο- μαι	κατεγέλασα			κατεγελάσθην
κεῖμαι, lie	κείσομαι				
κελεύω, bid	κελεύσω	ἐκέλευσα	κεκέλευκα	κεκέλευσμαι	ἐκελεύσθην
κλαίω, weep	κλαύσομαι	ἔκλαυσα		κέκλαυμαι	
κλέπτω, steal	κλέψω	ἔκλεψα	κέκλοφα	κέκλεμμαι	ἐκλάπην
κομίζω, convey, bring	κομιῶ	ἐκόμισα	κεκόμικα	κεκόμισμαι	ἐκομίσθην
κρίνω, judge	κρινῶ	ἔκρινα	κέκρῐκα	κέκρῐμαι	ἐκρῐθην
κτάομαι, get, ob- tain.	κτήσομαι	ἐκτησάμην		κέκτημαι	ἐκτήθην
κτείνω, kill	-κτενῶ	-ἔκτεινα	-ἔκτονα		
λαμβάνω, take	λήψομαι	ἔλαβον	εἴληφα	εἴλημμαι	ἐλήφθην
λανθάνω, lie hid, escape notice	λήσω	ἔλαθον	λέληθα		
λέγω,} φημί,} say	{λέξω {ἐρῶ	ἔλεξα εἶπον [1]	} εἴρηκα	εἴρημαι	{ἐλέχθην {ἐρρήθην
λείπω, leave	λείψω	ἔλιπον	λέλοιπα	λέλειμμαι	ἐλείφθην
μανθάνω, learn	μαθήσομαι	ἔμαθον	μεμάθηκα		
μάχομαι, fight	μαχοῦμαι	ἐμαχεσάμην		μεμάχημαι	
μέλει, concern (Impers.)	μελήσει	ἐμέλησε	μεμέληκε		
μέλλω, am about to	μελλήσω	ἐμέλλησα			
μέμφομαι, blame	μέμψομαι	ἐμεμψάμην			
μένω, remain	μενῶ	ἔμεινα			

[1] The 2nd Pers. of the Ind. uses Weak Aor. forms—εἶπας, εἴπατε.

Present.	Future.	Aorist.	Perf. Act.	Perf. Pass.	Aor. Pass.
(ἀνα) μιμνῄσκω, re-mind	-μνήσω	-έμνησα		μέμνημαι (I re-member)	ἐμνήσθην (I re-membered)
νέω, swim	νεύσομαι	ἔνευσα	νένευκα		
νομίζω, think, con-sider	νομιῶ	ἐνόμισα	νενόμικα	νενόμισμαι	ἐνομίσθην
οἶδα, know	εἴσομαι				
οἴομαι, ⎫ think οἶμαι, ⎭	οἰήσομαι				ᾠήθην
οἴχομαι, am gone	οἰχήσομαι				
(ἀπ) -ολλυμι, de-stroy, lose	-ολῶ	-ώλεσα -ωλόμην (intr.)	-ολώλεκα -όλωλα (intr.)		
ὄμνυμι, swear	ὀμοῦμαι	ὤμοσα	ὀμώμοκα		
ὀξύνω, sharpen	ὀξυνῶ	ὤξυνα	ὤξυγκα	ὤξυμμαι	ὠξύνθην
ὁράω, see	ὄψομαι	εἶδον	ἑόρακα	ἑόραμαι ὦμμαι	ὤφθην
ὀργίζομαι, become angry	ὀργιοῦμαι			ὤργισμαι	ὠργίσθην
ὁρμάομαι, start	ὁρμήσομαι			ὥρμημαι	ὡρμήθην
ὁρμίζω, moor (tr.)		ὥρμισα		ὥρμισμαι	ὡρμίσθην
ὁρμίζομαι, moor (in-trans.)	ὁρμιοῦμαι	ὡρμισάμην		ὥρμισμαι	ὡρμίσθην
ὀφείλω, owe		ὤφελον			
ὀφλισκάνω, incur charge of	ὀφλήσω	ὦφλον	ὤφληκα		
[παίω], ⎫ strike τύπτω, ⎭	πατάξω	ἐπάταξα		πέπληγμαι	ἐπλήγην
παραινέω, advise see ἐπαινέω					
παρέχω, provide	παρέξω παρασχήσω	παρέσχον	παρέσχη-κα	παρέσχημαι (Middle)	
πάσχω, suffer	πείσομαι	ἔπαθον	πέπονθα		

Present.	Future.	Aorist.	Perf. Act.	Perf. Pass.	Aor. Pass.
πείθω, *persuade*	πείσω	ἔπεισα	πέπεικα (tr.) πέποιθα (intr.)	πέπεισμαι	ἐπείσθην
πέμπω, *send*	πέμψω	ἔπεμψα	πέπομφα	πέπεμμαι	ἐπέμφθην
πέτομαι, *fly*	πτήσομαι	ἐπτόμην			
πίμπλημι, *fill*	πλήσω	ἔπλησα	πέπληκα	πέπλησμαι	ἐπλήσθην
πίπτω, *fall*	πεσοῦμαι	ἔπεσον	πέπτωκα		
πλέω, *sail*	πλεύσομαι	ἔπλευσα	πέπλευκα		
πράσσω, *do* (tr.) *fare* (intr.)	πράξω	ἔπραξα	πέπραχα (tr.) πέπραγα (intr.)	πέπραγμαι	ἐπράχθην
πυνθάνομαι, *ascertain*	πεύσομαι	ἐπυθόμην		πέπυσμαι	
πωλέω, ἀποδίδομαι, } *sell* {	πωλήσω ἀποδώσομαι	ἀπεδόμην	πέπρακα	πέπραμαι	ἐπρώθην
ῥήγνυμι, *break*	ῥήξω	ἔρρηξα	ἔρρωγα (intr.)		ἐρράγην
ῥίπτω, *throw, hurl*	ῥίψω	ἔρριψα	ἔρριφα	ἔρριμμαι	ἐρρίφθην
σκεδάννυμι, *scatter*,	σκεδῶ	ἐσκέδασα		ἐσκέδασμαι	ἐσκεδάσθην
σπείρω, *sow*	σπερῶ	ἔσπειρα	ἔσπαρκα	ἔσπαρμαι	ἐσπάρην
σπένδομαι, *make peace*	σπείσομαι	ἐσπεισάμην		ἔσπεισμαι	
σπουδάζω, *am busy*	σπουδάσομαι	ἐσπούδασα	ἐσπούδακα	ἐσπούδασμαι	ἐσπουδάσθην
στέλλω, *equip*	στελῶ	ἔστειλα	ἔσταλκα	ἔσταλμαι	ἐστάλην
στρέφω, *turn*	στρέψω	ἔστρεψα		ἔστραμμαι	ἐστράφην
σφάλλω, *cause to slip*	σφαλῶ	ἔσφηλα		ἔσφαλμαι	ἐσφάλην
σώζω, *save*	σώσω	ἔσωσα	σέσωκα	σέσωσμαι	ἐσώθην
τελέω, *accomplish*	τελῶ	ἐτέλεσα	τετέλεκα	τετέλεσμαι	ἐτελέσθην
τέμνω, *cut*	τεμῶ	ἔτεμον	τέτμηκα	τέτμημαι	ἐτμήθην
τίθημι, *place*	θήσω	ἔθηκα ἐθέμην	τέθηκα	[κεῖμαι]	ἐτέθην

Present.	Future.	Aorist.	Perf. Act.	Perf. Pass.	Aor. Pass.
τιτρώσκω, *wound*	τρώσω	ἔτρωσα		τέτρωμαι	ἐτρώθην
τρέπω, *turn, rout*	τρέψω	ἔτρεψα ἐτραπόμην	τέτροφα	τέτραμμαι	ἐτράπην
τρέφω, *nourish*	θρέψω	ἔθρεψα	τέτροφα᾽	τέθραμμαι	ἐτράφην
τρέχω, θέω, } *run*	δραμοῦμαι	ἔδραμον	{ δεδρά- μηκα		
τυγχάνω, *hit, happen*	τεύξομαι	ἔτυχον	τετύχηκα		
ὑπισχνέομαι, *promise*	ὑποσχήσομαι	ὑπεσχόμην		ὑπέσχημαι	
φαίνω, *show*	φανῶ	ἔφηνα	πέφαγκα (tr.) πέφηνα (intr.)	πέφασμαι	ἐφάνθην ἐφάνην
φέρω, *carry, bear*	οἴσω	ἤνεγκον [1]	ἐνήνοχα	ἐνήνεγμαι	ἠνέχθην
φεύγω, *flee*	φεύξομαι	ἔφυγον	πέφευγα		
φημί, see λέγω					
φθάνω, *anticipate*	φθήσομαι	ἔφθασα ἔφθην	ἔφθακα		
φοβέομαι, *fear*	φοβήσομαι			πεφόβημαι	ἐφοβήθην
χαίρω, *rejoice*	χαιρήσω				ἐχάρην
χράομαι, *use*	χρήσομαι	ἐχρησάμην		κέχρημαι	ἐχρήσθην
χρή, *it is necessary* Inf. χρῆναι	χρήσει	Past χρῆν ἐχρῆν			
ψεύδω, *deceive* (Middle = *lie*)	ψεύσω	ἔψευσα		ἔψευσμαι	ἐψεύσθην
ὠνέομαι, *buy*	ὠνήσομαι	ἐπριάμην		ἐώνημαι	ἐωνήθην

[1] The Indicative of this tense uses weak forms ἤνεγκας, etc., except in the 1st Sing. and 3rd Plur.

APPENDIX II

COMPOUNDS OF COMMON VERBS

ἄγω, *lead*.

εἰσάγω, *introduce, import*.

ἀνάγω, (1) *lead from coast to interior*.
    (2) *take to sea* (Middle, *put out to sea*).

κατάγω (1) *lead down to coast*.
    (2) *bring to land*.
    (3) *bring back from exile*.

προσάγω, (1) (mil.) *bring up to attack* (Dat. or πρός with Acc.).
    (2) Middle, *bring over to one's side*.

αἱρέω, *take* (Middle, *choose*).

ἀφαιρέομαι, *take away, steal* (double Acc.).

καθαιρέω, *destroy* (esp. *to raze a city*).

ἀναιρέομαι, *recover* (esp. *take up dead for burial*).

βαίνω, *go*.

ἀναβαίνω, (1) *go up from coast*.
    (2) *mount a horse*; ἀναβαίνειν ἐφ' ἵππον.

ἐμβαίνω εἰς ναῦν, *embark*.

ἐκβαίνω (or ἀποβαίνω) ἐκ νεώς, *disembark*.

διαβαίνω, *cross* (*a river*).

ὑπερβαίνω, *cross* (*a mountain*).

ἀποβαίνω (of things), *turn out*; ταῦτα καλῶς ἀπέβη.

συμβαίνω, *come to terms*.   Impersonally, *come about, happen*.

βάλλω, *throw*.

εἰσβάλλω εἰς, *invade*.

προσβάλλω, *attack* (Dat.).

περιβάλλω (gen. in Middle), *surround*. For Passive *use* περιπίπτω,
    e.g. νῆσον τείχει⎫
    or τεῖχος νήσῳ ⎭ περιβάλλεσθαι.

διαβάλλω, *set at variance, slander*.

μεταβάλλω, *change*.

ἐκβάλλω, *banish*.   For Passive use ἐκπίπτω.

παραβάλλομαι, *risk, hazard*.

γίγνομαι, *become.*

  ἐπιγίγνομαι (of time), *follow* ; τοῦ ἐπιγιγνομένου ἔτους.

  περιγίγνομαι, *survive, get the better of* (Gen.).

  προσγίγνομαι, *be added, join* (Dat.).

γιγνώσκω, *get to know.*

  ἀναγιγνώσκω, *read.*

  καταγιγνώσκω, *condemn* (Gen. *of person,* Acc. *of crime* or *penalty*)

  συγγιγνώσκω, *pardon* (Dat.).

  μεταγιγνώσκω, *change one's mind, repent.*

δίδωμι, *give.*

  ἀποδίδωμι, *give back* (Middle, *sell*).

  παραδίδωμι, *hand over, surrender* (trans.).

  προδίδωμι, *betray.*

  ἐνδίδωμι (intr.), *surrender, give in.*

  ἐκδίδωμι, *give in marriage.*

  μεταδίδωμι, *give a share of* (Gen.).

ἔρχομαι, *come, go.*   (ἔρχομαι and its Compounds have εἶμι for Future
      and ᾖα for Imperfect. The Verb εἶμι also supplies the Present
      Tense except in the Indic.)

  ἀπέρχομαι, *go away, go back.*

  συνέρχομαι, *assemble.*

  διέρχομαι, *go through, traverse* (of time, *elapse*).

  ἐπανέρχομαι, *return.*

  κατέρχομαι, *come back from exile.*

  ἔπειμι, *attack, charge* (Dat.).

  προσέρχομαι πρός, *approach.*

  παρέρχομαι, πάρειμι, *come forward* (*of a speaker*).

ἔχω, *have.*

  ἀπέχω, ⎫
  κατέχω, ⎬ *restrain.*   (p. 160.)

  ἀπέχω (intrans.), *be distant from* (Gen. or ἀπό with Gen.).

  ἀπέχομαι, *refrain.*   (p. 160.)

  κατέχω, *keep.*

  ἀνέχομαι, *hold out, endure* (with Part.).

  ἀντέχω, *hold out* (intrans.) ; ἀντέχομαι, *cling to* (Gen.).

  ἐπέχω, *wait.*

  μετέχω, *have a share of* (Gen.).

  παρέχω, *supply* (παρέχει μοι, *I have an opportunity*).

περιέχω, *surround.*
προσέχω (τὸν νοῦν), *attend to* (Dat.).

ἵημι, *send, let go.*
    ἀφίημι, *dismiss, let go.*
    μεθίημι, *let slip* ; *e.g.* μεθίημι καιρόν. Middle, *let go of* (Gen.).
    συνίημι, *understand.*
    ἐφίεμαι, *aim at, desire* (Gen.).

ἵστημι, *set up, place. Transitive tenses,* Pres., Imp., Fut., Wk. Aor.
    Intransitive tenses, Str. Aor., Perf., Plup.
    ἀφίστημι, *make to revolt.*
        (intr. tenses and Middle), *revolt.*
    καθίστημι, *set up, appoint.*
        (intr. tenses and Middle), *be appointed.*
    ἐξίστημι (with φρενῶν or τοῦ φρονεῖν or abs.), *drive out of wits.*
        (intr. tenses and Middle), *depart from, cease from* (Gen.), or
            to be out of one's wits.
    μεθίστημι, *change, remove.*
        (intr. tenses and Middle), *change, revolt.*
    ἐφίστημι (intr. tenses and Middle), *be in command of* (Dat.).
    ἀνθίστημι (intr. tenses and Middle), *resist* (Dat.).
    ὑφίστημι (intr. tenses and Middle), ⟨1⟩ *undertake, promise.*
                          (2) *hold one's ground, resist.*

λαμβάνω, *take.* Middle, *cling to, lay hold of* (Gen.).
    καταλαμβάνω, *overtake, come upon* ; *e.g.* κατέλαβον ἀποροῦντας,
        they found them in distress.
    συλλαμβάνω, *arrest, seize.*
    ὑπολαμβάνω *answer* (Gen. in Aor. Part. with verb of *saying*).

τίθημι, *place.* [Passive often κεῖμαι and compounds.]
    διατίθημι, *settle, dispose of.*
    προστίθημι, *add.*
    ἐπιτίθεμαι, *attack* (Dat.).
    συντίθεμαι, *make an agreement.*
    ὑποτίθεμαι, *suggest, advise* (Dat.).

φέρω, *bring.*
    διαφέρω, *differ from, be superior to* (Gen.).
    ἐπιφέρω πόλεμον, *wage war on* (Dat.).
    προσφέρω, *apply, use* ; προσφέρω βίαν τινι.
    συμφέρει, *it is expedient* (Dat.).

APPENDIX III

COMMON PROSE USAGES OF PREPOSITIONS

WITH ONE CASE

	ACCUSATIVE.	GENITIVE.	DATIVE.
ἀνά	ἀνὰ ποταμόν, *up stream.* ἀνὰ πᾶσαν τὴν ἡμέραν, *all day long.* ἀνὰ τρεῖς, *by threes (three deep).*		
εἰς	εἰσέβαλον εἰς τὴν Ἀττικήν, *they invaded Attica.* εἰς καιρόν, *at the right time.* εἰς διακοσίους, *up to two hundred.* εἰς τόδε ἥκω, *I have come for this purpose.*		
ὡς	ἐπέμφθη ὡς τὸν βασιλέα, *he was sent to the king* (only used of persons).		
ἀντί		εἰρήνην ἔχομεν ἀντὶ πολέμου, *we have peace instead of war.*	

GPC–P

	ACCUSATIVE.	GENITIVE.	DATIVE.
ἀπό		ἀπὸ τῆς βαρβάρου ἦλθεν, he came from the foreign country. ἀπ' ἐκείνης τῆς ἡμέρας, from that day. ἀφ' ἵππου μάχεσθαι, to fight on horseback.	
ἐκ		ἐκ Σπάρτης φεύγει, he is banished from Sparta. ἐκ τούτων, after this οἱ ἐκ δεξιᾶς, those on the right. ἐξ ἴσου, equally.	
πρό		πρὸ θυρῶν, before the door. πρὸ τῆς μάχης, before the battle.	
ἐν			ἐν ταῖς Ἀθήναις, in Athens. ἐν τοῖς Πέρσαις, among the Persians. ἐν τούτῳ, meanwhile. ἐν καιρῷ, at the right time. ἐν σπονδαῖς, in a time of truce.

	ACCUSATIVE.	GENITIVE.	DATIVE.
σύν			σὺν ἡμῖν, *in company with us.* [Not in Attic till Xenophon.] σὺν θεοῖς, *with the help of the gods.*

WITH TWO CASES

	ACCUSATIVE.	GENITIVE.
διά		διὰ τῆς χώρας πορεύονται, *they march through the country.* διὰ πολλοῦ, *at a great distance, after a long time.* διὰ πέντε ἐτῶν, *every five years.* διὰ φιλίας ἰέναι, *to be on friendly terms.*
	διὰ τοῦτο φεύγει, *he is exiled on account of this.* Lat. *propter.* διὰ πολλά, *for many reasons.*	δι' ἀγγέλου λέγειν, *to speak by means of a messenger.* Lat. *per.* διὰ τάχους, *quickly.*
κατά	κατὰ ποταμόν, *down stream.* κατὰ γῆν καὶ θάλασσαν, *by land and sea.* κατὰ δύναμιν, *to the best of one's ability.* κατὰ τοὺς νόμους, *in accordance with the laws.* τὸ κατ' ἐμέ, *as far as I am concerned.* καθ' ἡμέραν, *daily, day by day.*	τὰ κατὰ γῆς, *things below the earth.* κατὰ πέτρας πεσεῖν, *to fall from a rock.* κατὰ τῆς κεφαλῆς καταχεῖν, *to pour on the head.* λέγειν κατὰ τινος, *to speak against some one.* πόλιν κατ' ἄκρας διαφθεῖραι, *to destroy a city utterly.*

	ACCUSATIVE.	GENITIVE.
κατά	κατὰ Πίνδαρον, *according to Pindar* (in quotation). πόλιν ἑλεῖν κατὰ κράτος, *to take a city by storm.*	
ὑπέρ	ὑπὲρ Αἴγυπτον ἰόντι, *to one going beyond Egypt.* ὑπὲρ δύναμιν, *beyond one's power.*	λιμὴν καὶ πόλις ὑπὲρ αὐτοῦ, *a harbour and a city above it.* μάχεσθαι ὑπὲρ τῆς πατρίδος, *to fight for one's country.*

WITH THREE CASES

	ACCUSATIVE.	GENITIVE.	DATIVE.
ἐπί	ἐπὶ τοὺς πολεμίους, *against or towards the enemy.* τὸ ἐπ' ἐμέ, *so far as depends on me.* ὡς ἐπὶ τὸ πολύ, *for the most part.*	ἐπὶ τῆς τραπέζης, *upon the table.* ἐπὶ τῆς Νάξου, *towards Naxos.* ἐφ' ἵππου, *on horseback.* ἐπὶ τοῦ Κύρου, *in the time of Cyrus.*	ἐπὶ τῇ θαλάττῃ, *on the sea.* χαίρειν ἐπὶ τῇ φιλίᾳ, *to rejoice in friendship.* ἐπὶ τούτοις, *on these conditions.* ἐπὶ τῷ Κύρῳ, *in the power of Cyrus.*
μετά	μετὰ ταῦτα, *after this.*	μετὰ τούτων, *with these.*	(In poetry only.)
παρά	παρὰ τὸν βασιλέα, *to the king's court.* παρὰ τὸν ποταμόν, *along the river.* παρὰ νόμον, *contrary to the law.* παρ' ὀλίγον ἀπέθανε, *he all but died.*	παρὰ τοῦ βασιλέως, *from the king, from the king's court.*	παρὰ τῷ βασιλεῖ, *beside the king, in the presence of the king, at the king's court.*

	ACCUSATIVE.	GENITIVE.	DATIVE.
περί	περὶ τὴν Ἀττικήν, all round or all over Attica. οἱ περὶ τὸν Κριτίαν, Critias and his party. ὁπλῖται περὶ ἑκατόν, about 100 hoplites. εἶναι περί τι, to be engaged on a thing.	περὶ τῆς ἀρετῆς, concerning virtue. περὶ πολλοῦ ποιεῖσθαι, to reckon of great importance.	δακτύλιον ἔχειν περὶ τῇ χειρί, to have a ring on the finger.
πρός	πρὸς τὴν νῆσον, towards or to the island. πρὸς χάριν, with a view to pleasing. πρὸς βίαν, forcibly. πρὸς ταῦτα, therefore (with Imperatives).	πρὸς τῶν πολεμίων, from the enemy or (the result was) in favour of the enemy. πρὸς θεῶν, in heaven's name (in appeals).	πρὸς τῷ ποταμῷ, at or near the river. πρὸς τούτοις, in addition to this.
ὑπό	ἰέναι ὑπὸ τὸ σπήλαιον, to go down into the cave. ὑπὸ νύκτα, just before or about night.	ὑπὸ τοῦ βασιλέως ἐπράχθη, it was done by the king (agent.)	ὑπὸ τῷ τείχει, close under the wall. ὑπὸ τοῖς ἀνθρώποις, subject to men.
ἀμφί	οἱ ἀμφὶ Πρίαμον, Priam and his train. ἀμφὶ τὸν χειμῶνα, about winter.	(In poetry only.)	(In poetry only.)

Certain Adverbs are also used as Prepositions, and most of these take the Genitive Case, e.g. ἄνευ, without, μέχρι, until, ἕνεκα, on account of, πλήν, except, ἐγγύς and πλησίον, near, μεταξύ, between, ἐντός, εἴσω, within, ἐκτός, outside of.

The Adverb ἅμα, at the same time as, is followed by a Dative, e.g ἅμα τῷ ἦρι, at the return of spring. So ὁμοῦ, together with.

APPENDIX IV

PARTICLES

Those marked * cannot stand first in a sentence

ἄγε δή, φέρε δή, *come now, but come.*

ἀλλά, *but.*

οὐ μὴν ἀλλά, *not but what, nevertheless.*

οὐ μόνον . . . ἀλλὰ καί, *not only . . . but also.*

οὐχ ὅπως . . . ἀλλὰ καί, *not only . . . (not) . . . but also.*

ἄλλως τε καί, *especially.*

ἄρα, generally translated 'then,' 'so then,' expressing mostly regret and always slight surprise.

> *e.g.* μάτην ἄρ', ὡς ἔοικεν, ἥκομεν.
>
> *So then, we have come in vain after all !*

ἄρα, interrogative particle.

> ἆρ' οὐ; =nonne ?
>
> ἆρα μή ;=num ?

ἅτε (with participles), *inasmuch as.*

αὖ*, *on the other hand, moreover.*

γάρ*, *for.* In Dialogue often translated 'yes' or 'no.'

> *e.g.* ἀγωνιστέον ἄρα ἡμῖν; ἀνάγκη γάρ, ἔφη.
>
> *Must we then strive ? Yes, he said, it is necessary.*

γε*, *at least.*

γοῦν*, *at least, at any rate.*

πάνυ γε, *quite so.*

γε μήν*, *nevertheless, but yet.*

δέ*, *but, and.* Often used like Latin *autem* simply to connect sentences.

δ' οὖν*, *however that may be . . ., (ceterum).*

δή*. It is impossible to give any exact translation of δή. The examples below will explain some of its uses.

> τί δή; *what* then, pray *what* ?
>
> νῦν ὁρᾶτε δή, *now you* surely *see.*
>
> τότε δή, *then* indeed, *at that* very *time* (tum vero).
>
> μέγιστος δή, quite *the greatest,* confessedly *the greatest.*

οὗτος δὴ ὁ Σωκράτης, *this Socrates* forsooth (ironical).

μεθ' ὅπλων γε δή, above all *with arms.*

βλέψον. καὶ δὴ βλέπω, '*Look! Well, I am looking.*'

δήπου*, *doubtless, I presume.*

δῆτα* (emphatic form of δή). In questions = '*pray.*'

εἴθε, εἰ γάρ, *would that* (used to express wishes, pp. 78 and 176).

ἐφ' ᾧ, ἐφ' ᾧ τε (with Inf. or Fut. Ind.), *on condition that* (p. 100).

ἤ . . . ἤ, *either . . . or.*

ἦ μήν, used in oaths or solemn protestations.

> e.g. ἐγγυᾶσθαι ἦ μὴν παραμενεῖν.
>
> *To undertake solemnly to remain.*

καί, *and, even, also.*

$\left.\begin{array}{l} \text{. . . } \tau\epsilon \text{ . . . } \kappa\alpha\iota \\ \kappa\alpha\iota \text{ . . . } \kappa\alpha\iota \end{array}\right\}$ *both . . . and* (p. 45).

καὶ δή (to add a remark), '*and moreover,*' '*and too.*'

καὶ γάρ, *for truly.*

καίτοι, *however, and yet.*

μέντοι*, *however.*

. . . μέν . . . δέ, *on the one hand . . . on the other hand* (p. 45).

μὲν οὖν*, *nay rather* (without δέ necessarily following).

$\left.\begin{array}{l} \mu\acute{o}\nu o\nu \text{ } o\mathring{v} \\ \mathring{o}\sigma o\nu \text{ } o\mathring{v} \end{array}\right\}$ *all but.*

> e.g. ὅσον οὐ διεφθάρη ὁ στόλος.
>
> *The expedition was on the point of being destroyed.*

ὅμως, *however, nevertheless* (often ὅμως δέ or ἀλλ' ὅμως, *but yet*).

οὐδέ, *and not, not even.*

οὔτε . . . οὔτε, *neither . . . nor.*

οὖν*, *therefore, then.*

οὐκοῦν, *therefore.*

οὔκουν, lays stress on the negative, '*not . . . therefore.*'

που*, *possibly, I suppose.*

τοίνυν*, *therefore.*

ὡς (with participles), *on the ground that*—or to express purpose (pp. 94 and 122).

ὥσπερ (with participles), *as if* (p. 123).

ὥστε, *consequently* (p. 100).

APPENDIX V

THE CHIEF RULES FOR ACCENTS

I. In Greek there are two accents, the Acute (as on λόγος) and the Circumflex (as on πρᾶγμα).

The Acute accent on the last syllable of a word is changed to the Grave ` when another word follows, unless that word be an enclitic, in which case the Acute remains.

A word with the Acute on the last syllable is called Oxytone.[1]

A word with the Acute on the last syllable but one is called Paroxytone.

A word with the Acute on the last syllable but two is called Proparoxytone.

A word with the Circumflex on the last syllable is called Perispomenon.[2]

A word with the Circumflex on the last syllable but one is called Properispomenon.

GENERAL RULES

II. **Position of Acute and Circumflex.**—The Acute may stand on long or short syllables, the Circumflex only on syllables containing a vowel long by nature or a diphthong.

The Acute may stand on any of the last three syllables, the Circumflex only on the last or last but one. But if the last syllable is long, the Acute cannot stand on the last but two, nor the Circumflex on the last but one.

e.g. ἄνθρωπος, but ἀνθρώπου, λῦσον, λυθῶ.

---

[1] ὀξὺς τόνος = *acute tone.*

[2] περισπάω = *I draw in different directions.*

III. In words of which the last syllable is short and the last but one long by nature, if the accent is on the last but one it must be the circumflex.

e.g. τεῖχος, ποιεῖτε.

IV. **Contracted Syllables** have the Circumflex when the *first* of the two syllables was accented.

e.g. φιλέω, φιλῶ.

They have the Acute when the *second* syllable was accented.

e.g. φιλεέτω, φιλείτω.

They are unaccented if neither of the two syllables was accented.

e.g. φίλεε, φίλει.

V. **Enclitics.**—Certain words called Enclitics (*leaning words*) lose their accent through being pronounced in close connection with the preceding word.

Such are—

(*a*) All forms of the Indefinite τις.

(*b*) The Indefinite adverbs, πως, που, ποτέ, etc.

(*c*) The following cases of the Personal Pronouns, μέ, μου, μοι, σε, σου, σοι, ἑ, οὑ, οἱ.

(*d*) The Present Indicative of εἰμί, *I am,* and φημί, *I say* (except in the 2nd Pers. Sing.) [1]

(*e*) The Particles, τε, γε, τοι, νυν, περ.

---

[1] The whole present of εἰμί is accented when it denotes *existence.* The 3rd Pers. Sing. is accented on the first syllable in the following cases :—

    (*a*) When it denotes *existence, e.g.* οὐκέτ᾽ ἔστιν, *he is no more.*

    (*b*) In the sense, 'it is possible' where it = ἔξεστι.

    (*c*) When it begins a sentence.

    (*d*) After εἰ, καί, οὐκ, ὡς.

Rules for Enclitics.

(*a*) If the preceding word is proparoxytone or properispomenon, the accent of the enclitic is thrown back as
an acute on the last syllable.

> *e.g.* τοῦτό μοι ἔδωκέ τις.

(*b*) If the preceding word is paroxytone, an enclitic *of one
syllable* loses its accent with no other change, an enclitic *of two syllables* retains its accent.

> *e.g.* λόγος τις, λόγοι τινές.

(*c*) If the preceding word is perispomenon, the enclitic
loses its accent without other change ; if it is oxytone
it retains the acute accent. (See Rule 1.)

> *e.g.* ἀγαθός τις, *a certain good man.*
> ὁδῶν τινων, *of certain roads.*

(*d*) When several enclitics follow one another, each throws
its accent back, so that only the last is unaccented.

> *e.g.* εἴ ποτέ πού τι εἶδον.

VI. **Atonics.**—A few words have no accent, unless they
are followed by an enclitic or stand as the last word of a
sentence.

(*a*) The nom. of the Article, ὁ, ἡ, οἱ, αἱ.
(*b*) οὐ, ὡς (=*how*).
(*c*) εἰς, ἐν, ἐκ, ὡς (=*to*).
(*d*) εἰ, ὡς (=*when, as, that*).

VII. **Anastrophe** (throwing back).

(*a*) The dissyllabic prepositions throw back their accent to
the first syllable when they follow their case (except
ἀμφί, ἀντί, ἀνά, διά).

> *e.g.* τούτων πέρι, *concerning these things.*

(*b*) Oxytone words, except indeclinable words, become
paroxytone when the final vowel is elided.

> *e.g* δείν᾽ ἔπαθε (for δεινὰ ἔπαθε),
> but ἐπ᾽ αὐτοῦ.

ACCENTS ON VERBS

VIII. (1) **Generally the accent stands as far back as possible.**

  e.g. ἔλυσε, ἐλύθην, λῦσαι.

(*N.B.*—Final syllables in αι and οι are treated as **short** except in the Optative.)

  e.g. λῦσαι (Inf.), λύσαι (Opt.).

(2) Contracted forms are accented according to Rule IV. The following are treated as contracted forms:—

(*a*) The Subjunctive of all passive aorists.

  e.g. λυθῶ, πλακῶ.

(*b*) The Subjunctive and Optative of Pres. and Str. Aor. Act. and Mid. of verbs in -μι (except in -νυμι).

  e.g. τιθῶ, τιθεῖμεν, θῶ, θεῖσθε.

EXCEPTIONS

(1) The Str. Aor. is accented on the last syllable in the Inf. and Part. Act. and in the 2nd Sing. of the Imperative Mid., and on the last syllable but one in the Inf. Mid.

  e.g. λαβεῖν, λαβών, λαβοῦσα, λαβόν, λαβοῦ,[1] λαβέσθαι.

(2) The following Str. Aorists are oxytone in the Imperative:—

  εἰπέ, ἐλθέ, εὑρέ, ἰδέ, λαβέ.

(3) The following parts of verbs are paroxytone if the last syllable but one is short, properispomenon if it is long:—

(*a*) Wk. Aor. Inf. Act.

  e.g. τιμῆσαι, πλέξαι.

(*b*) All Infinitives in -ναι.

  e.g. τιθέναι, λελυκέναι, στῆναι.

(*c*) All Infinitives and Participles of the Perf. Pass.

  e.g. λελυμένος, τετιμῆσθαι.

---

[1] But ἀφίκου, ἐπιλάθου.

(4) All active Participles of verbs in -μι, and all others in -εις and -ως are oxytone.

e.g. τιθείς, λυθείς, λελυκώς.

(5) In compound verbs the accent may not go back:

(*a*) Beyond the augment.

e.g. παρέσχον, κατῆγον.

(*b*) Beyond the last syllable of the preposition.[1]

e.g. ἀπόδος, ἐπίσχες.

(*c*) Beyond the verbal part of Infinitives and Participles of verbs in -μι.

e.g. ἀποδούς, ἀποδόσθαι.

Or beyond the verbal part of 2nd Sing. Imp. Mid. of verbs in -μι compounded with a preposition of one syllable.

e.g. προθοῦ, but μετάδου.

NOUNS AND ADJECTIVES

(*N.B.* -αι and -οι, Nom. Pl., are treated as short.)

IX. (1) Generally the accent on the oblique cases remains on the same syllable as in the Nominative, as far as is permitted by the general rules (Rule II.).

e.g. ἄνθρωπος, ἄνθρωπον, ἀνθρώπου.

(2) All Genitives and Datives of oxytone words of the 1st and 2nd declension are perispomena.

e.g. ὁδός, ὁδοῦ, ὁδοί, ὁδῶν.[2]

(3) In the first declension the Gen. Plur. is perispomenon.

(4) In the 3rd declension the Gen. and Dat. of monosyllables are accented on the last syllable.[3]

e.g. χείρ, χειρός, χεῖρες, χειρῶν.

---

[1] But notice ἄπειμι, πάρεστι, ἄπιθι, etc.

[2] But in the Attic 2nd declension the acute is retained.

e.g. λεώς, λεώ.

[3] Except Participles θείς, θέντος, with τίς, τίνος; πᾶς, πάντων, πᾶσι; παίδων, and some others.

(5) In words like πόλις and πῆχυς the endings -εως, -εων are treated as one syllable.

e.g. πόλεως, πήχεων.

X. No complete rules can be given for accenting the Nominative Singular.   But the following rules are generally true.

(1) Oxytone are—Nouns in -ευς, e.g. βασιλεύς.

-ω, e.g. πειθώ.

-as (-αδις), e.g. φυγάς (φυγάδος).

-ις (Acc. Imparisyllabic), e.g ἐλπίς (Acc. ἐλπίδα).

Most Adjectives in -ρος, e.g. αἰσχρός.

-νος,   ἱκανός.

-ης,   ἀληθής.

-υς,   ἡδύς.

-ικος,   πρακτικός.

Verbal Adjectives in -τος,   λυτός.

Adj. meaning 'good' or 'bad,' ἀγαθός, κακός.

(2) Paroxytone.   Most Nouns in -ια,   e.g. δειλία.

Verbal Nouns in -τωρ,   ῥήτωρ.

Patronymics,   Ἀλκιβιάδης.

Verbal Adj. in -τεος,   λυτέος.

(3) Proparoxytone.   Nouns in -εια except those from Verbs in -εύω,   } ἀλήθεια, but δουλεία.

(4) The accent goes back as far as possible in

Verbals in -μα,   e.g. πρᾶγμα.

Neuters in -ος,   μέγεθος.

Nouns in -ις (Acc. -ιν),   δύναμις.

Comparatives and Superlatives, καλλίων, ἄριστος.

Adjectives in -ιμος,   φρόνιμος.

GENERAL VOCABULARY

A

abandon, ἀπολείπω

ability, to the best of, κατὰ δύναμιν

able, be, {δύναμαι / οἷός τέ εἰμι

about concerning, περί, Gen.

about, to be about to, μέλλω

about (of numbers), μάλιστα or ὡς

abroad, to be abroad, away from home, ἀποδημέω

absent, to be, ἄπειμι

accomplish, πράσσω, ἐκπράσσω, ἐκτελέω
> without accomplishing one's purpose, ἄπρακτος

according to, κατά, Acc.

account,—on account of, διά, Acc., ἕνεκα, Gen.

accuse, αἰτιάομαι. See p. 68. ἐγκαλέω. Voc. 152

Achelous (river), Ἀχελῷος

acquit, ἀπολύω. See p. 68

Acropolis, Ἀκρόπολις

act rightly, ποιεῖν τὸ προσῆκον

add, προστίθημι

addition, in addition to, πρός, Dat.

address, exhort, παρακελεύομαι, Dat.

admire, θαυμάζω. See p. 70

admit, confess, ὁμολογέω

advance, προχωρέω

advantage,—it is to the advantage of, συμφέρει. See p. 128

adversary, ἐναντίος

adverse, ἐναντίος

adversity, be in adversity, δυστυχέω

advice, give, συμβουλεύω, Dat.

advise, πείθω, Acc., παραινέω, συμβουλεύω, Dat.

Aeneas, Αἰνείας, -ου

Aeschines, Αἰσχίνης, -ου

afraid, be, δέδοικα, φοβέομαι

after (Prep.), μετά, Acc.
> after this, μετὰ ταῦτα, ἐκ τούτων
> (Conj.), ἐπειδή, ἐπεί, ἀφ' οὗ, ἐξ οὗ. See p. 150

afterwards, ὕστερον, μετὰ ταῦτα
> not long afterwards, οὐ πολλῷ ὕστερον

again, αὖθις, πάλιν

against (motion), ἐπί, Acc.

Agamemnon, Ἀγαμέμνων, -ονος

agree, come to terms, συμβαίνω

agreement, terms, τὰ ῥητά

Alcibiades, Ἀλκιβιάδης, -ου

Alcmaeon, Ἀλκμαίων, -ωνος

Alexander, Ἀλέξανδρος

all, πᾶς

all but, ὅσον οὐ

allow, ἐάω, Acc. ἐπιτρέπω, Dat.
> it is allowed, ἔξεστι, πάρεστι, Dat.

ally, σύμμαχος
> to be one's ally, fight for one, συμμάχομαι, Dat.

almost, σχεδόν, ὅσον οὐ
alone, μόνος
already, ἤδη
also, καί
although, καίπερ. See p. 122
always, ἀεί
ambassadors, πρέσβεις
ambush, ἐνέδρα
Amphion, 'Αμφίων, -ωνος
Amphipolis, 'Αμφίπολις, -εως
ample, ἱκανός
ancestor, πρόγονος
anchor,—weigh anchor, αἴρω
anger, ὀργή
angry, to be angry with, ἀγανακτέω,
    ὀργίζομαι, Dat., δι' ὀργῆς ἔχειν,
    Acc.
announce, ἀγγέλλω, ἀπαγγέλλω
annul, καταλύω
another, ἄλλος
answer, ἀποκρίνομαι, ὑπολαμβάνω
    in answer, ὑπολαβών
anticipate, φθάνω. See p. 123
appear, φαίνομαι
    appear to be, be manifestly.
        See p. 123
applaud, ἀναθορυβέω
appoint, καθίστημι. Voc. 79
approach, προσέρχομαι.
    See p. 230
Arcadian, 'Αρκάς, -άδος
archer, τοξότης
Archimedes, 'Αρχιμήδης, -ου
ardour, σπουδή
Argives, 'Αργεῖοι
arise (happen), γίγνομαι
Aristides, 'Αριστείδης, -ου
arm (Verb), καθοπλίζω
arms, ὅπλα
army, στράτευμα, στρατός, στρατία
    (as opposed to fleet) πεζός
arouse, ἐγείρω

array, arrange, τάσσω
    arrange a line of battle,
        παρατάσσομαι, ἀντιτάσσομαι
arrest, συλλαμβάνω
arrive, ἀφικνέομαι
arrow, τόξευμα
art, τέχνη
Artaxerxes, 'Αρταξέρξης, -ου
as, ὡς, as if, ὥσπερ (see p. 123) ;
    as . . . as, οὕτως . . . ὡς ; as
    . . . as possible, ὡς, with
    superlative ; as soon as, ἐπεὶ
    τάχιστα
ascertain, πυνθάνομαι, γιγνώσκω
ashamed, to be, αἰσχύνομαι
Asia, 'Ασία, f.
ask (a question), ἐρωτάω [Aorist
    ἠρόμην]
    (request), αἰτέω
assault, προσβολή
    with one assault, μιᾷ ὁρμῇ
assemble, συνέρχομαι
assembly, ἐκκλησία
    hold an a., ἐκκλησίαν ποιεῖν
assert, φάσκω
assist, βοηθέω, Dat., ὠφελέω, Acc.
assistance, βοήθεια
associate with, φοιτάω παρά,
    Acc.
Athens, 'Αθῆναι. Voc. 18
Athenian, 'Αθηναῖος
attach, προστίθημι
attack, ἐπιτίθεμαι, προσβάλλω,
    ἐπέρχομαι, ἐμπίπτω, Dat.
    (Noun), προσβολή
attempt, πειράομαι, Gen. or Inf.,
    ἐπιχειρέω, Dat. or Inf.
attend to, προσέχω (τὸν νοῦν), Dat.
    care for, θεραπεύω
Attica, ἡ 'Αττική
authorities, οἱ ἐν τέλει
avenge, τιμωρέω. Voc. 75

247

avoid, ὑπεξίσταμαι, ὑποστρέφω
await, δέχομαι, προσδέχομαι
awaken, ἐγείρω
away, to be, ἄπειμι

B

Babylon, Βαβυλών, -ῶνος, f.
bad, κακός, πονηρός
badly, poorly, φαύλως
baggage, σκεύη, n. pl.
band (crowd), ὄχλος
banish, ἐκβάλλω (for Passive use
    ἐκπίπτω)
barbarian, βάρβαρος
base, αἰσχρός
battle, μάχη ; *(by sea)* ναυμαχία
    join battle with, μάχην συν-
    άπτω πρός, Acc.
    *(esp. of fighting at close
    quarters),* ἐς χεῖρας ἔρχομαι,
    Dat.
bay, κόλπος
be, εἰμί, *or with Adverbs* ἔχω, e.g.
    εὖ ἔχειν, *to be well*
be, be sufficient ὑπάρχω
bear, φέρω
    (endure), φέρω, ὑπομένω
beat (defeat), νικάω
beautiful, καλός
become, γίγνομαι
befall, συμβαίνει, Dat.
before, πρίν. See p. 150
before (Adv.), πρότερον, τὸ πρίν
before that, πρὸ τοῦ
beg (entreat), παραιτέομαι [68, 123
begin, ἄρχω *or* ἄρχομαι. See pp.
beginning, ἀρχή
behalf,—on behalf of, ὑπέρ, Gen.
behave to, treat, χράομαι, Dat.
believe, πείθομαι, πιστεύω, Dat.
benefit. Voc. 65

besiege, πολιορκέω
betray, προδίδωμι
better,—to be better than,
    διαφέρω, Gen.
bind, δέω
birth. γένος
bite, δάκνω
bivouac, αὐλίζομαι
blame, μέμφομαι, Dat. ;
    ἐν αἰτίᾳ ἔχω, Acc.
blameworthy, to blame, αἴτιος
bold, θρασύς, τολμηρός
boldness, τόλμα
boast, κομπάζω
book, βίβλος
booty, λεία
both, ἀμφότεροι, ἑκάτεροι.
    See p. 135
both . . . and, καὶ . . . καὶ . . ᴑ
    or τε . . . καὶ . . .
boy, παῖς
Brasidas, Βρασίδας, -ου
brave, ἀνδρεῖος
bravely, ἀνδρείως
bravery, ἀνδρεία
bread, ἄρτοι
breadth, εὖρος. See p. 23
break (a treaty, etc.), λύω, παρα
    βαίνω
    (a line), παραρρήγνυμι
breakfast, ἄριστον
    get breakfast, ἀριστοποιέομαι
bribe, δῶρον
bridge, γέφυρα
briefly, διὰ βραχέων
bring (of things), φέρω, προσφέρω
    κομίζω
    (of persons), ἄγω
    down, καταφέρω
    in, εἰσκομίζω
    back, ἀπάγω
    back from exile, κατάγω

bring out, ἐκφέρω
　　up, τρέφω
　　upon, ἐμβάλλω
broad, εὐρύς. See p. 23
brother, ἀδελφός
build, οἰκοδομέω
　　(*ships, etc.*), κατασκευάζω
　　to be built round, περιβάλ-
　　λεσθαι, Dat.
bull, ταῦρος
burdensome, ἐπαχθής
burn (transitive), καίω, κατακαίω
　　(intransitive), καίομαι
bury, θάπτω
buy, ὠνέομαι. See p. 70
by (*near*), πρός, Dat.
　　(*agent*), ὑπό, Gen. (and see p.
　　　　　　　　　　　　　　　[18]

C

Cadmus, Κάδμας, -ου
Cadmea (*citadel of Thebes*),
　　Καδμεία, f.
call, καλέω, προσκαλέω
call together, συγκαλέω
Callias, Καλλίας, -ου
camp, στρατόπεδον
can, δύναμαι
capable of, ἱκανός (with Inf.)
captain, λοχαγός
　　(*of ship*), τριήραρχος
captive, αἰχμάλωτος
Carduchi, Κάρδουχοι
care (*take*), φυλάσσομαι, ἐπιμελέ-
　　ομαι. See p. 98
carefully, ἐπιμελῶς
careless, ῥάθυμος, ἀμελής
carelessness, ἀμέλεια
carry, φέρω
carry out (*a decree, etc.*), περαίνω
Carthage, Καρχηδών, -ονος
Carthaginian, Καρχηδόνιος
catch, καταλαμβάνω

cattle, κτήνη, n. pl.
cause, αἰτία
cautiously, εὐλαβῶς
cavalry, ἱππῆς
cavern, σπήλαιον
cause to be, καθίστημι
cease, παύομαι. See pp. 68, 123
centre, τὸ μέσον
certain, σαφής
　　a certain, τις (enclitic)
chance, τύχη
charge, ἐπέρχομαι ; (Noun), προσ-
　　βολή. See p. 231
cheer, θαρσύνω
chief (*men*), οἱ πρῶτοι
child, παῖς
choke, ἀποπνίγω
choose, αἱρέομαι, ἐξαιρέομαι, ἐκλέγω
Cilicians, Κίλικες
Cimon, Κίμων, -ωνος
citadel, ἀκρόπολις
Cithaeron, Κιθαιρών, -ῶνος
citizen, πολίτης
city, πόλις, ἄστυ
clearly, σαφῶς
Cleon, Κλέων, -ωνος
clever, δεινός
cling to, ἔχομαι, Gen.
cloak, χλαῖνα
closely, continuously, συνεχῶς
clothes, ἐσθής
coast, αἰγιαλός
Colchis, Κολχίς, -ίδος
cold (Noun), ψῦχος
collect (trans.), ἀγείρω, συναγείρω
　　(*levy*), ἀθροίζω
colony, ἀποικία
come, ἔρχομαι. See p. 231
come,—to be come, ἥκω
　　to help, βοηθέω, Dat.
　　forward (*to speak*),
　　　　παρέρχομαι. See p. 231

come down (esp. to the sea), κατέρχομαι
   back from exile, κατέρχομαι
   on (=to ensue), ἐπιγίγνομαι
command, κελεύω, Acc. ; προστάσσω, Dat.
   (in the army, ' pass the word '), παραγγέλλω, Dat.
   be in command of, ἡγεμονεύω, Gen. ; ἐφέστηκα, Dat.
common, κοινός
companion, ἑταῖρος
compel, ἀναγκάζω
complain, δεινὸν ποιέομαι
complete, ἐκτελέω, ἐξεργάζομαι
comrades (Voc.), ὦ ἄνδρες
conceal, κρύπτω. See p. 74
concerned, as far as I am concerned, τὸ ἐπ' ἐμέ
condemn, κατακρίνω, καταγιγνώσκω. See p. 68
condition (on condition that), ἐφ' ᾧτε. See p. 100
confess, ὁμολογέω
confidence, θάρσος
confident, to be, θαρρέω
confiscated, to be, δημόσιο·· γίγνεσθαι. Voc. 162
consider, deliberate, βουλεύομαι
Conon, Κόνων, -ωνος
conquer, νικάω, Acc. ; κρατέω, Gen.
conscious, am conscious of, συνοῖδα ἐμαυτῷ. See p. 52
consider, think, νομίζω
   deliberate, βουλεύομαι
consult, συμβουλεύομαι, κοινόομαι, Dat.
   (an oracle), χράομαι, Dat.
contest, ἀγών, ἅμιλλα
continent, ἤπειρος
continue, διατελέω. See p. 123
contrary to (the law, etc.), παρά, Acc.

converse, διαλέγομαι
convict, ἐλέγχω
Corinth, Κόρινθος, f.
corn, σῖτος
country, χώρα
   (native land), πατρίς
courage, ἀνδρεία
   be of good courage, εὐθυμέω
courageous, ἀνδρεῖος
cowardice, κακία, δειλία
cowardly, coward, κακός, δειλός
craft, δόλος
create, cause to be, καθίστημι (transitive tenses)
Cretans, Κρῆτες
crime, commit a crime, ἀδικέω
crisis, καιρός
cross, διαβαίνω
   (a mountain), ὑπερβαίνω
crowd, ὄχλος
crown, στέφανος
cruel, ὠμός
cry out, βοάω
cut, τέμνω
   off, ἀποτέμνω
   cut off, i.e. intercept, ἀπολαμβάνω
Cyclops, Κύκλωψ, -ωπος
Cyprus, Κύπρος, f.
Cyrus, Κῦρος

D

danger, κίνδυνος
   be in danger of, κινδυνεύω, Inf.
dangerous, δεινός
dare, τολμάω
daring, τόλμα
Darius, Δαρεῖος
dark, σκοτεινός
darkness, σκότος
dart, βέλος
daughter, θυγάτηρ

dawn, ἔως
    at dawn, daybreak. Voc. 20
day, ἡμέρα
day,—by day, all day, etc. See p. 23
    day by day, every day, καθ'
        ἡμέραν
    day before, προτεραία
    day after, next day, ὑστεραία
    to-day, τήμερον
    on the same day, αὐθήμερον
dead body, νεκρός
dear, φίλος
death, θάνατος
    put to death. See *kill*
deceive, ἐξαπατάω
decide, διακρίνομαι, or use δοκεῖ
    decide previously (of senate),
        προβουλεύω
decree (of senate at Athens),
    προβούλευμα
deed, ἔργον
deep, βαθύς
    four deep, etc., ἐπί, Gen.
defeat, νικάω
    to be defeated, ἡσσάομαι
defend, ἀμύνω (see p. 14) φυλάσσω ;
    speak in defence of oneself),
        ἀπολογέομαι
delay (trans.), κωλύω
    (intrans.), μένω, ἐπέχω
deliberate, βουλεύομαι
delighted, be delighted, ἥδομαι
Delphi, Δελφοί, m. pl.
Demosthenes, Δημοσθένης, -ους
deny, οὔ φημι, ἀπαρνέομαι. See
    p. 160
deprive, ἀποστερέω
descend (esp. to the sea), κατέρχομαι
desert (Noun), ἡ ἔρημος (χώρα)
    (trans.), ἀπολείπω
    (intrans. of soldier), αὐτομολέω
    (evacuate, leave empty), ἐρημόω

deserve, ἄξιος εἶναι, Gen.
desire, ἐπιθυμέω, Gen.
desist from, παύομαι, Gen.
    or Part.
despair, ἀθυμέω, ἀθύμως ἔχω
despatch, ἀποστέλλω
despise, ὀλιγωρέω, καταφρονέω,
    Gen.
destroy, ἀπόλλυμι, διαφθείρω
    (a city), καθαιρέω
determine, βουλεύομαι, or use δοκεῖ.
    Voc. 46
die, ἀποθνῄσκω, τελευτάω
different, in different directions,
    etc. Use ἄλλος . . . ἄλλοσε,
    etc. See p. 135
difficult, χαλεπός
difficulties, τὰ χαλεπά
    to be in difficulties, ἀπορέω
    with difficulty, σχολῇ
direction, in the direction of, ἐπί,
    Gen. ; πρός, Acc.
    in different directions,
    use ἄλλος . . . ἄλλοσε.
    See p. 135
    in all directions, πανταχόσε
    from all directions, πανταχόθεν
disaster, συμφορά
discontented, to be, δεινὸν ποιοῦμαι
discover, εὑρίσκω, μανθάνω
discuss, διακρίνομαι περί, Gen.
disembark, ἀποβαίνω
disgraceful, αἰσχρός
disheartened, ἄθυμος
dismiss, ἀφίημι
    (from one's thoughts), ἐάω
disobey, ἀπειθέω
display, show, φαίνω, ἀποδείκνυμι
    show off, ἐπιδείκνυμαι
dissatisfied with, to be, χαλεπῶς
    φέρω
distance, at a distance, διὰ πολλοῦ

distant, to be, ἀπέχω, Gen. or ἀπό with Gen.

distress, to be in, ἀπορέω

ditch, τάφρος

divulge, μηνύω

do, ποιέω, πράσσω

doctor, ἰατρός

Dorieus, Δωριεύς, -έως

down (Prep.), κατά. See p. 235

drachma, δραχμή

draw up, drag up, ἀνέλκω

draw up, array, τάσσω

dread, δέδοικα, δέδια

dream,—in a dream, ὄναρ

drive, ἐλαύνω

drive out, ἐκβάλλω

duty, τὸ προσῆκον

dwell, οἰκέω

E

each, ἕκαστος; (*of two*) ἑκάτερος. See p. 135

each time, ἑκάστοτε

eagerly, προθύμως

eagerness, σπουδή

ear, οὖς

early, πρώ

earth, γῆ

easy, ῥᾴδιος

eat, ἐσθίω

eclipse, ἔκλειψις

Egypt, Αἴγυπτος, f.

either . . . or, ἤ . . . ἤ

elder, πρεσβύτερος

elect, αἱρέομαι, χειροτονέω

embark, ἐμβαίνω εἰς, Acc.

empire, ἀρχή

encamp, στρατοπεδεύομαι, αὐλίζομαι

encourage, παραμυθέομαι, Acc.
    encouraged, θαρρέω

end (trans. or intrans.), τελευτάω
    end one's life, τελευτάω

endure, ὑπομένω
    (*punishment, etc.*), ὑπέχω

enemy, πολέμιος, ἐχθρός
    (*a private enemy*), ἐχθρός

engaged, to be en- } σπουδάζω, Acc.
gaged on,   } εἶναι περί, Acc.

enough (Adj.), ἱκανός

enquire, ἐρωτάω

enraged, to be enraged, ὀργίζομαι

enrich, πλουτίζω

enslave, καταδουλόω

ensue, ἐπιγίγνομαι

enter, εἰσέρχομαι εἰς. See p. 231

entreat, παραιτέομαι

envy, ζηλόω. See p. 70

Ephesus, Ἔφεσος, f.

Ephialtes, Ἐφιάλτης, -ου

Ephors, ἔφοροι

Epigoni, Ἐπίγονοι

equal, ἴσως
    on equal terms, ἐξ ἴσου

equip, παρασκευάζομαι

escape, ἐκφεύγω

especially, μάλιστα, ἄλλως τε καί . . .

esteem highly, περὶ πολλοῦ (πλείονος, πλείστου) ποιεῖσθαι

evacuate, ἐξέρχομαι ἐκ

even, καί
    not even, οὐδέ

evening, ἑσπέρα
    towards evening, πρὸς ἑσπέραν

everywhere, πανταχοῦ
    (*in all directions*), πανταχόσε

evil, κακός
    (*evil tidings, etc.*), τὰ κακά

exceedingly, μάλα, σφόδρα

except, πλήν (as Prep. governs Gen.)

excessively, λίαν
exhaust, κατατρίβω
exhort, παρακελεύομαι, Dat.
exile (Verb), ἐκβάλλω
exile (person), φυγάς
exile (banishment), φυγή
expedient, it is, συμφέρει, Dat.
expedition, στρατεία
experience, ἐμπειρία
experienced, ἔμπειρος
    (having skill), ἐπιστήμων
explain, ἐξηγέομαι
extreme, ἔσχατος

F

faithful, πιστός
fall, πίπτω
fall on, attack, ἐμπίπτω, Dat.
fall down, καταπίπτω
falsely, ψευδῶς
famine, λιμός
famous, famed, γνώριμος, ἐπιφανής
fare badly, κακῶς πράσσω
fast, ταχύς (Adv. ταχέως)
father, πατήρ
fear, φοβέομαι
feast, ἑορτή ; (Verb, εὐωχέομαι)
few, ὀλίγοι
field, ἀγρός
fight, μάχομαι, Dat.
find, εὑρίσκω
    find out, ascertain by enquiry,
        πυνθάνομαι
    learn, get to know by observa-
        tion, etc., γιγνώσκω
finish (cause to cease), παύω
    (cease), παύομαι. See pp. 14,
        123
    (trans. or intrans.), τελευτάω
    (accomplish, complete), ἐκ-
        τελέω, ἐξεργάζομαι
fire, πῦρ

fire, set on fire, ἅπτω, καίω
firm, βέβαιος ; (Adv. βεβαίως)
first, πρῶτος ; (Adv. πρῶτον)
    to arrive first, etc., φθάνω.
        See p. 123
fish, ἰχθύς
fit out, παρασκευάζω
fitting, it is, πρέπει, Dat.
flank,—on the flank, κατὰ κέρας
fleet, αἱ νῆες or τὸ ναυτικόν
flight,—put to flight, τρέπω
flower, ἄνθος
fly, (run away), φεύγω
    (in the air), πέτομαι
follow, ἕπομαι, Dat.
    (pursue), διώκω
following, next, ἐπιγιγνόμενος
    the following, as follows, etc.,
        τάδε, ὧδε. See p. 133
folly, μωρία, ἄνοια
food, σῖτος
foolish, μῶρος, ἄφρων
foot, πούς
for (on behalf of), ὑπέρ, Gen. ;
    (for the sake of), ἕνεκα, Gen.
forbid, οὐκ ἐάω, ἀπαγορεύω (Aor.
    ἀπεῖπον). See p. 160
force, βία
    by force, βίᾳ, κατὰ κράτος
forces (mil.), δύναμις or see army
    with all his force, πανστρατίᾳ
foreign, βάρβαρος
    land, ἡ βάρβαρος
forest, ὕλη
forget, ἐπιλανθάνομαι. See p. 68
former. Use πρίν
the former, . . . the latter, ἐκεῖνος
    . . . οὗτος. See p. 133
formerly, πάλαι, πρότερον
forsooth, ἄρα, δῆτα. See p. 238
fort, τείχισμα
fortify, τειχίζω, περιτειχίζω

fortunate, εὐτυχής

free, ἐλεύθερος

free (Verb), ἐλευθερόω, λύω

freedom, ἐλευθερία

friend, φίλος

friendly, εὔνους

    to be on friendly terms, διὰ φιλίας ἰέναι, Dat.

from, ἀπό, ἐκ ; (*of persons*) παρά, Gen.

front,—in front, ἐκ τοῦ ἔμπροσθεν

frontier, ὅρος

fruit, καρπός

fulfil a promise, ὑπόσχεσιν ἀποδίδωμι

full, πλέως

funeral pyre, πυρά

furiously, προπετῶς

furlong, στάδιον

future, μέλλων ; *for the future,* τὸ λοιπόν ; *any time in the future,* τοῦ λοιποῦ

G

games, ἀγῶνες (pl. of ἀγών, contest)

garrison, φρούριον, φρουροί

gate, πύλη

gather (*fruit, etc.*), συγκομίζομαι

general, στρατηγός

    to be general, στρατηγέω

generous, ἐλευθέριος

get, κτάομαι

get up, Intrans. tenses or Mid. of ἀνίστημι

gift, δῶρον

give, δίδωμι

    back, ἀποδίδωμι

    up, παραδίδωμι

    in marriage, ἐκδίδωμι

    a share of, μεταδίδωμι.

    See p. 70

give advice, συμβουλεύω, Dat.

glad,—to be glad, ἥδομαι

    See pp. 72, 123

gladly, ἡδέως

glorious, καλός

glory, κλέος, δόξα

gnat, κώνωψ

go. See ἔρχομαι, p. 231 and compounds of βαίνω, p. 230

    away, ἀπέρχομαι. See p. 231

    out, ἐξέρχομαι. See p. 231

    down, καταβαίνω

    about among, φοιτάω

    to be going to, μέλλω

god, θεός

gold, χρυσός

golden, χρυσοῦς

good, ἀγαθός

    do good to, εὖ ποιέω. See p. 74

good-will, εὔνοια

Gorgon, Γοργώ

government, οἱ ἐν τέλει

graceful, χαρίεις

graciously, ἡπίως, εὐμενῶς

grateful, to be, χάριν οἶδα, χάριν ἔχω. See p. 70

great, μέγας

greatly, πολύ, σφόδρα

Greece, Ἑλλάς, -άδος

Greeks, Ἕλληνες

grief, πένθος

ground, on the ground that, because, ὡς. See p. 122

grow, αὐξάνομαι

guard (Noun), φύλαξ

guard, φυλάσσω

    off one's guard, ἀπροσδόκητος

guest, ξένος

guide, ἡγεμών

    (Verb), ἡγέομαι, Dat.

guilty, αἴτιος

    be guilty of, ὀφλισκάνω

H

half, ἥμισυς.   Voc. 74

hall, αὐλή

halt, ἀναπαύομαι

hand, χείρ
    fall into the hands of, ὑπο-
    χείριος γίγνομαι, Dat.
    fight hand to hand, εἰς χεῖρας
    ἔρχομαι

happen, take place, γίγνομαι.   Also
    τυγχάνω— See p. 123.   συμ-
    βαίνει (Impers.), Dat.

harbour, λιμήν

hardly, μόλις, σχολῇ

hardship, πόνος

harm, βλάπτω, κακὰ δρᾶν, κακὰ
    ποιεῖν (see p. 74), ἀδικέω
    (Noun), βλάβη, κακόν

hasten, σπεύδω (Voc. 83); (in-
    trans.), ἐπείγομαι

hate, μισέω
    be hated by, hateful to, ἀπεχ-
    θάνομαι, Dat.

have, ἔχω, or ἐστί with Dat.

head, κεφαλή

hear, ἀκούω.   See p. 68

height, ἄκρον

height,—at the height of, ἐν ἀκμῇ

Hellespont, Ἑλλήσποντος

help, βοήθεια

help, βοηθέω, Dat. ; ὠφελέω, Acc.

herald, κῆρυξ

Hercules, Ἡρακλῆς, -έους

herdsman, ποιμήν, βουκόλος

here, ἐνθάδε, αὐτοῦ

hereupon, ἔνθα δή

hero, ἥρως

hide, κρύπτω.   See p. 74

high-minded, ἐλευθέριος

hill, λόφος

hinder, κωλύω.   See p. 160

hire, μισθόομαι

historian, συγγραφεύς

hither, δεῦρο

hold, ἔχω, κατέχω
    (cling to), ἔχομαι, Gen.

hold out, endure, ἀντέχω
    hold one's ground, ἀνθίσταμαι

home, οἶκος.   Voc. 18
    to be abroad, away from home,
    ἀποδημέω

Homer, Ὅμηρος

honour, τιμή, δόξα

honour (Verb), τιμάω

honourable, καλός

hope, ἐλπίς

hope (Verb), ἐλπίζω.   See p. 51

hopeless, ἀνέλπιστος
    (of things) to be hopeless,
    ἀνελπίστως ἔχειν

hoplite, ὁπλίτης

horn, κέρος

horse, ἵππος
    on horseback, ἐφ' ἵππου

host, πλῆθος

hostage, ὅμηρος

house, οἶκος, οἰκία

how (with Adjectives and Ad-
    verbs), ὡς
    (Interrogative), πῶς, etc.
    See p. 59

how much, how many.   See p. 59

however, μέντοι (2nd word), ὅμως
    (may be 1st word)

hunger, λιμός

hungry, to be, πεινάω

hunt, θηρεύω

hurl, βάλλω, ῥίπτω
    down, κατακυλίνδω

I

idle, to be idle, ῥαθυμέω

if, εἰ, ἐάν. See p. 112
    in questions (=*whether*), εἰ,
      πότερον. See p. 62 and
      note
ignorant, be ignorant, ἀγνοέω
ill, to be ill, νοσέω
imitate, τὰ ὅμοια πράσσω, Dat.
immediately, εὐθύς
immense (*of numbers*), ἀναρίθμητος
immortal, ἀθάνατος
impious, ἀσεβής
important, to consider important,
    περὶ πολλοῦ ποιεῖσθαι
impossible, ἀδύνατον
imprison, εἴργω, καταδέω
in, ἐν, Dat.
inasmuch as, ἅτε. See p. 122
increase, αὐξάνω, αὔξω
    (intr.), αὐξάνομαι
independent, αὐτόνομος
indignant, to be indignant, δεινὸν
    ποιέομαι, χαλεπῶς φέρειν
induce, πείθω
infantry, πεζοί
inform. Use ἀγγέλλω
inhabit, ἐνοικέω
inhabitants, οἱ ἔνοικοι, οἱ ἐνοι-
    κοῦντες
injure, ἀδικέω, βλάπτω, κακὰ δράω.
    See p. 74
innocent, ἀναίτιος
instead of, ἀντί, Gen.
instruct, give orders to, προστάσσω,
    Dat.
    teach, διδάσκω
intend, διανοέομαι, ἐν νῷ ἔχω
into, εἰς, Acc.
invade, εἰσβάλλω εἰς
involved in, to be, καταστῆναι εἰς
Ionian, Ἰόνιος
island, νῆσος
Italy, Ἰταλία

J

Jason, Ἰάσων, -ονος
Jocasta, Ἰοκάστη
journey, ὁδός
    (Verb), πορεύομαι
judge, κριτής
    (=*juryman*), δικαστής
jurymen, δικασταί
just, δίκαιος
just (*lately*), ἄρτι

K

keep, ἔχω, κατέχω
    safe, σῴζομαι
    one's word, τῇ πίστει ἐμμένω
kill, ἀποκτείνω. (For Passive use
    ἀποθνῄσκω, lit. I *die*)
kindly, ἠπίως, εὐμενῶς
king, βασιλεύς
kinsman, συγγενής
know, οἶδα. See p. 52
    not to know, ἀγνοέω
    know how to, οἶδα, or ἐπίσ-
      ταμαι, with Inf.
    am conscious of, συνοῖδα
      ἐμαυτῷ. See p. 52
known, famous, γνώριμος

L

lack, scarcity, ἔνδεια, ἀπορία
Laconia, ἡ Λακωνική
land, γῆ
    native land, πατρίς
    by land, κατὰ γῆν
last (Verb), διατελέω
last, ὕστατος
    at last, τέλος or τὸ τέλος
late, ὀψέ
    later,—in later times, χρόνῳ
      ὕστερον
    too late, ὀψέ

laugh to scorn, καταγελάω
   to be a laughing-stock, καταγέλαστος εἶναι
law, νόμος
lazy, ῥάθυμος
lead, ἄγω, Acc. ; ἡγέομαι, Dat.
   (*of a road*), φέρω
leader, ἡγεμών
leadership, ἡγεμονία
leap, εἰσάλλομαι.   Voc. 140
learn, μανθάνω
least,—at least, γε
leave, leave behind, λείπω, καταλείπω
leave, depart from, ἀπέρχομαι.
   See p. 231
left, ἀριστερός, εὐώνυμος
   on the left (*wing*), ἐπ' ἀριστερᾷ
less (Adv.), ἧσσον
lest   See p. 98
leisure, σχολή
Lemnos, Λῆμνος
Lesbian, Λέσβιος
let slip, παρίημι
letter, ἐπιστολή
levy, ἀθροίζω
lie, ψεύδομαι
lie (*down*), κεῖμαι
life, βίος
light-armed troops, πελτασταί
like, ὅμοιος
limb, μέλος
linger, διατρίβω
lion, λέων
listen to, ἀκροάομαι, ἀκούω, Gen.
   of person
live in, dwell in, οἰκέω, ἐνοικέω ἐν
   live, be alive, ζάω
   pass one's time, διάγω
   live on, survive, ἐπιβιόω
living creature, ζῷον
long, μακρός; (*of time*), μακρός, πολύς

long, no longer, οὐκέτι, μηκέτι
   how long ? πόσον χρόνον :
   as long as, ὅσον χρόνον
look at, προσβλέπω
loose, λύω
lose, ἀπόλλυμι
loss,—be at a loss, ἀπορέω
loud, μέγας
love, φιλέω
low, low-lying, πεδινός
Lysander, Λύσανδρος

M

Macedonian (Adj.), Μακεδονικός
mad, μανικός
madness, μανία, ἄτη (= *infatuation*)
magistrates, οἱ ἐν τέλει
magnificent, εὐπρεπής
mainland, ἤπειρος
maintain, abide by, ἐμμένω, Dat.
majority, οἱ πολλοί
make, ποιέω
   be made, appointed, intrans.
   tenses and Mid. of καθίστημι
man, ἀνήρ (vir), ἄνθρωπος (homo)
man (Verb), πληρόω
manner, τρόπος
many, πολλοί
Marathon, Μαραθών.   See p. 20
march, πορεύομαι
marine, ἐπιβάτης
market, ἀγορά
marry (*of man*), γαμέω, Acc.
   (*of woman*), γαμοῦμαι, Dat.
marsh, λίμνη
marshy, λιμνώδης
master, δεσπότης
   (*teacher*), διδάσκαλος
master, be master of, κρατέω, Gen.
meadow, λειμών
means, τρόπος

meanwhile, ἐν τούτῳ

Medea, Μήδεια

meet, ἐντυγχάνω, Dat.

    go to meet, ἀπαντάω, Dat.

men of old, etc. See p. 1

mercenary, μισθοφόρος

    mercenary force, τὸ ξενικόν

merchant ship, ὁλκάς

message, ἀγγελία

messenger, ἄγγελος

middle, μέσος. Voc. 77

Milesians, Μιλήσιοι

Miltiades, Μιλτιάδης, -ου

Minos, Μίνως, -ωος or -ω

Minyae, Μίνυαι

miserably, ἀθλίως

missile, βέλος

mistake, make a mistake, be mistaken, ἁμαρτάνω

moment, occasion, καιρός

    for the moment, πρὸς τὸ παρόν

money, χρήματα, ἀργύριον

    (large sum of), πολλὰ χρήματα

monster, θηρίον

month, μήν

moon, σελήνη

moreover, πρὸς τούτοις

morning, ἕως

most (the majority), οἱ πολλοί

most of all, μάλιστα

mother, μήτηρ

mother city, μητρόπολις

mountain, ὄρος

much, πολύς

music, μουσική   [p. 130

must, δεῖ, or Verbal Adj. See

my, ὁ ἐμός. μου

Mycenae, Μυκῆναι

Mytilene, Μυτιλήνη

N

name, ὄνομα

    (Verb), ὀνομάζω

nay, nay rather (making a correction), μᾶλλον δέ, μὲν οὖν. See p. 238

near, ἐγγύς

nearly, σχεδόν

necessary, ἐπιτήδειος

    it is necessary, δεῖ. See p. 128

necessity, of necessity, ἀνάγκῃ

need, δέομαι, ἀπορέω, Gen.

negotiate, πράσσειν πρός, Acc.

neither, οὐδέτερος. See p. 135

never, οὐδέποτε, μηδέποτε

nevertheless, μέντοι, ὅμως

new, νέος

    =fresh, καινός

news, τὰ ἀγγελθέντα

next, following, ἐπιγιγνόμενος

Nicias, Νικίας, -ου

night, νύξ

    by night, etc. See p. 23

noble, ἀγαθός, γενναῖος

nobody, no one, οὐδείς

noise, ψόφος   [ῥέω

nonsense,—to talk nonsense, φλυαρέω

nose, ῥίς

not at all, in no respect, οὐδέν

nothing, οὐδέν

notice,—without being noticed, etc., λαθών. See p. 123

number, πλῆθος

O

obey, πείθομαι, Dat.

obol, ὀβολός

observe,—not observed by, λαθών, etc. See p. 123

obtain, κτάομαι

Oedipus, Οἰδίπους, -οδος

officers, οἱ ἄρχοντες

often, πολλάκις

old,—men of old, οἱ πάλαι

old man, γέρων

Olympian games, τὰ Ὀλύμπια

Olynthus, Ὄλυνθος, f.
    territory of, ἡ Ὀλυνθιακή
on, ἐπί, Gen. ; ἐν, Dat.
on account of, διά, Acc.
on behalf of, ὑπέρ, Gen.
one, εἷς
one another, ἀλλήλους.   See p. 135
one of two, etc.   See p. 135
one . . . the other, ὁ μὲν . . . ὁ δέ.
    See p. 40
once, ἅπαξ
    at once, εὐθύς
    once upon a time, ποτέ
only (Adj.), μόνος : (Adv.), μόνον
open, ἀνοίγνυμι
opponent, ἐναντίος
opportunity, καιρός
    the opportunity comes, offers,
       παρέχει (Impersonal), Dat.
oppose, ἐναντιόομαι, Dat.
oppress, πιέζω
or, ἤ
oracle, χρηστήριον
orator, ῥήτωρ
order, κελεύω   [p. 94
    in order that, ἵνα, etc.   See
organise, συσκευάζω
origin, ἀρχή
other, ἄλλος.   See p. 135
ought, δεῖ, χρή.   See p. 128
outcry, κραυγή
overcome, περιγίγνομαι, κρατέω,
    Gen.
overtake, καταλαμβάνω
overthrow, raze (a city), καθαιρέω
overthrow, subdue, καταστρέφομαι
own.   See p. 41
ox, βοῦς

P

pain, feel pain, ἀλγέω
pancratium, παγκράτιον
panic, φόβος

parasang (about 4 English miles),
    παρασάγγης
pardon, συγγιγνώσκω, Dat.
parent, γονεύς
pass, intrans. of time, διέρχομαι
    pass the word along, παραγγέλλω
    pass through, διαβαίνω
past, in the past, ἐν τῷ παρελθόντι
    χρόνῳ
patriotic, φιλόπολις
Pausanias, Παυσανίας, -ου
pay, μισθός
pay (tribute), φέρω
peace, εἰρήνη
    make peace, σπονδάς, εἰρήνην
       ποιοῦμαι, or σπένδομαι
    keep peace, remain at peace,
       εἰρήνην ἄγω
Peloponnesus, Πελοπόννησος, f.
pelt, βάλλω
penalty, δίκη
    pay the penalty, δίκας διδόναι
    exact the penalty, δίκας λαμ-
       βάνειν παρά, Gen.
people, δῆμος
    (=people generally), οἱ ἄν-
       θρωποι
perceive, αἰσθάνομαι.   See p. 52
perforce, ἀνάγκη
perhaps, ἴσως
Pericles, Περικλῆς, -έους
perilous, σφαλερός
perish, ἀπόλλυμαι, ἀποθνήσκω
permit, ἐάω
persecute, διώκω
Perseus, Περσεύς, -έως
Persia, ἡ Περσική
Persian, Πέρσης, -ου, Μῆδος
persuade, πείθω
pestilence, λοιμός
Philip, Φίλιππος
philosopher, φιλόσοφος
Phineus, Φινεύς, -έως

Phoenicians, Φοίνικες
pious, εὐσεβής
pirate, λῃστής
pity, οἰκτίρω. See p. 70
  (Noun), ἔλεος
place, τόπος, χωρίον
plague, λοιμός
plain, πεδίον
plain,—it is plain that I, etc.,
  δῆλός εἰμι with Part. or φαίνομαι
  with Part.
plainly, σαφῶς
Plataea, Πλαταιαί
Plataeans, Πλαταιῆς, -έων
pleased,—to be pleased, ἥδομαι,
  Dat. See p. 123
pleasant, pleasing, ἡδύς
pleasure, ἡδονή
plot against, ἐπιβουλεύω, Dat.
plunder, booty, λεία
poet, ποιητής
point—on the point of, all but,
  ὅσον οὐκ
politics, τὰ τῆς πόλεως πράγματα
Polynices, Πολυνείκης, -ους
Polyphemus, Πολύφημος
ponder, φροντίζω
poor, πένης
poorly, badly, φαύλως
Poseidon, Ποσειδῶν, -ῶνος
position (military), χωρίον
    take up a position, intrans.
    tenses of καθίστημι
possess, κέκτημαι
possession—be in possession of,
  κρατέω, Gen.
possessions, κτήματα, χρήματα
possible, it is, ἔξεστι, πάρεστι,
  Dat.
postpone, ἀναβάλλω
Potidaea, Ποτίδαια, f.
power, δύναμις, κράτος, ῥώμη
  in power of, ἐπί, Dat.

powerful, δυνατός
praise, ἔπαινος
  (Verb), ἐπαινέω
prefer, προαιρέομαι
prepare, παρασκευάζω
presence, in presence of, παρά,
  Dat.
  (over against), ἐναντίον, Gen.
present, δῶρον
present, to be, πάρειμι
    present condition of affairs,
    τὰ παρόντα
    present danger, etc., τὸ αὐτίκα
    δεινόν
    for the present, ἐν τῷ παρόντι,
    πρὸς τὸ παρόν
    at the present moment,
    τὸ παραυτίκα
    the present (time), τὸ νῦν
preserve, σῴζομαι
press,—be hard pressed, πιέζομαι
prevent, κωλύω, εἴργω
    nothing prevents, etc., οὐδέν
    ἐμποδών ἐστιν, etc.
    See p. 160
prison, δεσμωτήριον
prisoner, δεσμώτης
  (of war), αἰχμάλωτος
private, ἴδιος
  privately, ἰδίᾳ
prize, ἆθλον
probably, κατὰ τὸ εἰκός
promise, ὑπισχνέομαι. See p. 51
properly, ἐπιεικῶς
property, κτήματα, χρήματα
prophet, μάντις
propose. See advise
prosper (of persons), εὐτυχέω
  (of things), προχωρεῖν, κατορ-
  θοῦσθαι
provide, πορίζω, παρέχω
provisions, τὰ ἐπιτήδεια
provoke, παροξύνω

prudent, σώφρων, φρόνιμος
publicly, δημοσίᾳ
pull, ἐπισπάω
punish, κολάζω, ζημιόω, τιμωρέο-
    μαι: δίκας λαμβάνω παρά,
    Gen.
    be punished, δίκας δίδωμι
punishment, ζημία
pursue, διώκω
put back to shore, κατάγομαι
put in (of ships), προσέχω εἰς
put to flight, τρέπω
put off, ἀναβάλλω
Pydna, Πύδνη, f.
Pylos, Πύλος
pyre, πυρά
Pyrrhus, Πύρρος
Pythia (priestess of Apollo), Πυθία

Q

queen, βασίλεια
quick, ταχύς (Adverb ταχέως)
quiet, keep quiet, ἡσυχάζω, ἡσυχίαν
    ἔχω

R

race, γένος
rank (of army), τάξις
ransom, λύομαι
rashly, ἀσκέπτως
rather than, μᾶλλον ἤ
ratify, κυρόω
raze, καθαιρέω
reach, προσέρχομαι πρός, Acc.,
    ἀφικνέομαι πρός, Acc.
read, ἀναγιγνώσκω
ready, ἕτοιμος
reality,—in reality, ἔργῳ, ἀληθῶς
reap the fruits of, κομίζω τοὺς
    καρπούς
reasonable, to be, εἰκὸς εἶναι
rebel, intrans. tenses of ἀφίστημι

rebuke, ἐπιτιμάω, Dat.
receive, λαμβάνω, δέχομαι
recover, ἀναλαμβάνω
reduce, subdue, καταστρέφομαι
    (bring over to one's side),
    προσάγομαι
reflect, φροντίζω, ἐνθυμέομαι
refrain, ἀπέχομαι. See p. 160
refuge,—take refuge in, καταφεύγω
refuse, οὐκ ἐθέλω, οὔ φημι
regard,—with regard to, περί, Gen.
reinforcements, βοήθεια, βοηθοί
rejoice, χαίρω, ἥδομαι. See p. 123
relate, ἐξηγέομαι
release (for ransom), ἀπολυτρόω
remain, μένω, καταμένω, ἐπιμένω
remember, μέμνημαι, Gen.
remind, ἀναμιμνήσκω
remove (trans.), the trans. tenses
    of μετανίστημι
    (intrans.), the intrans. tenses
    of μετανίστημι
repent, μεταμέλει. See p. 128
reply, ἀποκρίνομαι, ὑπολαμβάνω
report, ἀγγέλλω, ἀπαγγέλλω
reproach, ὀνειδίζω
repulse, ἀποκρούομαι
reputation, δόξα
request, αἰτέω
resist, ἀμύνομαι. See p. 14
    ἀνθίσταμαι, Dat.
resolutely, θαρραλέως
resolve, use δοκεῖ. See p. 128
resources, χρήματα
responsible, αἴτιος
rest, the rest, οἱ ἄλλοι
rest (Verb), ἀναπαύομαι
restore, give back, ἀποδίδωμι
restrain, ἀπέχω, κατέχω, κωλύω.
    See p. 160
result, ἀποβαίνω
retreat, ἀναχωρέω
    retreat before, ὑπεξέρχομαι

return, ἐπανέρχομαι, ἥκω
    (*esp. from exile*), κατέρχομαι.
    See p. 231
revolt, ἀφίσταμαι.   Voc. 57
    cause to revolt, ἀφίστημι
reward, μισθός
Rhodian, Ῥόδιος
rich, πλούσιος
riches, πλοῦτος
ride, ἐλαύνω
right, just, δίκαιος
right (hand, etc.), δεξιός
    on the right wing, ἐπὶ δεξιᾷ
risk, run the risk of, κινδυνεύω
    (Inf.)
risk (stake), παραβάλλομαι
river, ποταμός
roar, βρυχάομαι
rob, ἀφαιρέομαι, double Acc. ;
    ἀποστερέω, double Acc., or Acc.
    of *person*, Gen. of *thing*
robber, λῃστής
Romans, Ῥωμαῖοι
room, θάλαμος
rope, σχοινίον
round, περί, Acc.
rout, τρέπω
rule, ἄρχω, Gen.
    (Noun), ἀρχή
rulers, οἱ ἄρχοντες, οἱ ἐν τέλει
run, τρέχω
run,—at a run, δρόμῳ
    run forward, προθέω
    about, διαθέω

S

sacrifice, θύω
safe, ἀσφαλής, Adv. ἀσφαλῶς
    get safe to, escape safely to,
    σῴζομαι εἰς
safety, ἀσφάλεια
    in safety, ἐν ἀσφαλεῖ

sail, πλέω
    away, ἀποπλέω
    out, ἐκπλέω
    (*set sail*), αἴρω
sailor, ναύτης
sake, for the sake of, ἕνεκα, Gen.
Salamis, Σαλαμίς, -ῖνος, f.
same, ὁ αὐτός
    at the same time as, ἅμα,
    Dat.
sand, ψάμμος
Sardis, Σάρδεις, -εων
satrap, σατράπης
save, σῴζω
say, λέγω, etc.   Voc. 41
scarcely, μόλις
scatter (trans.), διασκεδάννυμι ;
    (intrans.), διασπείρομαι or δια-
    σκεδάννυμαι
scout, κατάσκοπος
Scythians, Σκίθαι
sea, θάλασσα ; (*open sea*), πόντος ;
    by sea, κατὰ θάλασσαν
sea-coast, παραλία
second, δεύτερος
    a second time, τὸ δεύτερον
secretary, ἐπιστολεύς
secretly, λάθρα, or use λανθάνω.
    See p. 123
see, ὁράω
seek, ζητέω
seem, δοκέω, φαίνομαι
seems good, δοκεῖ
seize, συλλαμβάνω
self, αὐτός.   See p. 38
sell, ἀποδίδομαι, πωλέω
senate, βουλή
send, πέμπω
    back, ἀποπέμπω
    out, ἐκπέμπω
    forward, προπέμπω
    for, μεταπέμπομαι, προσκαλέω
separate, ἀπαλλάσσω.   See p. 68

serve, ὠφελέω
    (as a soldier), στρατεύω
set free, λύω, ἀφίημι
set out (see start)
set sail, αἴρω
set up, ἵστημι, transitive tenses
settle, διατίθεμαι: (by discussion),
    διακρίνομαι
shame, αἰσχύνη
shameless, ἀναίσχυντος
share, μετέχω. See p. 70
    give a share of, μεταδίδωμι
sharp, ὀξύς
shepherd, ποιμήν
shield, ἀσπίς
ship, ναῦς
shoot, βάλλω
    (arrows), τοξεύω
shore, αἰγιαλός
show, ἀποδείκνυμι
shrink from, ἀποκνέω
shudder at, ἀποκνέω
shut up (imprison), εἴργω
sick (to be), νοσέω
side,—on the side of, μετά, Gen.
    to be on the side of, fight for,
        συμμάχομαι, Dat.
from all sides, πανταχόθεν
siege, πολιορκία
    take by siege, ἐκπολιορκέω
sight,—catch sight of, καθοράω
silver, ἄργυρος
simultaneously, ἅμα
since (of cause), ὅτι, ἐπεί. See p. 90
    (of time), ἐξ οὗ. See p. 150
sing, ᾄδω
single, ἁπλοῦς
sister, ἀδελφή
skilful, ἐπιστήμων ; Adv. ἐπιστη-
    μόνως
skilful in, ἐπιστήμων, Gen.
skill, τέχνη
skin (wineskin, etc.), ἀσκός

slave, δοῦλος
slavery, δουλεία
sleep, ὕπνος
    (Verb), καθεύδω
slothful, to be, ῥᾳθυμέω
slow, βραδύς ; Adv. βραδέως
small, μικρός
smoke, καπνός
snow, χιών
so, οὕτως
    (consequently), οὖν, 2nd word ;
        ὥστε, 1st word
    to be so, οὕτως ἔχειν
so great, τοσοῦτος
so greatly, τοσοῦτο(ν), Adv. Acc.,
    or ἐς τοσοῦτον
so that (consequence), ὥστε.
    See p. 100
Socrates, Σωκράτης, -ους
soldier, στρατιώτης
Solon, Σόλων, -ωνος
some . . . others, οἱ μὲν . . . οἱ δὲ . . .
sometimes, ἐνίοτε
son, υἱός
soon, δι’ ὀλίγου, οὐ διὰ πολλοῦ, τάχα
sophist, σοφιστής
sortie, ἐκδρομή
soul, ψυχή
spare, φείδομαι, Gen.
Sparta, Σπάρτη
Spartans, Λακεδαιμόνιοι
Spartan aristocracy, Σπαρτιᾶται
speak, λέγω
    speak to, converse with,
        διαλέγομαι, Dat.
    speak evil of, κακὰ λέγειν.
        See p. 74
    speak well of, εὖ λέγειν.
        See p. 74
spear, αἰχμή
speedily, ταχέως, διὰ τάχους
spend, ἀναλίσκω, δαπανάω
    (of time), διάγω

spring, ἔαρ
   on the return of spring, ἅμα
     τῷ ἦρι
stade, στάδιον.   Voc. 20
stand, ἕστηκα
   up, intransitive tenses and
   Middle of ἀνίστημι
start, ἄπειμι, ἀφορμάομαι ;
   (*of armies, etc.*), αἴρω
state, πόλις, τὸ κοινόν
stature, μέγεθος
steadily, βεβαίως
steal, κλέπτω
still, ἔτι
   (=*nevertheless*), μέντοι, ὅμος
stone, λίθος
   made of stone, λίθινος
stop (trans.), παύω, κωλύω.
   See p. 160
   (intrans.), παύομαι.
     See pp. 14 and 123
storm, χειμών
storm (Verb), κατὰ κράτος (βίᾳ)
   αἱρέω
strange, δεινός
   (*foreign*), βάρβαρος
stranger, ξένος
stratagem, δόλος
stream, ῥοῦς (ῥόος)
street, ὁδός
strength (*to have*), ἰσχύω
strive for, ἐρίζω περί, Gen.
strong, ἰσχυρός
subdue, καταστρέφομαι
subject, ὑπήκοος, Gen.
succeed (*of things*), προχωρεῖν, κατ-
   ορθοῦσθαι
success, without success, ἄπρακτος
successful, εὐτυχής
such, τοιοῦτος
   such a thing, τὸ τοιοῦτον
   to such a pitch of, ἐς τοσοῦτο,
     with Gen.

suddenly, ἐξαίφνης, ἄφνω
suffer, πάσχω
sufficient, ἱκανός
   to be sufficient, ἀποχρῆν (ἀπο-
     χράω)
suicide, commit suicide, βιάζεσθαι
   ἑαυτόν
summer, θέρος
   in summer, etc.   See p. 23
summon, καλέω, προσκαλέω, μεταπέμπομαι
   summon home from exile,
     κατάγω
sun, ἥλιος
   at sunset, ἅμ' ἡλίῳ καταδύντι
superior, κρείσσων
   be superior to, διαφέρω, Gen.
suppliant, ἱκέτης
supremacy, ἡγεμονία
surely (**in** *questions*), πῶς οὐ ;
   See p. 58 *n.*
surrender (trans.), παραδίδωμι
   (intrans.), ἐνδίδωμι
surround, περιέχω, κυκλόω
survive, περιγίγνομαι, Gen.
Susa, Σοῦσα, n. pl.
sustenance, τροφή
swear, ὄμνυμι.   See p. 51
sweet, ἡδύς
swim, νέω
   out, ἐκνέω
sword, ξίφος
Syracuse, Συράκουσαι
Syracusan, Συρακόσιος

T

take, λαμβάνω, αἱρέω.   (In Passive
  sense ἁλίσκομαι is also used)
   (*receive*), δέχομαι
   take place, happen, γίγνομαι
talk, λέγω
   talk nonsense, φλυαρέω
task, ἔργον

teach, διδάσκω
tell, λέγω, *etc.* Voc. 41
  a story, μυθολογέω
temple, νεώς
terms, on these terms, etc. ἐπί, Dat.
  come to terms, συμβαίνω
  bring to terms, ἀναγκάζειν περὶ
  ἀπαλλαγῆς πράσσειν
terrible, δεινός
terrify, φοβέω, ἐκπλήσσω
thank, be thankful, χάριν ἔχω.
  See p. 70
Thebes, Θῆβαι
Thebans, Θηβαῖοι
Themistocles, Θεμιστοκλῆς, -έους
then, τότε, ἐνταῦθα
  =*therefore,* οὖν (2nd word),
  τοίνυν (2nd word)
  = *next,* ἔπειτα
there, ἐκεῖ
therefore, οὖν (2nd word) ; πρὸς
  ταῦτα (with Imperatives)
Thermopylae, Θερμοπύλαι
think, νομίζω, οἴομαι, ἡγέομαι
  (*think right*), ἀξιόω
  (*ponder*), φροντίζω
thither, ἐκεῖσε
Thrace, Θράκη
Thracian, Θρᾷξ
threaten, ἀπειλέω, Dat.
throng, ὄχλος
through, διά, Gen.
  (*all round, throughout*), περί,
  Acc.
  (*by means of*), Dat. or διά,
  Gen.
throughout, ἀνά, Acc. ; περί, Acc.
throw, βάλλω
  away, ῥίπτω
Thucydides, Θουκυδίδης, -ου
Thurians, Θούριοι
thus, οὕτως, ὧδε. See Voc. 59
tie, δέω

till (Prep.), μέχρι, Gen.
  (Conj.), ἕως, *etc.* See p. 150
time, χρόνος
time,—after a short time, δι᾽ ὀλίγου,
  οὐ διὰ μακροῦ
  in time, at the right time,
  ἐς καιρόν, ἐν καιρῷ
  in the time of, ἐπί, Gen.
  in later times, χρόνῳ ὕστερον
tired, to be, ἀποκάμνω
Tiresias, Τειρεσίας, -ου
Tissaphernes, Τισσαφέρνης, -ους
to, πρός, εἰς, Acc. ; (*of persons*) ὡς,
  Acc.
to-day, τήμερον
to-morrow, αὔριον, or ἡ αὔριον
too (*excessively*), λίαν. See p. 100
tooth, ὀδούς
touch, ἅπτομαι, Gen.
towards, πρός, Acc. ; ἐπί, Gen.
town, ἄστυ
train, παιδεύω
traitor, προδότης
treachery, προδοσία
treat, χράομαι, Dat.
treat well, badly, εὖ, κακῶς δρᾶν
  (Passive πάσχειν). See p. 74
treaty, σπονδαί
  make a treaty with, σπονδὰς
  ποιεῖσθαι πρός, Acc.
tree, δένδρον
trench, τάφρος
trial. See *try*
tribe, φῦλον
tribute, φόρος
Trojans, Τρῶες
trophy, τρόπαιον
Troy, Τροία
true, ἀληθής
trust, πιστεύω, Dat.
trustworthy, πιστός
truth, ἀλήθεια, τὸ ἀληθές
  speak truth, ἀληθεύω

try, πειράομαι
 (*put on trial*), κρίνω, ἐς κρίσιν
  καθιστάναι
turn away (intrans.), ἀποστρέφομαι
turn out, result, ἀποβαίνω
tyrant, τύραννος

U

Ulysses, Ὀδυσσεύς, -έως
unable,—be unable, οὐ δύναμαι,
 οὐκ ἔχω with Inf. ; οὐχ οἷός τέ
 εἰμι, etc., with Inf.
uncover, ἐκκαλύπτω
under, ὑπό. See p. 237
undergo, πάσχω, intrans. tenses of
 ὑφίστημι
understand, συνίημι
undertake, ἀντιλαμβάνω, Gen. ;
 ἐπιχειρέω, Dat.
unexpectedly, ἀπροσδοκήτως,
 or Adj. ἀπροσδόκητος
unfortunate, δυστυχής
unguarded, ἀφύλακτος, ἔρημος
unjust, ἄδικος
unobserved, λάθρα, or use λανθάνω.
 See p. 123
unpleasant, δυσχερής
unprepared, ἀπροσδόκητος
until (Prep.), μέχρι, Gen.
 (Conj.), ἕως (ἄν), etc.
  See p. 150
unwilling, ἄκων
up, ἀνά. See p. 233
uproar, θόρυβος
urge, πείθω
use, χράομαι, Dat.
useful, χρήσιμος
usual,—as was usual, κατὰ τὸ
 εἰωθός
utmost, ἔσχατος
utterly, κατ' ἄκρας

V

vainly, in vain, μάτην
vengeance,—take vengeance on,
 τιμωρέομαι
very, μάλα, σφόδρα
vexed, be vexed, δεινὸν ποιέομαι
victorious, to be, νικάω
victory, νίκη
virtue, ἀρετή
voice, φωνή
vote, ψηφίζομαι
voyage, πλοῦς

W

wait, μένω, ἐπέχω
wall, τεῖχος
wander, πλανάομαι
want (Noun), ἀπορία, ἔνδεια
 (*need*), *be in want*, δέομαι,
  ἀπορέω, Gen.
war, πόλεμος
 be at war, πολεμέω
 make war upon, πόλεμον ἐπιφέρω, Dat.
warn, νουθετέω
waste (*time*), διατρίβω
watch, τηρέω
water, ὕδωρ
wave, κῦμα
way, ὁδός
 (*manner*), τρόπος
weak, ἀσθενής
weapon (*missile*), βέλος
weep, κλαίω
welcome, ἀσπάζομαι
well (Adv.), εὖ
 to be well (*of things*), καλῶς
  ἔχειν
well, φρέαρ
what, what sort of. See p. 59
whatever, of whatever kind, ὁποῖος.
 See p. 148

when, ἐπεί, ἐπειδή, ὅτε.   See p. 150
   and Voc. 136 n.
   (Interrogative), πότε ;
whenever, ὁπότε, εἴ ποτε.   See
   pp. 148, 150
where (Relative), οὗ, ὅπου
   (Interrogative), ποῦ ;
   where from, whence, πόθεν, etc.
   See p. 59
   where to, whither, ποῖ, etc.
   See p. 59
wherever, ὅπου, εἴ που.   See p. 148
wherefore, τί ; διὰ τί ;
whether, πότερον, εἰ.   See p. 62
   and note
while, ἕως.   See p. 150
whither, οἷ, ὅποι
   (Interrogative), ποῖ ;
who.   See p. 59
whoever, ὅστις, εἴ τις.   See p. 148
whole, πᾶς, ὅλος
why ? τί ; διὰ τί ;
wife, γυνή
wild beast, θηρίον
willingly (to be), ἐθέλω
   willingly, ἑκών
   willingly at least, ἑκὼν εἶναι
win, φέρομαι, κτάομαι
wind, ἄνεμος
wine, οἶνος
wing (of army), κέρας
   on the right (left) wing, ἐπὶ
   δεξιᾷ (ἀριστερᾷ)
winter, χειμών
   in winter, etc.   See p. 23
wisdom, σοφία ; (good sense), φρόνησις
wise, σοφός, φρόνιμος

wish, βούλομαι, ἐθέλω
with, μετά, Gen.
   often translated by ἔχων,
   ἄγων.   See p. 123
without, ἄνευ, Gen.
woman, γυνή
wonder (at), θαυμάζω
wooden, ξύλινος
word, λόγος
work, ἔργον
world, γῆ
worn out, to be, ἀποκάμνω
worsted, to be, ἡσσάομαι
worthy, ἄξιος
wound, τραῦμα
   (Verb), τραυματίζω, τιτρώσκω
wrap up, ἐγκαλύπτω
wreck, ναυάγιον
write, γράφω, συγγράφω
   poetry, ποιέω
writer, historian, συγγραφεύς
wrong, κακός, ἀδικός
   do wrong to, ἀδικέω

X

Xenophon, Ξενοφῶν, -ῶντος

Y

year, ἔτος, ἐνιαυτός
   every year, ὅσα ἔτη, κατὰ ἔτος
   twice a year, δὶς τοῦ ἐνιαυτοῦ
yet, ἔτι
   not yet, οὔπω
yield (trans.), παραδίδωμι
   (intrans.), ἐνδίδωμι
young, νέος
youth, νεανίας

INDEX

A

THE END